D0900455

Black
Academic
Libraries
and
Research
Collections

Black Academic Libraries and Research Collections

An Historical Survey

Jessie Carney Smith

GREENWOOD PRESS

Westport, Connecticut • London, England

Contributions in Afro-American and African Studies, Number 34

Acknowledgments

The following material is quoted with permission:

The quote on pages 14-15 is from the Carnegie Commission on Higher Education, *From Isolation to Mainstream; Problems of the Colleges Founded for Negroes, A Report and Recommendations* (New York: McGraw-Hill Book Company, 1971).

The quote on pages 231-32 is from *Materials By and About American Negroes* (Atlanta: Atlanta University, School of Library Service, 1967). Papers presented at an institute sponsored by the Atlanta University School of Library Service with the cooperation of the Trevor Arnett Library, October 21-23, 1965. Edited and with an introduction by Annette Hoage Phinazee.

Library of Congress Cataloging in Publication Data

Smith, Jessie Carney.
  Black academic libraries and research collections.

  (Contributions in Afro-American and African studies ; no. 34)
  Bibliography: p.
  Includes index.
  1. Afro-American university and college libraries. 2. Afro-Americans—Library resources—United States.
I. Title. II. Series.
Z675.U5S64   027.7   77-71857
ISBN 0-8371-9546-2

Library of Congress Catalog Card Number: 77-71857
ISBN: 0-8371-9546-2
ISSN: 0069-9624

First published in 1977

Greenwood Press, Inc.
51 Riverside Avenue, Westport, Connecticut 06880

Printed in the United States of America

To Ricky

Contents

Tables and Illustration

FIGURE

Preface

In the spring of 1968, the Council on Library Resources announced the beginning of a fellowship program for mid-career librarians which would provide a new avenue for professional development. The program allowed a limited number of recipients to explore particular research projects relevant to their own interests which would be helpful to their careers, their institutions, and the library profession in general. It was under the CLR Fellowship Program that this study of black college libraries was undertaken.

The initiation of the Council's Fellowship Program paralleled a resurgent interest among educators throughout the nation in the development of black higher education facilities and resources. An example of this interest may be seen in the concern of the Southern Association of Colleges and Schools, which is the accrediting agency for institutions in the Southern states where the greatest number of black colleges and universities are found. While some of these institutions had been approved by the Association prior to the late 1960s, others had not. The Association expressed concern for both types of institutions by providing consultant service for those seeking approval as well as for those seeking reaccreditation.

Activities of agencies such as the Southern Association involved, to some extent, an analysis of library programs, facilities, and services in these institutions. When library programs were identified as weak and potentially ineffective, the Association either failed to accredit the institution or gave it provisional status until library deficiencies could be corrected. Clearly, this action was indicative of the Association's genuine concern with proper development of libraries to support the educational programs in their institutions. As will become apparent, many of the institutions included in this study were negligent in the development of library programs over the years. It was not until pressure was exerted by the accrediting agency that any noticeable support was provided in some of these institutions. The point is further underscored in the self-study reports which many of these libraries prepared expressly for the accrediting agency.

While simultaneously serving as consultant to the Southern Association and as university librarian in a predominantly black college, this investigator recognized a pressing need for a detailed, in-depth analysis of library programs, facilities, and services in the black colleges. Several studies of black college libraries have been undertaken over the years, as Chapter 2 indicates. These studies, however, are either outdated, limited to particular types or aspects of libraries, or generally lacking in the scope necessary for an in-depth analysis of black academic libraries. They do provide important background materials for the present study by identifying a number of problems which black libraries have faced throughout their history and by pointing out the interest of other individuals and agencies in the development of these libraries. Many agencies and individuals have found it helpful to consult these studies before embarking on proposal-writing projects or fund-raising activities which might lead to greater financial support.

Since this study was proposed in 1968, its potential usefulness has increased. Such agencies as the Southern Association of Colleges and Schools, the U.S. Office of Education's Bureau of Libraries (as it was known then), the Office for Advancement of Public Negro Colleges, the Council on Library Resources, and the United Negro College Fund have continuously endorsed the idea of the study and have expressed a keen interest in its results. Both presidents and librarians of institutions examined in the study have expressed interest in obtaining copies of the final report so that they might have a fuller picture of the overall development of black college libraries as well as a means of comparing the development and operation of their own libraries to those in the other black colleges.

Library educators, acknowledging the need for more background material on all types of libraries, have expressed an expectation that this report will give them a greater knowledge of contemporary problems in black academic libraries. This interest has been compounded by the continuing concern of agencies with the study of minorities in general.

This study is one of the few that have dealt with the history of black colleges and the development and status of their libraries. Although many of the black colleges have been under attack in recent years because of poor quality educational programs and faculties and inadequate physical facilities, they continue to educate sizable numbers of black students who complete a college degree. The need for maintaining adequate library facilities and services becomes obvious. Of equal importance is the need for a thorough and up-to-date analysis of library programs within these institutions with a view toward providing impetus for strengthening them as required.

The investigator is indebted to a number of individuals and organizations for cooperation, counsel, and assistance provided from the inception of the idea to the completion of the work. As accolades are given, the reader should bear in mind that they do not appear in order of importance. Such an order would have been impossible to establish, for each individual and organization has played a unique part in this undertaking.

Realizing, however, that this project could not have been undertaken without financial support, the investigator is deeply appreciative of the efforts of the Council on Library Resources in making this study possible. Under a grant of $12,500 provided by the Fellowship Program of the Council, the full expenses of this study have been met. The Council and its staff, particularly Fred Cole, Foster Mohrhardt, and Edith Lesser, have been most encouraging, cooperative, and patient during the preparation of this work. Even when the original time schedule for the completion of the project was not met, the Council continued to provide encouragement and support. The investigator only hopes that the Council appreciates her continuing and keen interest in the development of black college libraries, as well as the depth of the study and the amount of time required to do it justice. It has been difficult to meet the schedules of librarians in institutions visited and, at the same time, while on leave from the position of University Librarian at Fisk University for nearly three full semesters, to attend to matters in the Fisk library which continued to require personal attention. Additional-

ly, during the intervening months, the investigator continued her activities
in various professional organizations, which weighed heavily on her time
and energy.

Thanks are extended to three persons who played important parts in
the study from the very beginning: Robert B. Downs, then Dean of Library
Administration at the University of Illinois; David D. Kaser, then Director of Libraries, Cornell University; and Stephen J. Wright, then President
of the United Negro College Fund. Dr. Downs was especially helpful in
analyzing the questionnaire instrument and making suggestions for its improvement, giving helpful hints on conducting a study of libraries, and
providing bibliographies and tools that would be useful to the investigator in the development of the study. Dr. Kaser offered a wealth of information that was useful in preparing the questionnaire and in conducting
the research. Dr. Wright provided invaluable support based on his experiences as former President of Fisk University and as a leader of an important organization concerned basically with black colleges, the United Negro College Fund.

Librarians, library staffs, presidents, and faculty members of institutions involved in the study have provided valuable assistance to one degree or another. The investigator is especially grateful to those librarians
who responded to the questionnaire, despite the tremendous amount of
time required to complete it, and for their continued interest in the project. Whether or not an institution responded to the questionnaire, the
investigator always received a warm welcome when visits were made to
the institutions; she appreciates the generous amount of time given to
her during the visits. She realizes also that great demands are now being
made on librarians, library staffs, presidents, and faculties, and that some
of the librarians were already too overworked to take the time required
to complete the questionnaire.

Special thanks are extended to the Southern Association of Colleges
and Schools, which made available the self-study reports from many of
the institutions included in the study. The reports provided much of the
background information on the institutions that was omitted from the
questionnaire, gave information on the libraries in these institutions, and
provided data on some of the libraries that failed to respond to the questionnaire. These reports helped the investigator gain a broader picture of
the institutions accredited by the Southern Association.

The President of Fisk University at the time of the study, James R. Lawson, was especially helpful, cooperative, and understanding throughout the research period. By providing a leave of absence for nearly three semesters, by making available unlimited time to conduct the research and write the final report, and by expressing an active interest in the study, Dr. Lawson has played a vital part in making this research possible.

While its members may not realize it, the library staff of Fisk University, particularly one of the Associate Librarians, Ann A. Shockley, has played its part in the completion of this study. Because Ms. Shockley assumed many of the administrative duties that normally would have required the investigator's attention, and because the staff continued to make library operations run smoothly in her absence, free time was available in which the investigator could conduct the research. The staff's loyal support and words of encouragement were extremely beneficial.

Special thanks are extended to Jean Cazort, also Associate Librarian at Fisk; Susan Haddock and Meredith Haddock, then members of the Fisk library staff; Rutherford H. Adkins, Interim President, Fisk University; and Jack Dalton, Director, Library Development Center, Columbia University, who read the manuscript and gave helpful suggestions for writing the final report.

Finally, the investigator is especially grateful to Vallie P. Pursley of the Fisk library staff, who served as secretary to the project from its beginning through the final typing of the manuscript. Her cooperation, dedication, reliability, and loyalty have been especially appreciated during these trying times.

1

Introduction

Studies of libraries in black academic institutions present an image in conflict with norms established by such agencies as the American Library Association and the Southern Association of Colleges and Schools. Immediately, one may wonder whether or not these norms should apply when evaluating black college libraries, which serve a population whose characteristics are so vastly different from those of traditionally white colleges and universities. In addition, some question might be raised regarding the function of the black college library and the role that it has played in the education of black students in the past.

Clearly, those agencies that in the past have had primary concern for the function and development of the library as an educational unit in the academic institution are in a position to set standards and pass judgment on various types of libraries. They have studied countless library programs to measure their effectiveness and have provided various types of support for library development. In cases where academic libraries are involved, their primary concern has been with the library's role in the educational process. They give attention to the various elements that help determine that role and the extent to which the library serves that role. These elements include financial support, library staffs, resources, buildings, use of resources by faculty and students, equipment, and so forth. Whether or not the library is in a black institution, it has the responsibility of providing these elements of a library program. When all or a part of these elements are underdeveloped, as has been the case in far too many black libraries, the need for improved library programs is greatly accentuated.

The purpose of this study is to analyze library programs, facilities, and services in black academic institutions and to provide historical data as well as current information on their development. It examines library programs in terms of requirements set forth by evaluation agencies and attempt to determine the extent to which these libraries meet established standards. The study brings into focus the strong as well as the weak elements of library programs. It further attempts to identify the specific requirements and functions of the black college library over and above those generally set forth in established standards. By putting into proper perspective the traditional as well as the present condition and function of the black academic institution itself, the study attempts to examine the library in terms of the demands placed on it by the institution.

This study places particular emphasis upon black materials found in libraries in black academic institutions. Realizing that some of the best collections of black materials are located in the black academic libraries, this study attempts to identify the strengths of these collections and to determine their effectiveness in curricular and research activities. It seeks to determine the history of these collections, their scope and content, their administrative organization, the quality and number of staff members serving the collections, the housing and preservation of the collections, the services provided, the financial support received, and projections for the future of these collections.

This study will yield many-faceted results: it will give suggestions for financial support from foundations; it will provide useful data for the various college accrediting agencies; it will provide information on special black collections that are of use to scholarship at a higher or on a national level; it will provide information which might be instrumental in influencing administrators in these institutions to support their libraries more adequately; it will provide an opportunity for comparing developments in these libraries to new developments in librarianship as a whole; it will provide the library profession with data on a group of libraries which is seldom identified; and it will give to administrators in these libraries some recommendations for improving their services and resources.

The scope of this investigation is limited to the eighty-eight four-year or graduate level institutions listed in McGrath's *The Predominantly Negro Colleges and Universities in Transition,* and one additional institution which reached four-year degree-granting status after the McGrath report was published.[1] While some of the institutions included in this study are no longer predominantly black, they were, nevertheless, invited to participate in the study. With this in mind, then, the study focuses on the predominantly as well as the historically black college library. It embraces both publicly and privately supported colleges and universities and seeks to compare the development of libraries in the two types of institutions.

In conducting this study, the investigator used the survey method. It is still a useful process for providing pertinent and precise information about existing situations, and the resulting data can be applied for comparison studies and in identifying trends.

A detailed three-part questionnaire, accompanied by a covering letter, was mailed to the head librarian in each of the institutions. A copy of the letter was sent to the president of each of these institutions in order to inform him that the survey was in progress and to seek his support as necessary. In many instances, the presidents were keenly interested in the study and prompted their librarians to respond to the questionnaire.

After the questionnaires were distributed, visits were made to eighty-two of the libraries, regardless of whether or not their questionnaires had been returned or whether or not they intended to participate in the study. While visits to the remaining seven institutions were anticipated, they were not made because of difficulties in scheduling. It was felt that on-site visits as well as interviews with head librarians, library staffs, presidents, deans, and some faculty members would provide valuable information which could not be obtained through the questionnaire. In some instances, photographs were taken of the interiors as well as the exteriors of the buildings.

The questionnaire was extremely detailed and lengthy, and the investigator is aware of the burden that its completion placed on the librarians and their staffs. This fact may account for the failure of some of the librarians to respond to the questionnaire. In addition, when visits were made to the libraries, interviews with librarians, presidents, and other persons were extremely time consuming for them. Not infrequently, the institutions were involved in self-studies for their accrediting agencies or were involved in other activities which placed heavy burdens on their time. Nevertheless, all were cooperative and interested in allotting what time they could to the interviews.

The questionnaire served a dual purpose: it provided data required by the investigator, and it assisted some of the librarians in collecting data needed for self-studies or evaluative reports in which they were engaged.

One library, Morgan State, used the section on black collections to help measure its own strengths and to establish an organizational structure which it could follow in the administration and operation of its special black collection.

Site visits provided one full day at each institution. When sizable collections of black materials were found, two full days were spent at the institution. These visits frequently provided an opportunity for the exchange of ideas on library operations, which yielded mutual benefits. As this investigator obtained information needed for the study, librarians frequently sought suggestions which they might follow in their programs. In several instances, the investigator read self-study reports that were in progress and made suggestions that might be useful to the institutions or to their libraries. In other instances, conferences were held with members of the library committee for the self-study as they were preparing for visits by the accrediting agency, and suggestions were given to them.

After the various interviews were held, library facilities were toured, and the library collections were examined in some detail. When new facilities were planned, written library-building programs were consulted, if available, and the architects' drawings and blueprints for the buildings were studied. When requested, critiques were given of the building plans. This activity was especially meaningful since the investigator had recently experienced writing a library-building program, planning the equipping of a new facility, and subsequently occupying the facility.

As mentioned previously, the questionnaire which was prepared to collect data for the study was extremely detailed. Part A of the questionnaire sought general background information on the institutions, their curricular and research programs, enrollment figures, number of faculty members and projections for the educational program for the next ten years. General information on the library was also sought in this section of the questionnaire and involved library administration policies, staff qualifications, salaries, collections, facilities, services and programs, budget, library education programs, and projections for the future of the library in all its aspects.

Parts B and C of the questionnaire gave special attention to black materials in these libraries. Part B attempted to investigate black materials that were physically incorporated into the general library collections, while Part C was concerned with the physically separated collections or special collections of black materials. Libraries were asked to complete either part, depending upon their specific situation.

As the report indicates, some libraries failed to respond to the questionnaire. Some libraries did respond to certain questions but provided incomplete information or responded with information which was difficult to analyze and/or interpret. As a result, descriptions of certain areas of these libraries, particularly special collections of black materials, may be incomplete. Information which was unavailable through questionnaires was frequently gathered from other sources and is given in as complete detail as possible.

Data collected through the questionnaire were analyzed through use of a computer. In doing this, a data bank was prepared so that the study can be updated periodically with minimum difficulty, particularly where statistical information is involved. In addition, a profile of each institution which responded to the questionnaire is available through the data bank. The investigator proposes to update the study within five years in order to determine the extent of growth in black libraries by that time.

This study was also designed to serve as a prototype for ten-year follow-up surveys. Information provided in the data bank may well function as a point of departure for the follow-up surveys. The writer proposes to draw upon this information in 1979 to update the study at the end of the ten-year cycle.

Since the study was completed, significant developments have taken place in black academic institutions and their libraries. Rather than attempt to rewrite the work at this time, examples of important developments that relate to particular issues raised are given through footnotes. In many instances, changes that have occurred are likely to have made such an impact on black academic institutions and their libraries that some of the recommendations given at the end of this study have now been addressed, while additional recommendations might be needed to focus on more recent problem areas. Such changes further support the need for follow-up surveys to update the work and to provide a continuing analysis of these institutions and their libraries. The work concludes with examples of issues that need to be addressed in the follow-up study.

NOTE

1. Earl J. McGrath, *The Predominantly Negro Colleges and Universities in Transition* (New York: published for the Institute of Higher Education by the Bureau of Publications, Teachers College, Columbia University, 1965), pp. 172-77.

2

Historical Perspective of the Black College

Studies of the black college in the United States frequently identify Lincoln University in Pennsylvania (1854) and Wilberforce University in Ohio (1856) as the oldest black colleges. Bowles and DeCosta find this identification defensible, considering "that these two institutions were the first to remain in their original location, to state or imply the awarding of baccalaureate degrees as their aim, and to develop completely into degree-granting institutions."[1]

Long before this date, however, various attempts were made by such groups as the American Colonization Society and the Conventions of the Free People of Color to sponsor institutions which would provide higher education for black people. Some of these early efforts resulted in the founding of a school for black youth at Pasippany, New Jersey, established by advocates of colonization in 1817; a school for black boys, initiated in Philadelphia County, Pennsylvania, in 1832 and realized in 1839, which was subsequently known as the Institute for Colored Youth and eventually became Cheyney State College; Avery College, Allegheny City, Pennsylvania in 1849; the academy established by Myrtilla Miner in the District of Columbia in 1851 to train young women to teach; and Ashmun Institute in Pennsylvania, now Lincoln University, incorporated in 1854.[2] These early institutions were designed primarily to prepare black youth to serve as teachers and ministers.

In the ensuing years, a number of institutions were founded for the specific purpose of educating black people. Included were those founded and/or supported by religious-oriented groups such as the American Missionary Association, political organizations such as the Freedmen's Bureau, which worked closely with the AMA, and black as well as northern white religious denominations such as Baptists, Methodists, Colored Methodist Episcopals, Presbyterians, Roman Catholics, and Seventh-Day Adventists.

Still others were founded as publicly supported institutions, receiving their financial backing primarily from the states in which they were founded. Of this latter group, a number were established by the Morrill Act of 1890, sometimes referred to as the Second Morrill Act or the Second Land-Grant Act, which made it possible for states to establish or to maintain separate black land-grant colleges in southern and border states.

Shortly after the Civil War and long before the Second Morrill Act was passed, three states apportioned funds which they received for their land-grant institutions to privately supported black institutions in their states, designating them as land-grant colleges. These states were Mississippi, where funds were awarded to Alcorn; Virginia, where funds were awarded to Hampton Institute and subsequently, in 1920, to Virginia State College; and South Carolina, where funds were awarded to Claflin University and transferred to a state-supported institution subsequently known as South Carolina State College. A total of ten black colleges which were privately supported before the Second Morrill Act was passed received land-grant funds as their state allocation for the education of black people. Kentucky apportioned funds to Kentucky State Industrial School from the Morrill Act of 1862, without compulsion of law; yet it was not until 1879 that the state actually made the funds available for land-grant purposes.[3] Thus the states' provision of land-grant funds for the education of black people shortly after the Civil War, and the Morrill Act of 1890 requiring that land-grant funds be equitably divided for white and black colleges, marked an early trend toward the "separate but equal" doctrine as applied to higher education.

Figure 1 illustrates patterns followed in the emergence of the black colleges, covering the period from before 1840 to 1960.

Most of the black colleges were established after the Civil War. Their founding, administration, and curricular offerings, however, clearly reflected the political, economic, and social conditions of that time. The same holds true for the patterns of their development. Their founding became

FIGURE 1

THE FOUNDING BY DECADE OF EIGHTY-NINE FOUR-YEAR, DEGREE-GRANTING BLACK INSTITUTIONS

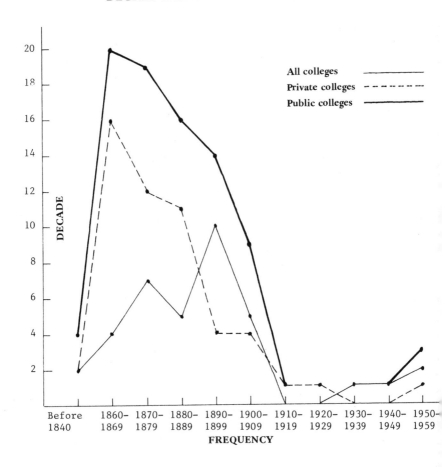

necessary simply because society as a whole failed to respond to the needs of the black population. White academic institutions in southern and border states where these colleges were founded made no provision for the black population. In the South, where large numbers of black people had a new-found freedom as a result of the Emancipation Proclamation, virtually nothing was being done to prepare them to live during the transitional period. In their radically changed condition, they were forced to make a place for themselves in the face of great economic and social adversity.

The American Missionary Association, whose interests had always been social as well as religious, had long been concerned with improving the condition of black people in America. It acted as an anti-slavery crusader and as a relief agency during and immediately following the Civil War. It later provided educational relief and support for black people by establishing and operating a chain of schools throughout the South. Its educational endeavors included the founding of Berea College in Kentucky. Though not founded as a separate black institution, the college was significant to black higher education in that it admitted black students. In 1861, the AMA established its first institution for the specific purpose of providing education for black people, Hampton Institute in Hampton, Virginia.

Other AMA-founded institutions which followed Hampton were Atlanta University in Georgia, Talledega College in Alabama, Fisk University and LeMoyne (now LeMoyne-Owen College) in Tennessee, Straight (now merged with New Orleans University to become Dillard University) in Louisiana, Tougaloo in Mississippi, and Tillotson (now Huston-Tillotson) in Texas.

The Freedmen's Bureau, a federally sponsored agency with great power over the affairs of newly freed black people, either founded, encouraged, or substantially aided in the development of Howard University in the District of Columbia, St. Augustine's College in North Carolina, Lincoln Institute in Missouri, and Storer College in West Virginia (now merged with Virginia Union). While the bill creating the Bureau in 1865 made no provisions for educating black people, by 1866 education for black people was one of its authorized functions.[4] The Bureau also encouraged, aided, and protected the work of church denominational boards and benevolent organizations in educational activities for freedmen.

Toward the close of the Civil War, the missionary spirit of northern white churches and their denominational boards resulted in the founding and support of black educational institutions in southern states. For example, the Freedmen's Aid Society of the Methodist Episcopal Church founded and/or supported Clark College, Atlanta, Georgia; Claflin University, Orangeburg, South Carolina; Shaw University, Holly Springs, Mississippi;[5] Bennett College, Greensboro, North Carolina; and Wiley College, Marshall, Texas. Institutions founded and/or supported by the American Baptist Home Mission Society were Shaw University, Raleigh, North Carolina; Benedict College, Columbia, South Carolina; Morehouse College, Atlanta, Georgia; Jackson College, Jackson, Mississippi; and Virginia Union University, Richmond, Virginia.

Boards of other northern denominations also succeeded in developing institutions of higher education for black people in the South. Among these were the Committee of Missions for Freedmen of the Presbyterian Church, North, which founded Scotia Seminary (now Barber-Scotia College), Concord, North Carolina, and Biddle Memorial Institute (now Johnson C. Smith University), Charlotte, North Carolina; the Board of Freedmen's Missions of the United Presbyterian Church, which founded Knoxville College, Knoxville, Tennessee; the Sisters of the Blessed Sacrament of Pennsylvania of the Roman Catholic Church, founders of Xavier College in New Orleans; and the United Christian Missionary Society of the Disciples of Christ, founders of Jarvis Christian Institute, now Jarvis Christian College, Hawkins, Texas.

The black church and its denominational boards, long recognized as a source of leadership in black communities, established and maintained a number of schools for black people. Some of the black church schools were founded before the Civil War but were developed into colleges only after the war's end.[6] These churches included the Cincinnati Conference of the Methodist Episcopal Church, which established Wilberforce University in Tawawa Spring, Ohio;[7] the African Methodist Episcopal Church, which established Allen University in Columbia, South Carolina, Paul Quinn College in Waco, Texas, Edward Waters College in Jacksonville, Florida, and Morris Brown College in Atlanta, Georgia; the African Methodist Episcopal Zion Church, which founded Livingstone College in Salisbury, North Carolina; the Colored Methodist Episcopal Church, which founded Lane College in Jackson, Tennessee, Paine College in Augusta, Georgia, Texas College in Tyler, Texas, and Miles College in Birmingham, Alabama; and the Negro Baptist Conventions, which founded such institutions as Arkansas Baptist College in Little Rock, Arkansas, Shaw Uni-

versity in Raleigh, North Carolina, Virginia College and Seminary in Lynch-
burg, Virginia, and Morris College in Sumter, South Carolina.

For the most part, the curricula in these institutions founded by black
religious denominations aimed at preparing persons for the ministry as
well as training teachers to help educate a struggling black society.

Political and legal factors contributed to the founding of publicly supported black educational institutions, including land-grant, normal, and
teacher-training institutions, or to the strengthening and possible public
control of privately supported colleges. Among these were Florida Agricultural and Mechanical College, Tallahassee; Southern University, Baton
Rouge, Louisiana; Alcorn Agricultural and Mechanical College, Lorman,
Mississippi; North Carolina Agricultural and Technical College, Greensboro; Tennessee Agricultural and Industrial State College, Nashville;[8]
Winston-Salem Teachers College, Winston-Salem, North Carolina; and
Cheyney Training School, Cheyney, Pennsylvania. The land-grant institutions in this group established courses in agriculture, mechanical arts,
and home economics to provide skills for thousands of untrained black
people as well as to prepare teachers to train persons in these fields.

Later in their development, some of the black colleges offered programs for preparation in medicine and related fields. While only Meharry
Medical College and Howard University continue programs for the preparation of dentists and physicians, medical education was once also provided at Shaw University, Raleigh, North Carolina, and New Orleans Medical School.[9]

Thus, since their inception, black colleges and schools have undergone
marked changes. The period from 1854 to 1870 may be characterized as
the pioneer period in which black educational institutions were founded
by white leaders, churches, missionary groups, and philanthropists, and
by black religious groups. The second period, the developmental era, covered the years 1870 to 1890 and also marked the beginning of black land-
grant colleges. Of primary importance was the effort of black people to
establish and administer their own institutions.

The third period, the rapid growth era, covered the years 1890 to 1930
and was characterized by the development of normal schools, teachers'
colleges, and publicly and privately supported institutions with a strong
orientation toward teacher training.[10]

The fourth and final period, from 1930 to the present time, may be
called the acceleration period. It is marked by changes in title from nor-

mal schools to colleges and from colleges to universities, the merging of institutions, a changing emphasis in curriculum, the emergence of programs in the sciences, the development of liberal arts programs, emphasis on graduate programs and preparation for graduate work, cooperative programs with black as well as predominantly white institutions, and a change in the racial composition of student bodies so that a few of these institutions, including West Virginia State College and Lincoln University (Missouri), are no longer predominantly black.

THE PRESENT-DAY BLACK COLLEGE

Educators are in disagreement over the role of the black college in the past and the part that it could play in shaping education in the future. As these arguments continue, it cannot be disputed that these colleges have educated and continue to educate an appreciable number of black student who seek college degrees. Many educators predict that the major source of educational opportunity for black students in the foreseeable future will continue to be in the black colleges.

A recent Carnegie Commission report on higher education in black institutions states that these colleges are experiencing a marked transitional period as they vie for students and faculty, undertake bold action to meet their mounting problems, and seek to become viable institutions within the American system of higher education. Specifically, the report identified twelve major themes of concern which might be paraphrased and presented here:

1. Black colleges have always had as a goal the achievement of a society in which economic, political, and social status are not determined by race.
2. These colleges have made contributions in the preparation of teachers, ministers, and other professional personnel despite substantial difficulties resulting from legally forced segregation.
3. Colleges founded for black people must now compete with other institutions for faculty and students.
4. These colleges are diverse and have little in common except their dedication to educating black people and to the solution of newer problems of transition within an integrated society.
5. In their period of transition, some of these colleges face the prospec

of considerable expansion in enrollment, with the aggregate enrollment possibly doubling by the year 2000.

6. New directions for these colleges will be toward more comprehensive programs to include more liberal arts, teacher education, and preparation for new occupations. Some preparation for advanced graduate work as well as compensatory instruction for poorly prepared students will be required.

7. Black colleges are in a unique position to provide various types of community service programs, and their contributions will be gratefully accepted.

8. These colleges are in a unique position to record and analyze the black experience in America.

9. Black colleges may look toward increased opportunities for cooperative programs, joint appointments of faculties, and joint use of facilities with historically multiracial institutions. Graduate programs in the latter institutions may need to seek prospective students from the black colleges.

10. In spite of increased federal and state appropriations, black colleges are experiencing special financial problems in the 1970s.

11. These colleges have a high proportion of students from low-income families. Over the next decade, they should receive special assistance from the proposed National Foundation for Higher Education to provide for planning comprehensive and innovative instructional programs.

12. Effective use of resources is needed in the black colleges. Merger programs between small, yet compatible, institutions should be considered.[11]

In summing up the present status of the traditionally black college, Bowles and DeCosta state that the purpose of black education now, as in the past, is not clearly understood—whether its purpose is preparation for life in black or white America. As they view black education in America today, they believe that it is between two worlds. On this issue, they remark that

it has not achieved full entrance to the world of white mass education with its increasingly mechanized operations and standards and the fierce but muted competition for place and status. Nor has it entirely left behind the world of the segregated Negro community with its standards and methods following the formal models of white education but adapted to the tolerances and expedients of an isolated culture.[12]

The present study of the traditionally black college library examines the institutions that responded to the questionnaire in an effort to gather background data on educational programs that might help put the role and status of the library into perspective. Of the eighty-nine questionnaires distributed, responses were obtained from sixty-five, or 73 percent of the institutions. The responses received represent the wide geographical distribution of the colleges themselves. The eighty-nine four-year degree-granting institutions are located primarily in the southern states, although a few lie outside the South. In addition to the District of Columbia these institutions may be found in Pennsylvania, Ohio, Missouri, and Oklahoma, and in the border states of Delaware and Maryland.

Of the sixty-five respondents included in this study, twenty-seven are publicly supported, while thirty-eight are supported by private funds. In terms of date of establishment, the reporting institutions are among the oldest as well as the youngest black colleges. Included are Wilberforce University (founded in 1856), Lincoln University in Pennsylvania (founded in 1854), and Southern University in New Orleans, founded as recently as 1959. The publicly supported institutions include fourteen of the seventeen black colleges that were either established or maintained as separate black land-grant institutions—Alabama Agricultural and Mechanical University, Alcorn Agricultural and Mechanical College, Arkansas Agricultural and Mechanical College,[13] Florida Agricultural and Mechanical State University, Kentucky State College, Langston University, Lincoln University (Missouri), North Carolina Agricultural and Technical State University, Prairie View Agricultural and Mechanical College, Savannah State College, South Carolina State College, Southern University, Virginia State College, and West Virginia State College. The three remaining institutions are Delaware State College, Tennessee State University, and the University of Maryland, Eastern Shore.

Regional accreditation agencies for the states in which these institutions are found are the Southern Association of Colleges and Schools, the North Central Association of Colleges and Secondary Schools, and the Middle States Association of Colleges and Secondary Schools. At the time of the study, fifty-two of the institutions reporting were accredited by the Southern Association, seven were accredited by the North Central Association, and two were accredited by the Middle States Association. The remaining four institutions were unaccredited by these agencies.

The sixty-five reporting institutions offer undergraduate degrees in a variety of areas. As might be expected, some, if not all, of the land-grant institutions offer educational programs and degrees in such areas as agriculture, animal husbandry, industrial education, home economics, and nursing. Common among the degree areas offered in these institutions— whether they are land-grant, public, or private colleges—were mathematics, business administration, health and physical education, music, areas in the social sciences, economics, psychology, sociology, areas in the natural sciences, English, elementary education, secondary education, and art. Increasingly, the institutions have become more liberal arts oriented, with a strong emphasis on teacher-training programs. Such areas in the sciences as biology, chemistry, and physics have been receiving greater attention in these institutions either through the offering of degrees, the strengthening of faculty, the upgrading of facilities, or special training programs (for example, summer institutes).

One institution in this group, Simmons Bible College, offers degrees in such purely religious fields as religious education and Bible. A strong religious orientation remains in programs at Jarvis, Oakwood, and Xavier, and particularly at Morris, Livingstone, and Virginia Union, where some preparation for the ministry is offered. At Virginia Union, some liaison between religious and nonreligious programs is sought. As the college bulletin indicates, the aim of the program is

> to develop intelligent Christian leadership through a close articulation between its liberal arts college and its graduate school of religion, preparing ministers thoroughly trained not only in theology but in the broader social concepts necessary to an understanding of current social and economic problems.[14]

Although the graduate program in theology at Virginia Union is administered separately, this educational aim provides an important link between the graduate and undergraduate programs.

Twenty of the sixty-five institutions offer the master's degree in one or more areas. The common area among these institutions is education. Other subjects frequently found at these schools are mathematics, chemistry, guidance and counseling, history, English, and business education or administration.[15] Four of the institutions—Alabama A & M, Prairie

View, North Carolina A & T, and Tuskegee—offer master's degrees in fields of agriculture, along with other subject areas. Degrees in fields of industrial education are offered at Alabama A & M, North Carolina A & T, Prairie View, and Cheyney State. Those institutions offering master's degrees in the largest number of areas are Atlanta (fourteen areas), North Carolina Central (twenty-two areas), North Carolina A & T (twenty-two areas), and Prairie View (twenty areas).

Five of the twenty institutions offering master's degree programs are privately supported. Included in this group are Atlanta, Fisk, Hampton, Tuskegee, and Xavier. Atlanta University offers no degrees below the master's level. Specifically, it offers the doctoral degree in biology and counseling and guidance.[16] Atlanta also offers the master's degree in biology but not in guidance and counseling.

Professional degrees other than medicine are offered in twelve of the sixty-five institutions. Library science degrees are offered at Alabama A & M, Atlanta, and North Carolina Central; social work at Atlanta; pharmacy at Florida A & M, Texas Southern, and Xavier; nursing and engineering at Florida A & M, North Carolina A & T, and Tuskegee; religion at Simmons, Morris, Livingstone, and Virginia Union; and law at North Carolina Central and Texas Southern.

Twenty institutions offer vocational certificates and/or associate arts degrees. Generally, these awards are made in the areas of nursing education, secretarial training, law enforcement, air conditioning and refrigeration, graphic arts, electricity, automobile mechanics, brick-masonry, tailoring, and other vocational areas. While the AA degree or certification is awarded in traditional trades areas, newer trades subjects (for instance, electronics, computer technology, and law enforcement) have been added in some of these institutions. Privately as well as publicly supported institutions are among this group. Some of these programs are in adult education, offered during evening courses; others are regular day programs for students who may or may not intend to enroll in a four-year, degree-granting program.

Special programs—including Upward Bound, prelaw, premedicine, undergraduate level library education, courses for farm workers, Headstart, radio broadcasting, and other areas—are provided in eleven of the institutions reporting. While some of the institutions confused special programs with vocational certificates and others failed to report Upward Bound programs that are known to exist, responses to this part of the questionnaire point out at least some of the nondegree programs that are offered in the black colleges.

Thirty-seven of the sixty-five institutions maintain special research programs during either the summer term, the academic year, or both periods. Eighteen of the thirty-seven responding to this question were privately supported institutions. Special research programs are generally heavily weighted toward the sciences, particularly programs for teachers of biology, chemistry, or mathematics. Of special interest in the area of black studies are a program at North Carolina A & T entitled the African/ Afro-American Studies Program and two at Fisk, Afro-American Research and the Research Program on Problems of the Negro Community.

The institutions were asked to give brief projections for their educational programs during the next ten years. The resulting projections call for the addition of graduate programs in five institutions, revised and/or expanded graduate programs in four institutions, inauguration of interdisciplinary programs in three institutions, and revised and/or expanded curricular programs at the undergraduate level in fourteen institutions. Other projections involved upgrading to university status, obtaining accreditation by the regional agency, expanding enrollments, expanding the physical plant, innovating teaching methods, introducing programmed learning, and extending the campus to include branches in other cities.

Two of the institutions reported that they planned to remain essentially liberal arts colleges. Eighteen of the schools gave no projections, some stating that the institution was in the process of revising its mission for the future.

In terms of full-time equivalent enrollment of undergraduate students, sixty-five reporting institutions had a total of 108,791 students as of fall, 1969. Graduate students totaled 5,363 in the same year, with the largest single group of 1,407 at Atlanta University, whose entire enrollment was graduate. In terms of total enrollment, the largest institution reporting was Southern University, with 8,385 full-time equivalents, and the smallest Simmons, with 119 full-time equivalents.

Statistics reported in *Fall Enrollment of Higher Education, 1969*, showed a total of 153,763 students in the eighty-nine four-year, degree-granting black colleges.[17] The largest of these was Southern University, which reported an enrollment of 9,222 on three campuses. The largest enrollment reported on a single campus was 8,550 at Howard University, while the smallest was 64 at Virginia Seminary. Further analysis showed that 5.6

percent of those students enrolled in the four-year black colleges were at Howard in the fall of 1969. Of the 7,435,000 students enrolled in all colleges and universities in the United States as of fall, 1969, 153,763, or 2.1 percent, were enrolled in the four-year black colleges.

From the sixty-five institutions reporting enrollment figures for this study, 77,323 students, or 68 percent, were in publicly supported institutions, while 36,831, or 32 percent, were in privately supported ones. In terms of enrollment, the largest publicly supported institution reporting was, as previously mentioned, Southern University, with 8,385 students, while the smallest was Elizabeth City State University, Elizabeth City, North Carolina, with an FTE of 1,039 students. The largest privately supported institution reporting was Tuskegee, with 3,000 students, and the smallest in this group was Simmons, with an FTE of 119 students.

Full-time equivalent faculty members in the institutions reporting totaled 7,287 in the fall of 1969. Of this figure, 340, or 4.7 percent, were at Tuskegee, the privately supported institution with the largest number of faculty members. Simmons, also privately supported, had a low of 12 FTE faculty members at that time. Of publicly supported institutions, Southern University represented the largest number of FTE faculty, with 516, while Elizabeth City represented the smallest number, with a total of 72. Aggregate faculty in the publicly supported institutions totaled 4,619, while the aggregate faculty in private institutions totaled 2,668.

SUMMARY

At a glance, black colleges began their development prior to the Civil War for the specific purpose of providing higher education to black people, although it was not until the end of the war that they became more stable and offered degree programs. Black and white religious denominations, a political organization, religious-oriented groups, and the states themselves were responsible for founding these institutions. Their emergence, administration, and curricular offerings clearly reflected the political, economic, and social conditions of the time. During their existence, they have changed from normal schools to colleges, from colleges to universities. Some have merged, and all have incorporated new areas of concentration into curricular programs. Increasingly, there has been an emphasis on liberal arts programs, the sciences, and graduate education, even to the level of the doctorate. Certification and associate arts degrees in vocational areas are available in some of these institutions either as adult education programs or as skill programs for persons who concentrate below the bachelor's degree level.

This report supports evidence found in other studies indicating that an appreciable number of black students enrolled in institutions of higher education today are found in the black colleges. Programs geared toward educating black Americans must necessarily focus on these colleges, where a large concentration of black students may be found.

NOTES

1. Frank Bowles and Frank A. DeCosta, *Between Two Worlds: A Profile of Negro Higher Education* (New York: McGraw-Hill Book Company, 1971), p. 20.

2. Carter G. Woodson, *The Education of the Negro Prior to 1861* (Washington, D.C.: Associated Publishers, 1919; New York: Arno Press and *New York Times,* 1968), pp. 258-70.

3. Dwight Oliver Wendell Holmes, *The Evolution of the Negro College* (New York: Teachers College, Columbia University, 1934), pp. 150-52.

4. Ibid., pp. 37-38.

5. The present name of this institution is Rust College. The original name is not to be confused with Shaw University in Raleigh, North Carolina.

6. Holmes, *The Evolution of the Negro College,* p. 67.

7. The university came under the auspices of the African Methodist Episcopal Church in 1863. *Wilberforce University Bulletin* 52 (November 1969), p. 10.

8. By the late 1890s, Knoxville College had expanded its curricular offerings to include agriculture and industrial arts. "At the turn of the century . . . [the College] was granted a charter by the State of Tennessee for agricultural, industrial and mechanical training, and the State contributed to the financial support of the College from 1902 to 1912 when this training was taken over by the Tennessee Agricultural and Industrial College at Nashville."*Knoxville College Bulletin, 1967-68* (Knoxville, 1968), p. 19.

9. From 1895 to 1900, Knoxville College maintained a department of medicine and awarded a number of M.D. degrees. Students admitted to the program were required to meet the standards for admission set forth by the Association of American Medical Schools. The medical unit and other specialized areas of training were gradually discontinued, so that by 1931, Knoxville College had become exclusively a liberal arts college. Lois N. Clark, telephone conversation, November 1, 1976. Since this study was completed, Morehouse College has begun to develop a new medical school.

10. U.S., Department of the Interior, *Survey of Negro Colleges and Universities* (Washington, D.C.: Government Printing Office, 1928), pp. 32-34.

11. Carnegie Commission on Higher Education, *From Isolation to Mainstream; Problems of the Colleges Founded for Negroes, A Report and Recommendations* (New York: McGraw-Hill Book Company, February 1971), pp. 1-3.

12. Bowles and DeCosta, *Between Two Worlds*, p. 213.

13. The present name of this institution is the University of Arkansas at Pine Bluff.

14. *Virginia Union Bulletin* 64, no. 3 (Richmond, December 1968), p. 6.

15. Since the study was completed, increasing numbers of institutions are offering master's degrees in urban planning and other new areas.

16. The only other black academic institution that offered the doctorate at the time of the study was Howard University. Meharry Medical College (in addition to its degrees in medicine) and Texas Southern University have since added the doctorate.

17. U.S., National Center for Educational Statistics, *Fall Enrollment in Higher Education, 1969, Supplementary Information: Institutional Data* (Washington, D.C.: Government Printing Office, 1971).

Studies, Research, and Improvement Programs for Black Academic Libraries

The history and development of the black academic institution is generally easier to trace than is that of its library. As was shown in Chapter 2,
the black college dates from the period preceding the Civil War, although
it was not until after the war that it came to be recognized. Nearly all of
these institutions were founded prior to 1900, but it was not until 1917
that noticeable attention was given to the status of black academic education through publication of the first extensive survey of black higher
education.

STUDIES AND RESEARCH

Between 1917 and 1942, three major surveys of black colleges and
universities were undertaken under the supervision of the United States
Bureau of Education, the final one under the sponsorship of the newer
United States Office of Education. The 1917 survey, *Negro Education:
A Study of the Private and Higher Schools for Colored People in the United States,* covered all types and grades of black institutions and made specific recommendations for improving them.[1] Where libraries were concerned, the survey showed that facilities maintained exclusively for black
people in the South were very inadequate. It suggested that, in the past,
investigation of library facilities had been incidental to the study of education for black people. Of an estimated thirty-five library buildings avail-

able to black people in the South, twenty were owned and maintained by private schools, while fifteen were public libraries operated by cities.

Of 635 private and higher schools maintained for black people, the report found that only 27 were known to provide a collection of books which even by liberal standards, could be described as a library. Of this group, 2 schools reported collections of between 25,000 and 30,000 books, 5 between 15,000 and 25,000 books, and 18 between 5,000 and 15,000 books. Collections in 11 of these libraries were reported as fair, that is, arranged and administered in a manner which would facilitate their effective use. Collections in practically all other libraries examined were "so unsuitable as to be almost worthless, the discarded refuse of garrets and overcrowded storerooms, which should have gone to the paper mill, but [were] sent to these poor children through mistaken kindness."[2] Rooms housing these collections were cold and uninviting, the books submerged in dust; and frequently doors were unlocked merely to impress the occasional visitor.

A few institutions which received grants from the Carnegie Corporation of New York, or from Andrew Carnegie himself, to support library-building programs were:

A and M College	Normal, Ala.	$16,540
Atlanta University	Atlanta, Ga.	25,000
Cheyney Institute	Cheyney, Pa.	10,000
Fisk University	Nashville, Tenn.	20,000
Howard University	Washington, D.C.	50,000
Knoxville College	Knoxville, Tenn.	10,000
Tuskegee Institute	Tuskegee, Ala.	20,000
Wilberforce University	Wilberforce, Ohio	17,950[3]

In most cases, the colleges were required to raise an endowment in an amount equal to the Carnegie donation. The new structures frequently provided space for library operations, offices, and classrooms.

A second study, *Survey of Negro Colleges and Universities,* was published in 1928 and analyzed the control, government and finance, educational services, enrollment, faculty, and physical plants in black institutions of higher education.[4] Included in the study were twenty-two publicly supported institutions; nine independently owned, governed, and controlled institutions; thirty-one privately supported institutions that were owned and controlled by northern white denominational church boards; and seventeen privately supported institutions governed and owned by black churches.

The study cited a need for more and improved higher education and gave strong recommendations for improving these institutions in all areas. Citing the library as a part of the educational equipment, the survey pointed out the serious handicaps which professors faced if this aspect of the program was deficient. In particular, the survey found that

> a study of the libraries . . . reveals one of the most serious present deficiencies. Of the 79 institutions, only 15 have libraries of 10,000 or more volumes. There are 8 libraries with from 10,000 to 15,000 volumes, 2 with from 15,000 to 20,000 volumes, and 5 with 20,000 or more. The most extensive library has 55,000 volumes. On the other hand, there are 7 institutions which either have no library or have such small or poor collections that they are not worthy of the name.[5]

In many cases, the size of library collections equaled only minimum standards for junior colleges. Even here, in many instances a large number of useless works were included in the collections as a result of donations from retired clergy and other persons. Few public documents were included in the collections.

In assessing the service of the library to the institution, the study revealed that many faculty members and administrators failed to understand clearly the purpose of the library. In this connection, the study found that

> undue restriction in the hours in which the library was open to students and teachers tended to nullify its utility to a great extent and to disassociate its use from the formation of reading and study habits. Frequently also use of library facilities by college students is greatly limited because high-school students crowd the space in study hours scheduled in the reading room. Only in a few cases was it fully appreciated that the college library is just as much a workshop for the teacher as for the student, and that books and professional magazines are not to be limited merely to student needs.[6]

Little attention was given in the study to the physical plant which housed the library. The study showed, however, that in some of these institutions the libraries were in quarters which were inaccessible. Furthermore, some of these libraries were frequently locked and unavailable for use and were opened only on certain occasions by the president of the institution.

Improved library service during the years preceding the survey was noted. The study showed a growth in expenditures for library support between 1922 and 1923 and between 1926 and 1927. During this five-year period, "sixteen colleges increased their expenditures from 55 to 99 percent, 8 from 100 to 199 percent, 10 from 200 to 299 percent, and 5 over 300 percent."[7] The greatest proportion of increased expenditure was noted in the smaller institutions.

Several colleges showed pride and wisdom in book selection practices and in the provision of suitable quarters. Some of the libraries were providing longer hours of service, and students were making greater use of these facilities and services. The institutions were beginning to recognize the need for employing well-trained librarians to the extent that, at the time of the study, forty-three had secured some library education.

The third and final survey, prepared by the United States Office of Education and titled *National Survey of the Higher Education of Negroes,* was published in 1942.[8] It aimed at determining what types of programs were needed in higher education and studying the educational programs and services then available in the black colleges. Like the two previous studies, it provided a strong basis for upgrading and improving the black colleges as a whole, particularly in the summaries and conclusions given in the various parts of the survey.

A considerable portion of the study was devoted to library facilities and services. It set forth the purposes and methods used in studying the library and examined collections, personnel, expenditures, housing, and library use.

In order to collect statistical information, a library statistical report form was sent to each black college and university listed in the *Education Directory* of the United States Office of Education. Sixty-eight of the institutions responded, and their returns formed the basis for the statistical information given in the report. A representative sample of thirty-five institutions served as a second source of information and provided qualitative data regarding periodical holdings, reference materials, and other items. A group of twenty-five institutions was selected for visits by members of the survey staff in order to obtain information regarding facilities and library functions.

In summary, it was found that

the libraries at the Negro institutions of higher education, when taken as a whole, are inadequate for the service which they should perform. There are a few libraries which compare favorably in book collections, personnel, finances and building with the good libraries of other groups of institutions; but the vast majority of the Negro-college libraries are weak in all these elements.[9]

At the time of the survey, the average number of volumes in these libraries, regardless of type, was very low. The land-grant colleges had an average of 15,388 volumes, while the teachers' colleges reported an average of only 8,991 volumes. In the four-year, publicly controlled institutions, the average number of volumes was 17,617 while the privately controlled schools averaged 22,863 volumes. The report concluded that, in terms of size, these libraries were decidedly below the standard recommended for good library service.[10]

In further analyzing the collections, the survey showed that the black libraries housed a reasonably good collection of basic reference sources even though, in quality, they fell below the standards recommended by the North Central Association institutions. Periodical holdings were exceedingly incomplete, with many titles lacking. Interestingly, in terms of holdings of black books, periodicals, and newspapers, these libraries surpassed other institutions used for comparative purposes.[11]

The majority of the black academic libraries were receiving less than their share of institutional budgets. In terms of actual budgets for library purposes, they were expending amounts insufficient to enable them to function properly in the educational programs. Using 7 percent as the portion of total educational expenditures that should be allotted for library purposes, most of these institutions fell short of the desired level. The study showed that "in the case of outlays per student for books, the Negro land-grant colleges averaged $5.43, the teachers' colleges, $3.94, and the four-year privately controlled colleges, $5.20."[12] An average of $12.50 was expended in a group of twenty white colleges studied for comparative purposes. In the black colleges, the average salary expenditure per student was $5.69 in the land-grant institutions; $5.01 in the teachers' colleges; $8.16 in the four-year, publicly supported colleges; and $9.71 in the four-year, privately supported colleges. These figures compared to the $17.10 average expended in a select group of twenty other institutions.[13]

In terms of library personnel, the colleges were operating libraries with too few staff members to provide adequate service. Teachers' colleges, which had smaller enrollments, also had smaller staffs. The four-year, privately controlled institutions provided the highest average number of total staff. It was felt that staffs in these libraries had a relatively high degree of professional training.

Library quarters were considered very satisfactory in several of the institutions, with some of them bordering on excellent. On the whole, however, it was felt that the libraries in the black institutions were housed in inadequate quarters. Space, accessibility, arrangement, and equipment were inadequate and hampered the provision of good library service.

The study concluded that black college students made good use of their libraries, even though many of the libraries were inadequate. Such arrangements as direct access to materials, browsing rooms, and dormitory collections, which normally encourage library use, were lacking in the black college libraries. In order to function as effective educational units in the future, it was recommended that these libraries receive increased budgets for materials, personnel, equipment, and capital outlays for improved facilities or the construction of new quarters.

Between 1946 and 1971, a series of articles and research reports discussed problems in black academic libraries. Some, though not all, of these publications were prepared by individuals who were concerned with the development of these libraries.

A. P. Marshall examined the professional requirements in black colleges in 1952 and found that of the forty-one institutions reporting, many had no vacancies and did not expect any in the immediate future. Those reporting vacancies showed a total of fifty-one, which ranged from top level positions to general library assistants. Skills in typing and a knowledge of education, social science, humanities, French, Spanish, science, and journalism were required to fill these vacancies. In regard to salaries offered to librarians, 39 percent of the institutions were above minimum standards of the ALA.

Twenty-six colleges reported that recent library school graduates would be acceptable for their positions, while four preferred not to accept them. In three libraries, the matter of sex was an issue; preference was given to men in one instance, while two colleges preferred women. Concerning race as a factor in the employment of librarians, seventeen colleges reported that it would be a factor, while ten indicated that it would not.

The forty-one institutions reported a total of 137 trained librarians, with one institution reporting a high of 21 and another reporting 12. The majority of the institutions reported at least one professional staff person, with fewer reporting two or more.[14]

After the United States Bureau of Education reports on black higher education, the first major study concerning all aspects of black academic libraries was conducted by Earl J. McGrath in 1965.[15] Findings of the study helped to develop the interest of educators, governmental agencies, foundations, and others; and these groups were encouraged to examine higher education in general more closely and to give particular attention to black higher education and the education of black youth. Since its publication, the study has been cited frequently in documents relating to the black college or black libraries.

The McGrath study examined collections, facilities, personnel, the use of resources by students and faculty, and the administrative and financial support of black academic libraries. In general, the study revealed that

> the resources and services of Negro college libraries run the gamut from excellent to poor, but unfortunately the curve of quality is heavily skewed toward the lower end. Their problems are the problems of most small college libraries, but they are more prominent and more intense. The need for library resources and services is accentuated in most predominantly Negro colleges by their lack of sufficiently trained faculty members and their larger than normal proportion of poorly prepared students.[16]

In terms of material resources, McGrath found that of the sixty-one institutions supplying information regarding their library buildings, only 50 to 60 percent met standards set by the American Library Association for function, seating capacity, and housing the collection. These shortcomings

were true despite the fact that a number of the buildings were then relatively new, with 39 percent erected before 1945, 26 percent between
1945 and 1954, and 35 percent after 1955. Many of these library buildings failed to provide for such modern concepts of library service as facilities for group study, audiovisual materials, and areas for typing.

An analysis of library holdings showed that although several institutions
had excellent collections, the black college library in general lacked the
necessary basic collection. Between 30 and 60 percent of the titles on basic subject lists were likely to be absent from the collections.

Of the sixty senior colleges and universities reporting their holdings,
only twenty-two, or 36.6 percent, had collections in excess of 50,000
volumes. Fewer than 20,000 were found in five, while one had only 10,096
volumes. Many were adding large amounts of worthless material to their col
lections, swelling size while reducing overall quality. On the whole, these libraries rated substantially below others in size of collection, rate of growth,
and budget. The black institutions lacked their share of distinctive or excep
tional libraries.

The study showed that most of these libraries provided adequate materials for beginning courses but were lacking in books and journals required
for upper level courses and for the faculty. Audiovisual materials were also
lacking. A strong recommendation was given in this connection:

> The colleges need to increase their own rate of support for
> library collections. They could attract useful contributions
> to their collections while warding off useless gifts which
> only impose wasteful burdens on already limited resources
> by distributing to their alumni and patrons a carefully word-
> ed statement outlining in general terms the kinds of books
> most needed in their libraries. But drastic outside action should
> also be launched to strengthen the collections of Negro college
> libraries. [17]

Recommendations were made for awarding grants to enable most of these
libraries to update their collections and provide for major elements of their
programs. The use of competent consultants was recommended for the
areas of building planning, collection development, weeding the collection,
and utilization of staff.

In terms of human resources, McGrath found that the number of librarians in these institutions with reasonable professional competence was in-

adequate to meet staffing requirements. They were also handicapped by a lack of strong supporting personnel. Only 35 percent of the libraries responding met standards of the American Library Association for the number of trained personnel. It was strongly recommended that regional training workshops be held in order to provide ideas for improving and evaluating library services.

The study further recommended the establishment of a college library service center which would function as a purchasing and cataloging agency for black academic libraries, thereby providing economy and efficiency in processing. This recommendation has been partially implemented through the establishment of the Cooperative College Library Center in Atlanta, which will be discussed later in this report.

The survey pointed out that in the black college library, neither faculty nor students made heavy use of the facility and its resources. Book losses were heavy, frequently amounting to several thousand dollars annually. These problems were considered to be similar to those of most other college libraries; yet they were magnified in the poorly financed institutions.

McGrath found that reading interest and broad library experiences were lacking among students in the black colleges. It was recommended that stronger library orientation programs be established for these students.

In terms of financial support, McGrath concluded that black colleges were aware of their need to provide more adequate funds for library services, as was evidenced by their increase in per-student expenditures for libraries. These libraries require more extensive support as a greater variety of teaching techniques is employed and as their faculties attempt to keep pace with the advances in their fields.

In summing up the conditions of library services in most of the black colleges at that time, McGrath stated that

> the physical facilities are in general more adequate than the books, journals, films, and records they contain, or the number and training of the library staff. Their collections and staff need extensive strengthening to rectify a history of insufficient support and to help lift teaching and learning out of ritual and routine.[18]

In attempting to deal with specific major problems, the Commission on Higher Educational Opportunity in the South issued a statement in 1967 which was designed to serve as a springboard for action. This statement was aimed at stimulating equal and broader educational opportunities for this segment of the population, leading to improvements in instructional programs at the black colleges and encouraging the shaping of public policies which would forge a single, high quality educational system for the South as a whole.

The report found that libraries in the traditionally black colleges in the South were below accepted standards in terms of size of collection, education of staff, use of materials, and adequacy of physical facilities. Recognizing these deficiences as being of long standing, the report suggested that they have led, in recent years, to institutional policies of providing supplementary budgets for the support of libraries in many institutions. In this connection, the report makes the following recommendation:

> It is clear that, if library resources and other instructional equipment are to be raised to full equivalency, the provision of supplemental funds must be continued, probably for at least 10 years. It will not be adequate simply to meet the demands of normal development, or merely to match the expenditures for this purpose at comparable white institutions; the gap must be closed as rapidly as possible.[19]

A program to increase the use of libraries and their resources by both students and faculty was thought to require special attention in these libraries.

E. J. Josey examines the role of the black academic library in the "Future of the Black College Library," which appeared in September 1969.[20] The report shows that the development of black college libraries has been hampered by inadequate budgets, poor facilities, and limited numbers of staff persons. The meager funds which these libraries received over the years permitted librarians to assemble small collections which neither supported the instructional program nor enabled them to focus on materials for research and recreational reading.

Library facilities in many of these institutions were considered unsightly, small, and uncomfortable; they were unable to accommodate adequately the small collections which they housed.

Staffs in these libraries were small yet dedicated to service. Even so, their involvement in clerical assignments and pedestrian activities, which

was forced upon them because of insufficient numbers of library personnel, prevented them from engaging in more professional tasks.

By the time of the report, conditions in the black college libraries were
improving. Several new buildings were erected, larger budgets were provided, and collections were expanded. Library staffs were updating their competencies through institutes and other programs.

The report concluded that black libraries of the future must focus upon
unique library orientation programs to teach disadvantaged students to
maximize library benefits, providing personal assistance to these students
to help them overcome reading and study deficiencies, developing first-
rate collections, acquiring newer forms of media, and providing suitable
quarters for library functions. To accomplish these goals, the report suggested that the black library should receive sufficient additional funds
and should join regional cooperative programs which provide other benefits. The quality of the library in the black college may determine the future of the institution itself.

A second study, conducted in 1969 by Herman L. Totten, measured
the facilities and services in libraries of the United Negro College Fund
institutions against standards of the American Library Association.[21] In
"They Had a Dream: Black Colleges and Library Standards," Totten
found that of the thirty institutions responding, patterns of administration varied, with thirteen, or 44 percent, of the librarians reporting directly to the president and seventeen, or 56 percent, reporting to the dean of
the college or the vice-president of academic affairs.

Twenty-three, or 77 percent, of the respondents reported that their
head librarians served on the curriculum committee, while seven, or 23
percent, did not. In terms of budget, nineteen, or 63 percent, reported
that total library expenditures were 5 percent or more of the educational and general expenditures of the college. Only three, or 10 percent, of
the libraries spent $50,000 or more for books and related materials.

Three or more full-time professional staff members were provided in
twenty-four, or 80 percent, of the libraries reporting. Twenty-seven, or
90 percent, of the libraries indicated that they were inadequately staffed.
Nonprofessional, part-time, and clerical workers ranged from one to twelve.
Twenty, or 70 percent, of the institutions granted librarians faculty status,
while nine, or 30 percent, provided administrative status only.

Ten, or 36 percent, of the reporting institutions had collections of
50,000 volumes or more, while the number of periodical titles ranged

from 156 to 1,523. Seventeen, or 53 percent, indicated that their library collections were inadequate for the educational and research purposes of the faculty and students.[22]

Special attention was given to libraries in the thirty-three public black colleges in a survey published in July 1970 by the Office for Advancement of Public Negro Colleges.[23] The report was based on responses to a questionnaire prepared by the OAPNC staff and distributed to the thirty-three public black colleges and one branch campus. It was limited to a survey of collections, staff, facilities, and professional affiliations. The primary purposes of the survey were to determine the extent to which these libraries would be able to keep pace with institutional and program development and to identify major sources of support for collection development during the immediately preceding three years.

The findings revealed that only four of the publicly supported black academic institutions reported a number of volumes sufficient to meet standards of the American Library Association. Twenty-seven of these institutions showed numerical deficiencies ranging from a low of 1,500 volumes to a high of 620,262 volumes. In terms of the total numerical deficiency of volumes reported by twenty-seven institutions, the study showed 1,896,770, or an average of approximately 70,250 volumes per library.

The average number of volumes per FTE at these institutions ranged from 15.4 to 89.2, as compared to an average FTE rate of 46.1 in publicly and privately supported black academic institutions. Twelve of the public black colleges and universities exceeded the 46.1 average number of volumes per student.

In terms of staff, the report showed that the average number of professionals employed in the public black colleges was 9.6. All of the libraries met minimum standards of the American Library Association in terms of the number of professional staff required. Of the approximately 200 staff members with master's level degrees in library science or professional degrees in education, more than one-fourth of the librarians had received their training from Atlanta University. Nearly 11 percent of these librarians received their degrees from North Carolina Central University; 3.5 percent hold degrees from Case Western Reserve University; and approximately 60 percent hold degrees in library science from thirty other predominantly white institutions located primarily in the Northeast and Midwest. At each of the public black colleges, the head librarian holds membership in the American Library Association.

A survey of library facilities shows that eight of these libraries were constructed prior to 1950, and twenty-one were built in the 1950s and 1960s. One celebrated the opening of a new facility in February 1971, and one was scheduled to begin construction on a new facility in the fall of 1971. Fourteen of the libraries reported that they were severely limited in student-seating capacity.

Support for the development of library resources has come primarily through federal grants under Title II-A, Higher Education Act. While there was a wide variance in the amounts received, some of the institutions had obtained more than $50,000 in Title II funds since September 1967, with one institution receiving slightly more than $80,000. In most cases, however, it was reported that these funds were for catch-up purposes. One grant was made by the Ford Foundation to develop law and business library resources at Texas Southern University, while Jackson State College received a grant jointly from the National Endowment for the Humanities and the Council on Library Resources to support an innovative project titled LAMP (Literature, Art, Music, Philosophy). LAMP has been described as a creative-learning project relying heavily on library resources and involving faculty, students, and the library staff.[24]

An inventory of black academic libraries published by Casper L. Jordan in 1970 equals in importance the United States Office of Education surveys as well as the McGrath study. Of eighty-five black, four-year, degree-conferring institutions queried for the study, fifty-one responded. Information not obtained through questionnaires was received from other sources, and as a result, the Jordan report presents a fairly complete description of the black academic library.

In the fall of 1968, there were 92,911 students enrolled on a full-time basis in the fifty-one privately and publicly supported institutions reporting. A total of 4,290,915 volumes was held by these libraries, the smallest collection numbering 5,281 and the largest 575,347. Collections in approximately one-fifth of the institutions exceeded 100,000 volumes. The number of volumes per full-time student was 46.1, while the number of periodicals was 2.5.

Privately supported colleges among this group held an enrollment of 46,404, or about half of the total reported. They also accounted for nearly half of the 2,494,000 volumes held in all libraries reporting. The largest collection of materials held by any library in the survey, 575,357 volumes, was in a "privately supported" institution.[25] The average number of volumes per student in the privately supported libraries was 53.7, the highest in the total group reporting; and the highest per capita holding of periodicals, 14.4, was also found in this group.

Nearly half of all students enrolled in black institutions were found in the publicly supported ones. These institutions contained one-half of the total volume count in black libraries, ranging in size from 43,346 to 261,94 volumes. The average number of volumes per capita was 37.1. Jordan found that "on the whole, privately-supported colleges rated higher than those tha are publicly supported."[26]

Thirty-four of the institutions represented were, at the time of the study members of the United Negro College Fund. Two-thirds of these libraries failed to meet minimum standards for the size of collections. One met the standards, eight exceeded the standards, and two graduate institutions coul not be evaluated by these standards. It was estimated that nearly 676,000 volumes were needed in the UNCF libraries to bring them up to minimum standards for the size of collections.

Considering total operating budgets in all libraries reporting, the study found that expenditures per capita ranged from $36 to $153, as compared to a suggested adequate expenditure range of $50 to $80. Five libraries spent less than $50 per capita, twenty-one spent between $51 and $80 per capita, three spent $80 per capita, and twenty-six or more exceeded $80 per capita. Many of these libraries had received increased funds to enable them to reduce deficiencies in volume count. In another measure, these libraries spent from a low of 1.5 to a high of 10.3 percent of general university budgets for library purposes.

The number of professional staff members ranged from two to twenty-seven, with a range of nonprofessional staff members from one to forty-one. Only two libraries reported a ratio of two nonprofessionals for each professional, as suggested by ALA standards. The study showed that many black libraries relied heavily upon students as a source of manpower. The range in student employment was from 1,035 to 135,232 hours during the year, which suggested the desirability of translating some of the expenditures for student wages into employment of more nonprofessional personnel. The study also suggested that administrators in these colleges were reluctant to hire more supportive library staff and relied on students to meet library personnel needs.

A study of salaries paid to professional personnel in these libraries showe that they were noncompetitive in positions for recent library school graduates. The average salary offered to recent library school graduates in these institutions, as reported in the *Library Journal,* was exceeded by only three of the libraries included in this study. Even in terms of experienced employees in these libraries, the study found that, on the whole, salaries were not competitive with those of other institutions.

The Jordan study concurred with McGrath's findings that the physical facilities were generally more adequate than the resources which they contained or the number of personnel employed. The study concluded that this was true of both privately and publicly supported institutions, although UNCF libraries had a slight edge.[27]

In 1971, the Southern Association of Colleges and Schools and its Commission on Colleges published a collection of reviews and comments on activities of black colleges which would be representative of the sixty-seven such institutions accredited by the Association at that time. The report acknowledged the unique role that black colleges in the South have played in the history of American higher education by serving the educational needs of black youth. The report commented on their survival despite meager human and material resources, neglect, racism, and internal conflict.

The study gathered statistics from the late 1950s on thirty-nine institutions which it accredits and compared them to statistics from the late 1960s on forty-two institutions which it accredits. Both analyses included some of the same institutions, although three additional ones appeared in the 1960s group. In terms of libraries in these black institutions, attention was only given to holdings and expenditures.

Over the years in question, the study found that the black colleges experienced difficulties in providing sufficient funds from their educational and general budgets for library support. In spite of this fact, library holdings showed a 69 percent increase in number of volumes since the late 1950s. Median holdings at the undergraduate institutions studied exceeded 42,000 volumes at the time of the study, while the figure at graduate colleges exceeded 110,000 volumes. Annual additions to library holdings increased from 6 to 9 percent.

The study showed that there were significant increases in total library expenditures per full-time equivalent student, with graduate and private colleges spending a slightly higher amount than undergraduate and public ones. The report concluded that increased library holdings and improved library services were providing benefits for almost all black colleges at the time of the study.[28]

A brief comparison of the various studies of the black academic library as reviewed in this chapter will show that these libraries have experienced years of neglect and deprivation. Early studies in particular revealed consistent weaknesses, many of which have been compounded through the yea Although a few have been able to reach minimum standards of the American Library Association, far too many have not yet achieved this level of development. Together, however, the reports indicate that the libraries have made significant progress in terms of increasing size of collections, improving size of staffs, and improving their physical facilities in some instances.[29] These reports also emphasize the need for a more qualitative analysis of total library operations, facilities, and services. They also suggest the need for examining the library as it relates to the educational objectives of its institution. It is toward this end that the present study has been developed.

IMPROVEMENT PROGRAMS FOR BLACK ACADEMIC LIBRARIES

In the history of traditionally black academic libraries, a considerable number of programs have been inaugurated which were specifically designed to strengthen and upgrade their resources, facilities, and services. Significant among these have been the efforts of organized philanthropy, such as the Carnegie Corporation of New York, which provided funds for erecting library buildings at a number of the black colleges during the first quarter of this century. The General Education Board, which provided financial support for black colleges for various purposes, earmarked some of its funds for library development whenever an institution cited this as its most pressing need. In 1928-29, the Board authorized an appropriation of $400,000 toward the construction of a new library facility at Fisk University and also made available, over a period of three years, an appropriation of $35,000 for equipment, library materials, and expenses relating to an experimental program in teacher training.[30] The results of this grant are very much in evidence at Fisk today in its collection of retrospective titles.

At about the same time, the newly established Julius Rosenwald Fund provided funds for erecting buildings, purchasing equipment, meeting current expenses, and developing libraries in the black colleges. The Fund's direct contributions to the black colleges helped to strengthen them in what has already been cited as one of their weakest points, their libraries.

Black academic libraries have received the benefit of the Phelps-Stokes Fund, as reflected in their interest in improving black higher education through study and research. In helping to finance the *Survey of Negro*

Colleges and Universities, published by the United States Bureau of Education in 1928, the Fund permitted a useful study of black academic libraries as a part of the overall survey. This study provided invaluable information which served to stimulate greater support of library programs, facilities, and services.

In the ensuing years, a number of programs have been launched for the improvement of black academic libraries. At this point, however, attention will be called to some of the more recent activities aimed at improving black academic libraries as a whole or in smaller groups. These programs may be divided into five categories: (1) collection development; (2) collection and preservation of cultural heritage materials; (3) staff development; (4) technical services; and (5) general library improvement.

Several collection development programs have been launched by the United Negro College Fund, although these efforts are for the exclusive benefit of UNCF member libraries. In the middle 1960s, the Fund administered a program of financial support from the W. J. Kellogg Foundation, which provided a total of $15,000 to each member library over a three-year period for building library collections in the area of teacher education. At a time when many library budgets were woefully low, these grants provided a tremendous boost.

In fiscal 1970 and 1971, the William Kenan Trust Fund authorized the United Negro College Fund to provide nearly $3,000 in each year to strengthen library resources. While this amount was relatively small, it permitted many of the institutions to strengthen special areas in their collections. Some libraries used these funds to strengthen resources in black studies.

For a three-year period beginning in fiscal 1971, the United Negro College Fund made available to member libraries a total grant of $5,000 to be expended to strengthen resources in environmental studies. These funds permitted the libraries to develop collections in an area which is receiving considerable attention by various groups and individuals throughout the nation. Federal funds for collection development were severely limited during fiscal 1970 and 1971, with some of these libraries receiving no such support in fiscal 1971, and it is likely that without the grant the institutions would have been unable to allocate sufficient funds to develop their collections in environmental studies.

Seven notable programs have been initiated in the area of collection and preservation of cultural heritage materials. In October 1965, the Atlanta University School of Library Service, in cooperation with the Trevor Ar-

nett Library of Atlanta University, sponsored an institute on Materials by
and about American Negroes.[31] The conference also received the financial support of organized philanthropy, the Rockefeller Foundation. Major purposes of the institute were:

1. To provide an opportunity to review the present status of library
   materials by and about American Negroes and to explore ideas for
   future development.
2. To consider specific methods of implementing programs which will
   increase access to materials.
3. To establish or strengthen communication among librarians and
   scholars in order that library materials will be acquired and used
   more efficiently.[32]

The summary and recommendations of the conference stressed acquisitions, preservation, and communication as areas in which greater research
and/or activity were needed. A follow-up institute was also recommended.
Because the recommendations are particularly significant to the theme of
this study, especially to Chapter 5, they are being appended to this report.
The institute provided a wealth of ideas and information not only for the
participants but also for those who examined the published proceedings.
It marked a pivotal point in the collection, preservation, publication, and
organization of black materials and stimulated the development of other
institutes devoted to this subject area. The proceedings, or sections of it,
are cited frequently in the library literature discussing this topic.

A similar conference, Bibliographic and Other Resources for a Study
of the American Negro, was held at Howard University in the summer of
1968. Jointly sponsored by the National Endowment for the Humanities
and the Ford Foundation, it attempted to examine the state of bibliographic services in the field of black studies, provide a knowledge of various
kinds of resources for black studies, and indicate the availability of these
resources. A major outgrowth of the conference was the publication of
The Negro in the United States: A Working Bibliography, which incorporated recommendations from a number of the conference participants.[33]
Discussions at the conference and the subsequent publication of the working bibliography pointed up the dire need for greater bibliographical control of publications in the area of black history and culture.

The Ford Foundation recognized that black libraries housing significant amounts of research materials in black studies need to inventory,

process, and preserve these materials and make them more readily available for use. As a result, in the spring of 1969 it made initial grants available to Tuskegee Institute, Atlanta University, Fisk University, and subsequently Howard University in order to meet these needs.[34] The significance of the grants cannot be overemphasized, for they enabled these libraries to prepare their rich collections of black studies materials for greater use and helped to preserve some of the nation's most outstanding collections on this subject.

As result of the Ford grant, Atlanta University published a "Guide to Manuscripts and Archives in the Negro Collection of Trevor Arnett Library" in 1971. A timely publication, the guide presents a detailed description of the papers housed in the collection and is complemented by a detailed index. It also presents to scholars a wealth of resources which, when fully tapped, will disclose new areas of research.

In Alabama, where eight black academic institutions are members of the Alabama Center of Higher Education, a program has been developed to establish black archives and to place librarian-archivists on each of the eight ACHE campuses. The project, funded under Title III, United States Office of Education, and titled Collection and Evaluation of Materials about Black Americans, is directed through a CEMBA office in Birmingham which serves as a clearinghouse for materials collected throughout the state. The CEMBA office also aids in planning and coordinating activities related to black studies, black studies materials, and other areas on the ACHE campuses; holds conferences; and develops funding proposals for CEMBA activities as needed.

The specific activities of the CEMBA program of ACHE have been designated as follows:

> Collect materials relating to the eight ACHE institutions and establish archives on each ACHE campus.

> Collect materials relating to correspondence, diaries, memorabilia of individuals, etc., and sort, classify and professionally prepare these as archival materials available for widespread use through photoduplications.

> Prepare annotated union lists of Archival [sic] materials, books, serial and other Afro-American publications held

by ACHE institutions. These institutions will publicize
their holdings and will enable qualified staffs to make their
expertise available to larger audiences.[35]

The program, then in its third year, has already been instrumental in collect
ing a large amount of black materials in Alabama and in making them
available through CEMBA institutions. Much of the material collected
is still being processed.

Two library-training institutes in Black Studies Librarianship, supported under grants from Title-B, Higher Education Act, were held at Fisk
University in the summers of 1970 and 1971.[36] Although not designed
specifically to assist black academic libraries, the programs were successful in reaching a number of these libraries through the participation of
their staff members in the institutes. The two institutes had different
titles, "Institute on the Selection, Organization, and Use of Materials by
and about the Negro" and "Building Collections of Black Literature."
The major objectives of the two programs were similar: to prepare library
personnel to select, organize, and disseminate materials by and about blac
people; and to coordinate library services with the requirements of new
curricula and research in Afro-American culture, black studies, and programs for the disadvantaged. The institutes were specifically designed to
increase the accessibility of resource materials for research and study and
to integrate such materials into the mainstream of American life and culture.

Matters dealt with at the institutes included developing acquisition
policies for black materials, preparing bibliographies, initiating a core
collection of black bibliographical material at Fisk, developing cooperative acquisition programs, identifying special black collections in libraries, evaluating black materials, collecting materials, processing, administering special collections, and interpreting materials to users.

In addition to training library personnel, the institutes have had far-
reaching effects on library staffs in black academic institutions, where
many black materials are collected. These effects may also touch all libraries, for several publications are available to aid in promoting those
activities stressed in the programs.[37] Of equal importance to librarians
and scholars will be the proceedings of the institutes now being prepared.

In the summer of 1971, North Carolina Central University initiated a unique program titled the African-American Materials Project. Supported under a grant from the United States Office of Education, the project is designed to cover six states: North Carolina, South Carolina, Virginia, Georgia, Tennessee, and Alabama. Its original design was to cover the entire United States; however, limited funds required the program to be modified to a smaller scale. At the end of the initial program, AAMP expects to present a model which other states or groups of states might adopt for collecting African-American materials.

Specifically, AAMP is designed to describe, locate, and make accessible all types of African-American materials within the six states, whether they are housed in libraries or in other locations. Where monographic works are concerned, its emphasis is on locating pre-1950 imprints. AAMP will prepare union lists of holdings in the various states, giving location symbols for the various libraries or sources of materials.[38]

Of particular interest is the Black Oral History project initiated at Fisk University in the fall of 1969. The project received a financial boost from the National Endowment for the Humanities in the fall of 1971, when a grant was made available to strengthen the program.

The purpose of the Black Oral History program is to bridge gaps in black history and culture through interviews with persons who might reveal information directly related to the black experience in America. By collecting and preserving unwritten history, the program will provide materials which will supplement primary and secondary sources already available.

Staff development projects for the immediate benefit of black academic libraries were conducted by Atlanta University in fiscal 1968-69 and 1969-70. Through the request and financial support of the Ford Foundation, workshop and internship programs were conducted by the School of Library Service for twenty librarians employed in black academic libraries. The first workshop/internship program was devoted to technical services and the second to readers' services.

Librarians were invited to participate in a two-week workshop in Atlanta, in which lecturers and consultants discussed problems and innovations in librarianship. Participants were also given an opportunity to discuss problems of their own libraries and seek some solutions. At the end of the workshop periods, librarians were sent to model libraries of similar size, generally located outside the South, to serve a four-week internship during which they could gain firsthand experiences that might be useful to them in their libraries. A number of libraries from mainstream America agreed to participate in the program. After the internship period ended, the librarian/interns as well as the host librarians were invited to an evaluation conference held in Atlanta to discuss the merits and weaknesses of the program. The general conclusion of the evaluation conference was that both programs were highly successful in providing opportunities for mutual benefits by intern and host librarian.

The Hill Family Foundation participated in the second workshop/internship program by supporting the inclusion of five additional persons in the Atlanta program. Internship programs for these participants were confined to Minnesota, at the request of the Foundation. At the end of the internship programs, financial grants were awarded to the participants' libraries for strenghtening the book collections.

With the initiation of the Ford workshop/internship program, the Ford Foundation simultaneously funded a scholarship program for black students at the Atlanta University School of Library Service. Each year for three years, twenty students were selected to receive scholarships for study toward a master's degree. At the end of their studies, the participants were expected to return to any of the black academic libraries for a period of two years. This program may be looked upon as a deliberate effort to strengthen library staffs in the black colleges by making it possible for students to obtain graduate degrees in library science.

Both the workshop/internship program and the scholarship program have provided immeasurable benefits to library personnel in these colleges.[3] The programs represent a significant effort by foundations to provide strength in an area where the need was great and where the results could be far-reaching.

A major technical service program for black academic libraries was established in Atlanta in 1969 with the support of the United Board for College Development. Prior to the establishment of the Cooperative College Library Center, the Board funded a feasibility study in which the investigators attempted to analyze the current selection practices of Miles, Oakwood, Stillman, Talladega, and Tougaloo colleges and Tuskegee Institute, in which it had an interest. Attempts also were made to develop criteria for determining the cost of technical processes in these libraries, to study plans for future processing procedures, and to identify solutions for problems of meeting processing requirements. Among other findings, the study revealed that

> all of the libraries need more funds than are now available to them in order to purchase the quantity of materials required. Their full-time non-professional and professional staffs would have to be increased substantially, and their facilities would have to be enlarged or rearranged to process materials more efficiently and cheaply.[40]

Now expanded to include twenty black colleges and equipped to accommodate even more, the Center has proved to be of tremendous benefit to black academic libraries through the provision of processing services. In many of these libraries, technical service staffs have been freed to perform other tasks, while in others it has been unnecessary to employ personnel normally required in their technical service areas.

The Center has been instrumental in obtaining funds under Title II-A, Higher Education Act, to strengthen collections in libraries of the consortium. In the fall of 1971, the Center affiliated with the Ohio College Library Center, Columbus, to provide a faster and more economical means of reproducing catalog cards, thereby enabling the Center to increase its processing output.

Activities to generate general library improvement programs have been undertaken by the Federal Council for Science and Technology, Committee on Scientific and Technical Information, Task Group on Library Programs, Subcommittee on Negro Research Libraries. Organized in February 1970, the Subcommittee has the following purposes: "To develop recommendations designed to improve communication, to stimulate cooperation and to foster joint planning and programs between Negro research libraries and Federal agencies and other research libraries."[41]

To achieve its purposes, the Subcommittee attempted to improve the awareness and utilization of information resources and educational technology as a means of enhancing instruction and research, to recommend to the Task Group on Library Programs federal information problems as they affect Negro research libraries, to communicate the needs and programs of Negro research libraries, and to provide a forum for communicating developments in the information community to Negro research libraries.

The Subcommittee encouraged the preparation of proposals for three projects, of which one has been funded, another has been funded in the planning stage, and a third is in negotiation. The AAMP program at North Carolina Central, which has been described, was funded in the summer of 1971. A second program, titled Black Libraries and Community Action Project and designed to strengthen and support projects between black academic libraries and their communities, was funded in the planning stage only by the Center for Advanced Study of Technology, United States International University, Corvallis, Oregon. The third project, Center for Afro-American Bibliography, has yet to be funded.

In 1972, the Subcommittee held conferences with COSATI, the Federal Library Panel, representatives of the Association of Research Libraries, the Association of College and Research Libraries, and the ALA Black Caucus in order to explore problems of black academic libraries generally, to discuss problems of black research libraries, and to seek solutions to these problems. As result of the conferences, members of the various committees who met with the Subcommittee have encouraged and stimulated their organizations to lend support to these libraries.

In the fall of 1969, the 3M Company, through the assistance of the United Negro College Fund, made equipment and materials grants available to UNCF member libraries. The grants included a microfilm library of materials in black studies selected from the Schomburg Collection of the New York Public Library. Two microfilm reader-printers and sufficient software for a three-year period comprised a part of the grant.

According to the 3M Company, the purpose of this grant was to provide for the UNCF libraries a rich collection of materials which their faculties might use to develop or to strengthen instructional programs in black studies. Innovative teaching methods were stressed through the provision of materials on film and the necessary apparatus for their use.

While the microfilm materials obviously strengthened areas in the collection, the microfilm reader-printers were of great benefit to the libraries when used with other materials on film. Prior to receipt of this grant, many of the libraries were using old, outmoded equipment which discouraged the study of microfilmed materials. When questioned about the benefits of this grant, most librarians reported heavy use of the new microfilm collection and noted the usefulness of the new machinery in conjunction with their existing materials on film.

Organized in the fall of 1971, the United Negro College Fund Steering Committee on Library Development devotes its efforts to assessing the problems and needs of libraries in UNCF member institutions and to developing proposals to meet these needs. Initial attention was given to assisting those libraries that fall considerably below ALA standards for the size of collections through a program titled "Project Catch-up." Beyond this work, the Committee envisions preparing proposals seeking funds to enrich and greatly strengthen resources, facilities, and services in all UNCF libraries. In addition, the Committee advises UNCF program officers on matters directly affecting libraries in these institutions.

SUMMARY

Between 1917 and 1971, studies and research findings relating to black academic libraries have been made available through three major surveys that appeared between 1917 and 1942, a number of smaller studies, and more recently, surveys conducted between 1965 and 1970. Although varying in depth, the studies generally agree that in the history of black academic institutions, their libraries have consistently remained below minimum standards. Each study reported growth, development, and improvement; yet they agreed that these libraries have not reached the status that they need to achieve in order to support the instructional and research purposes of their institutions. Further, the studies generally suggest that substantial funds are needed to enable these libraries to overcome their deficiences.

Improvement programs for black academic libraries, whether for the benefit of individual libraries or groups of libraries, have been and continue to be numerous. No previous attempt has been made to record these activities or to measure their success. There is an immediate need for a clearinghouse which would record these activities, classify them, and attempt to disseminate information about black academic libraries to foundations, to other agencies, and to the black institutions themselves.

The present study will suggest other areas in which improvement programs may be needed in black academic libraries. This step is possible only after careful study has been made of the data obtained for the study.

NOTES

1. U.S., Department of the Interior, Bureau of Education, *Negro Education: A Study of the Private and Higher Schools for Colored People in the United States*, vols. 1 and 2, Bulletin 1916, nos. 38-39 (Washington, D.C.: Government Printing Office, 1917).

2. Ibid., vol. 1, p. 173.

3. Ibid.

4. U.S., Department of the Interior, Bureau of Education, *Survey of Negro Colleges and Universities,* sections of Bulletin 1928, no. 7 (Washington, D.C.: Government Printing Office, 1928), chaps. 1-3.

5. Ibid., p. 46.

6. Ibid., p. 47.

7. Ibid.

8. U.S., Office of Education, Federal Security Agency, *National Survey of the Higher Education of Negroes,* vols. 2-4, misc. no. 6 (Washington, D.C.: Government Printing Office, 1942).

9. Ibid., vol. 2, p. 105.

10. Ibid., p. 96.

11. Ibid., p. 106.

12. Ibid.

13. Ibid.

14. Albert P. Marshall, "Professional Needs in Negro Colleges," *College and Research Libraries* 13 (January 1952), p. 37.

15. Earl J. McGrath, *The Predominantly Negro Colleges and Universities in Transition* (New York: Bureau of Publications, Teachers College, Columbia University, 1965).

16. Ibid., p. 128.

17. Ibid., p. 130.

18. Ibid., p. 136.

19. Commission on Higher Educational Opportunity in the South, *The Negro and Higher Education in the South* (Atlanta: Southern Regional Education Board, 1967), p. 16.

(September 1969), pp. 3019-69.

21. The United Negro College Fund, founded in 1940, is a group of accredited, four-year, privately supported institutions which united to engage in joint fund-raising activities.

22. Herman L. Totten, "They Had a Dream: Black Colleges and Library Standards," *Wilson Library Bulletin* 44 (September 1969), pp. 75-79.

23. The Office for Advancement of Public Negro Colleges reduced its count of public black colleges to thirty-three when, on July 1, 1970,. Maryland State College in Princess Anne officially became the University of Maryland, Eastern Shore, and thus a branch of the state university system. Office for Advancement of Public Negro Colleges, *Advancement Newsletter* 2, no. 6 (Atlanta: Office for Advancement of Public Negro Colleges, July 1970), p. 6.

OAPNC subsequently issued a document which substantially updates the 1970 report and reflects trends and emerging developments in the historically black public colleges and universities. The total number of OAPNC institutions has increased again to thirty-four and includes three institutions within the Southern University System. These are the campuses at Baton Rouge, New Orleans, and Shreveport. Although the University of Arkansas at Pine Bluff is included, data on the University of Maryland, Eastern Shore, is omitted from the study because it is no longer an

OAPNC-affiliated institution. Office for Advancement of Public Negro Colleges, *A Contemporary Status Report of the Libraries of Historically Black Public Colleges and Universities,* compiled by the Office for Advancement of Public Negro Colleges, a division of the National Association of State Universities and Land-Grant Colleges, in cooperation with the American Association of State Colleges and Universities (Atlanta, September 20, 1976).

In the present report, Maryland State continues to be considered a black college because the study was conducted prior to the change in designation. The report will also refer to Arkansas A M & N rather than the University of Arkansas at Pine Bluff.

24. *Advancement Newsletter,* pp. 2-5.

25. Reference is made here to Howard University, which is privately controlled rather than privately supported. Howard receives a large percentage of its support from the federal government.

26. Casper LeRoy Jordan, "Black Academic Libraries: An Inventory," Occasional Papers no. 1 (Atlanta: Atlanta University, November 1970), p. 11.

27. Ibid., p. 30.

28. Southern Association of Colleges and Schools, *Black Colleges in the South: From Tragedy to Promise; An Historical and Statistical Review by the Commission on Colleges* (Atlanta: Southern Association of Colleges and Schools, 1971).

29. Additional studies, reference items, statistical accounts, and other reports have been completed or are in preparation and will give current data of this nature.

30. General Education Board, *Annual Report* (New York: General Education Board, 1929), p. 80.

31. *Materials by and about American Negroes,* papers presented at an institute sponsored by the Atlanta University School of Library Service with the cooperation of the Trevor Arnett Library, October 21-23, 1965, ed. and with an introduction by Annette Hoage Phinazee (Atlanta: Atlanta University, School of Library Service, 1967).

32. Ibid., pp. vi-vii.

33. Dorothy B. Porter, *The Negro in the United States: A Working Bibliography* (Ann Arbor: University Microfilms, 1969).

34. Since this study was undertaken, the Amistad Research Center at Dillard University has received a grant from the Ford Foundation to process its archival collection.

35. CEMBA *Newsletter,* "Collection and Evaluation of Materials about Black Americans; A Program of the Alabama Center for Higher Education," vol. 1, no. 1 (Normal, Alabama: January 26, 1971), p. 1.

36. A variety of institutes in black studies librarianship have been held at Fisk and at other black institutions since this study was completed.

37. These publications include Ann A. Shockley, *A Handbook for the Administration of Special Black Collections,* rev. and enl., prepared for the Institute in Black Studies Librarianship (Nashville: Fisk University Library, 1971); L. M. Collins, *Books by Black Americans,* prepared for the Institute on the Selection, Organization and Use of Materials by and about the Negro (Nashville: Fisk University Library, 1971); Jean Elder Cazort, *A Handbook for the Organization of Black Materials,* prepared for the Institute on the Selection, Organization and Use of Materials by and about the Negro (Nashville: Fisk University Library, 1971); Jessie Carney Smith, *A Hand-*

book for the Study of Black Bibliography, prepared for the Institute in Black Studies Librarianship (Nashville: Fisk University Library, 1971).

38. North Carolina Central University, Durham, African-American Materials Project, *News Feature* (Durham, August 1971). The pre-1950 imprints list was compiled by Geraldine O. Matthews and published under the title *Black American Writers, 1733-1949: A Bibliography and Union List* (Boston: G. K. Hall and Company, 1975).

39. In 1974, the Association of College and Research Libraries of the American Library Association announced an internship program for administrators in predominantly black college libraries. Funded through a grant from the Andrew W. Mellon Foundation and administered through Atlanta University, the three-year program attempts to accelerate the development of management abilities of librarians in black colleges, whether or not these librarians are in top management positions. For a period of nine months, interns are provided with experience in the management of strong and progressive academic libraries throughout the country. Several black librarians have participated in the program or are currently serving as interns.

Though not specifically designed for black librarians or black colleges, the Council on Library Resources now offers an internship for "mid-career librarians of exceptional management potential" titled Academic Library Management Intern Program. This program also has immediate potential benefit for black librarians.

Since the study was completed, other conferences and improvement programs have been directed toward black librarians or librarians in black academic institutions. Included are a colloquium on the Southeastern Black Librarian, sponsored by the School of Library Science, North Carolina Central University, and the Lawrence Livermore On-Line Information Retrieval Workshop, jointly sponsored by the Lawrence Livermore Laboratory and the Atlanta University School of Library Service.

40. Annette Hoage Phinazee and Casper L. Jordan, "Centralized Library Purchasing and Technical Processing for Six Colleges in Alabama and Mississippi: A Report," *College and Research Libraries* 30 (July 1969), p. 370.

41. Federal Council for Science and Technology, Committee on Scientific and Technical Information, Task Group on Library Programs, Subcommittee on Negro Research Libraries, *Proceedings of the First Conference* (Washington, D.C.: Subcommittee on Negro Research Libraries, February 1970), n.p.

4

Libraries in
the Black College

Library evaluation, particularly where groups of libraries are concerned, is difficult and sometimes contributes to misleading conclusions. Each library should be studied in terms of its relationship to its own institution, for it was created and exists to serve a particular educational program. The library may also be examined in terms of its relationship to libraries in institutions of similar size. Library standards have been created to provide guidelines for evaluation in an effort to measure the effectiveness of library programs, both as the library attempts to assess itself against the standards and as it assesses itself against other libraries. It is toward the application of these standards to library evaluation that library studies generally, and to some extent, this study, are directed.[1]

As was pointed out in Chapter 3, early studies of black academic institutions recognized the importance of assessing the status of libraries in these institutions. Organized philanthropy, also discussed in Chapter 3, did not disregard libraries. Indeed, it was through philanthropic support that many libraries in black academic institutions were promoted. This chapter is concerned primarily with the present status of library facilities, resources, and services. It will examine the backgrounds in which these libraries were developed; study their administrative structure; evaluate their facilities, services, and programs; review their economics; and make some projections regarding their development in the future.

Many librarians and other educators will argue that statistical data on libraries should be measured against that given in *Library Statistics of Col-*

leges and Universities (published annually or, in part, biennially by the United States Office of Education), in order to determine how individual libraries or groups of libraries compare to other libraries in institutions of similar size or characteristics. For example, the *Analytic Report* shows median operating expenditures, median total library staff (FTE), library expenditures as a percentage of total expenditures for educational and general purposes, and other data by type of institution (public or private) as well as by size and by degree-granting level (baccalaureate or graduate).

It is unnecessary to repeat this evaluation procedure where the black college libraries are concerned primarily because the Jordan study, cited in Chapter 3, provides this information. Consequently, the present study utilizes other approaches to evaluating black college libraries, including comparing them to each other and measuring them against standards of the American Library Association. Institutions in this study are generally identified as publicly or privately supported, which also facilitates comparisons by type of institution.

Attention must also be given to the geographical location of the black institutions. Situated primarily in the South, these schools must be given consideration based on the extent of their isolation from other institutions Especially in times of rigid segregation practices, students in the black colleges were restricted to the use of their own libraries and were unable to look toward libraries in neighboring white institutions to help meet their needs.

Slightly more than one-fourth of the black colleges are located in areas where no neighboring library of notable size is immediately available. Thus their collections are expected to serve nearly all of the students' educational and cultural requirements. Six of the black colleges are located in somewhat isolated areas yet have a neighboring black institution which may offer reciprocal arrangements in meeting faculty and student needs. These paired institutions are Central State and Wilberforce, in Wilberforce, Ohio; Rust and Mississippi Industrial, in Holly Springs; and South Carolina State and Claflin, in Orangeburg.

EARLY DEVELOPMENT

The early history of black academic libraries is frequently unavailable because early record-keeping practices were poor or because records were destroyed during the passing years. Findings show that the oldest library in the group examined for this study was founded at Virginia Union University in 1865, the year in which the university was established. The newest library in the group was that of Southern University, New Orleans, founded when the college was established in 1959.

Table 1 shows twenty libraries which were established prior to 1900. In addition to Virginia Union, libraries at Fisk, Barber-Scotia, Clark, Philander Smith, Tuskegee, Wilberforce, Virginia State, West Virginia State, and Voorhees were established at the same time their institutions were founded. With the exception of three institutions—Virginia State, West Virginia State, and North Carolina A & T—all of these libraries were in privately supported institutions.

Reports from the various libraries reveal interesting histories of their development. Florida A & M reported that prior to 1908, library resources were meager at what was then known as Florida State Normal and Indus-

TABLE 1

Black Academic Libraries Founded Prior to 1900

Date of Library Founding	Date of Institution Founding	Institution
1865	1865	Virginia Union
1866	1866	Fisk
1867	1867	Barber-Scotia
1869	1869	Clark
1870	1868	Hampton
1870	1865	Atlanta
1874	1869	Talladega
1876	1875	Knoxville
1877	1877	Philander Smith
1881	1881	Tuskegee
1882	1882	Virginia State
1883	1879	Livingstone
1887	1887	*Wilberforce/Central State
1891	1891	West Virginia State
1893	1890	North Carolina A & T
1896	1867	St. Augustine
1897	1873	Wiley
1897	1897	Voorhees
1898	1869	Claflin
1898	1854	Lincoln (Pa.)

*A separation in elements of Wilberforce University in 1947 resulted in the founding of Central State University.

trial School. This collection was destroyed by fire in 1905. Andrew Carnegie contributed $10,000 for the construction of a new library facility, which opened for service in 1908.

Prior to the merger of Sam Huston and Tillotson colleges, each maintained a small library collection. The Tillotson library was begun about 1909 and consisted mainly of donated literary works and a few reference books. Sam Huston College had much the same kind of beginning in the early 1920s. The two colleges developed their libraries to an acceptable level, and as a result, each received accreditation by the Southern Association of Colleges and Schools prior to the merger of the two institutions in 1952.

Faculty offices at Fisk University housed the very early library collections until the erection of Jubilee Hall in 1876. In that year, the library occupied an "apartment" in the new structure. Library buildings which also served other purposes were erected in 1908 and again in 1930, each making provisions for special black collections.

The building which presently houses the library at Virginia Union was the Belgian Exhibition Hall at the 1939 World's Fair. It was subsequently dismantled and shipped to the Union campus. In 1948, the library moved into the relocated and renovated structure.

Talladega opened its library in 1874 with 300 volumes. At that time, the library was located in a building which was purchased by the American Missionary Association in 1867 to house the entire college.

At St. Augustine's College, the Benson Library building was made possible through a gift of $1,600 from Mary Benson of Brooklyn, New York, in 1896. Construction was done primarily by members of the masonry class.

Prior to 1937, the book collection at North Carolina Central was housed in the administration building and was maintained by teachers during their "free" hours.

Livingstone reported a library collection of 3,000 volumes in 1884-85. A central library was established in 1890 by several donors, who also provided a new collection of books. Booker T. Washington, along with the college president and the bishop of the A. M. E. Zion church, appealed to Andrew Carnegie for funds to construct the first building. The structure was completed in 1908.

Other libraries reported that their collections were housed in basements, old gymnasiums, old hospitals, dormitories, and various other places prior to their removal to new library buildings, or to ones allocated to serve that purpose.

It is difficult to determine historical patterns regarding the establishment of libraries in the black institutions. It is reasonable to say, however, that a handful of institutions began their libraries on or near the date of their own establishment. This pattern was true in the 1800s and even into the 1900s, when Bethune-Cookman, Texas Southern, and Mississippi Valley were founded. These three institutions also began their libraries with the founding of the institution.

PRESENT STATUS

Administration and Evaluation

Library administration was centralized in each of the institutions examined, with a single head librarian having full responsibility for library operations and activities. Some of these responsibilities were frequently shared with associate or assistant librarians.

Librarians in the sixty-five institutions were directly responsible to deans, to vice-presidents, or to presidents of the institutions. Thirty-eight of the librarians were responsible to deans, including the dean of academic affairs, the dean of the college, the academic dean, the dean of instruction, and the dean of the faculty. Thirteen librarians were responsible to vice-presidents, while fourteen were responsible to presidents. No problems in these administrative organizations were reported.

Library committees were found to exist in each of the institutions, although some librarians reported that these committees were less active than they should be or that such committees were being reorganized to assist in preparing for a self-study. Fifty-six reported that the composition of the committee included students, while eight reported that no students served on the committee. Generally, reports indicated that these committees, when functioning, served in an advisory capacity to the librarian. In no case did they engage in policy-making activities.

The committee generally included representatives from each academic division or, in some cases, from each academic department. The head librarian, and frequently another member of the staff, served on the committee. Composition of the committee was determined by various methods: eighteen were appointed by the president, two by the president and the

dean, two by the vice-president, eight by the dean, three were elected by
the faculty, three were elected or appointed by the committee on committees, five were elected or selected by academic departments or academic divisions, one was appointed by the administration and the faculty sen-
ate, and two were elected or appointed by the faculty committee. Three
libraries indicated that members of their library committees were selected
by the administration. Eighteen respondents failed to indicate methods by
which their committees were formed. In the case of student members, ten
indicated that members were selected or appointed by the student government association, while one indicated that students were selected by the
student union.

An interesting method of selection was reported by Atlanta University,
which is omitted from the preceding grouping. At Atlanta, all head librarians in the University Center, which includes Atlanta University, Morehouse College, Spelman College, Morris Brown College, and Clark College,
were automatically members of the library committee. Each institution
was invited to send one additional representative.

Written policies governing library administration were available in twenty
four of the sixty-five institutions. Such policy statements as were sub-
mitted by librarians for review in connection with the study were in the
form of library handbooks. They served to introduce policies to library
personnel, including student assistants.

External evaluations were reported by fifty-nine of the sixty-five libraries. One indicated that it was evaluated in 1958, two in 1960, one in 1961,
one in 1962, one in 1964, two in 1965, three in 1966, five in 1967, ten in
1968, fifteen in 1969, fourteen in 1970, and four in 1971. Six of the libraries had not been involved in evaluative activities.

Fifty-seven of these libraries were subject to evaluation by the Southern
Association of Colleges and Schools. The Association has attempted to encourage black institutions in the South to strive toward accreditation. As
a result, the institutions have been required to conduct self-studies. It is
for this reason primarily that their libraries have undergone self-evaluation
in recent years. Prior to these evaluation visits by the Southern Association,
many of the institutions were unaccredited.

Personnel

Patterns of personnel development in the libraries differed, and positions varied in title as well as in number. Table 2 shows the types of pro-

fessional personnel employed in sixty-five historically black colleges as of September 1, 1969, and further indicates the total numbers of such persons employed. As the table shows, a variety of classifications were assigned to personnel in the libraries reporting. Because the definitions and descriptions of such positions as Assistant Librarian and Assistant Librarian for Readers' Services were unclear, both classifications are included in the chart. Such positions as Catalog Librarian and Assistant Catalog Librarian are grouped under the classification of Catalog Librarian.

TABLE 2
**Professional Positions Filled or
Budgeted in Black College Libraries,
September 1, 1969**

Position	Filled	Budgeted/ Unfilled	Total
Director/Head Librarian	33	2	35
Acting Director/Head	4		4
Assistant Director	3	2	5
Associate Librarian	6		6
Assistant Librarian	11		11
Assistant Librarian or Head of Readers' (Public) Services	2	1	3
Head of Technical Services	6	3	9
Readers' Services Librarian	4	1	5
Technical Services Librarian	4		4
Reference Librarian	22	6	28
Circulation Librarian	9	1	10
Catalog Librarian	26	11	37
Acquisitions	10	7	17
Periodicals	7	5	12
Serials	2	1	3
Archivist	1		1
Special Collections	1		1
Documents	2		2
Coordinator	1		1
Curriculum Librarian	2		2
Division of General Studies	1		1
Education	3		3
Liberal Arts	1		1
Reported but undefined	140	14	154
TOTAL	301	54	355
Total institutions reporting but unclassifiable	3		

Analysis of the chart shows that 301 professional positions were filled
in libraries in institutions reporting such statistics. In terms of positions
budgeted but unfilled in the year in question, thirty-seven libraries had
fifty-three budgeted vacancies. Twenty-four of these vacancies were in
privately supported institutions, while twenty-nine were in the publicly
supported institutions. One position of Library Director or Head Librarian was vacant in each type of institution.

The institutions reported a total of 229 subprofessional positions and
221 clerical staff members as of September 1, 1969. Privately supported
institutions reported 73 subprofessional and 89 clerical positions, with
libraries in nine privately supported institutions reporting that they had
no subprofessional positions. Publicly supported institutions reported
153 subprofessional and 132 clerical positions, with libraries in two publicly supported institutions reporting no subprofessional positions.

With 301 professional staff members and 450 subprofessional and
clerical staff members employed in the sixty-two libraries responding to
these questions, an overall ratio of 1.49 nonprofessional to professional
staff members is obtained. Table 3 shows the professional, subprofessional, and clerical positions in thirty-seven privately supported institutions
and gives the ratio of nonprofessional to professional positions. Table 4
gives the same information for twenty-seven publicly supported institutions. ALA standards state that the ratio of professional to nonprofessional staff persons varies according to the needs of the institutions; yet
professional staff should avoid assignments that are essentially clerical
in nature. The standards further state that as the library increases in size,
the ratio of nonprofessional to professional staff persons should increase.
The reporting libraries indicated that they preferred a ratio of two nonprofessional staff persons for each professional staff member. Tables 3
and 4 show that only seventeen of the libraries reporting have achieved
this ratio—eight in privately supported institutions and nine in publicly supported institutions.

Baumol and Marcus have reported regression equations for the size
of the professional staffs and for the size of the total staffs of libraries
in several classes of colleges and universities.[2] The Baumol-Marcus equations have been employed here to study the staff sizes of some libraries
included in this survey. All institutions which reported the number of
independent variables required by the regression equations have been
included. Tables 5 and 6 give the results of these calculations along with
the actual staff size reported by the institutions. The calculated values

TABLE 3
Ratio of Clerical to Professional Staff in Thirty-Seven Privately Supported Black College Libraries, September 1, 1969

Institution	Profes-sional	Subpro-fessional	Clerical	Ratio of Sub-professional and Clerical
Atlanta	10	2	4	.60
Barber-Scotia	2		1	.50
Benedict	6	4		.66
Bethune-Cookman	1	1	1	2.0
Bishop	6	5	4	1.5
Claflin	2	3	2	2.5
Clark	2	1		.50
Dillard		1	1	
Fisk	9	1	9	1.1
Florida Memorial	3	2	1	1.0
Hampton	5		10	2.0
Huston-Tillotson	4	2	1	.75
Jarvis Christian	4	2	2	1.0
Johnson C. Smith	3	7	1	2.6
Knoxville	4	2	2	1.0
Lane	3		4	1.3
LeMoyne-Owen	2	1	2	1.5
Lincoln (Pa.)	9	1	1	.22
Livingstone	4	1		.25
Morris	1	3		3.0
Morris Brown	3	2	1	1.0
Oakwood	2		1	.50
Paine	4		1	.25
Paul Quinn	3	2	1	1.0
Philander Smith	2	1	1	1.0
St. Augustine	4	3	1	1.0
Shaw	3	4	7	3.6
Simmons	2			
Stillman	2		2	1.0
Talladega	3		2	.66
Texas College	4	1	2	.75
Tougaloo	3	2	4	2.0
Tuskegee	8	9	3	1.5
Virginia Union	2.6	2	1	1.1
Voorhees	4	1		2.5
Wilberforce	3	3	2	1.6
Wiley	4	3	2	1.2
Xavier	7	1	5	.85
TOTAL	143.6	73	82	

TABLE 4

Ratio of Clerical to Professional Staff in Twenty-Six Publicly Supported Black College Libraries, September 1, 1969

Institution	Professional	Subprofessional	Clerical	Ratio of Subprofessional and Clerical
Alabama A & M	6	3	8	1.8
Alabama State	4	7	3	2.5
Alcorn	5	7	4	2.2
Arkansas A M & N	3	4	4	2.6
Central State	6	6	4	1.6
Cheyney	4	6	1	1.7
Elizabeth City	3	2	3	1.6
Fayetteville	4	2	5	1.7
Florida A & M	15	17		1.1
Fort Valley	5	6	4	2.0
Grambling	9	7	3	1.1
Jackson State	9	9	11	2.2
Kentucky State	3	4	4	2.6
Langston	2	4	1	2.5
Lincoln (Mo.)	5		5	1.0
Mississippi Valley	9	6	4	2.2
Norfolk State	6	3	7	1.6
North Carolina A & T	9	13	4	1.8
North Carolina Central	16	9	5	.87
Prairie View			2	
South Carolina State	7	2	2	.57
Southern	12	7	4	.91
Southern Univ. N. O.		4	3	
Texas Southern	7	9	18	3.8
West Virginia State	6	2	2	.66
Winston-Salem	5	8	2	2.0
TOTAL	168	153	132	

are not to be considered recommended values for the libraries under study. They should, however, serve as guidelines for the libraries in evaluating the nature and number of programs which they offer and the staffing level of those programs.

The adequacy of library staffs as indicated by the educational backgrounds and experiences of staff members was reported by the respondents. Three of the head librarians hold doctorate degrees, fifty-six hold

TABLE 5

**Staffing Levels of Libraries in Selected Public
Institutions: Actual Versus Baumol and Marcus Model**

Institution	Professional Staff *Actual Model*		Total Staff *Actual Model*	
Alabama A & M	6	5	17	14
Alabama State	4	5	14	14
Alcorn	5	4	16	15
Central State	1	9	16	22
Florida A & M	15	12	32	36
Fort Valley	5	4	15	15
Grambling	9	9	19	22
Kentucky State	3	4	11	16
Langston	2	5	7	14
Lincoln (Mo.)	5	5	10	14
North Carolina A & T	9	15	26	59
North Carolina Central	16	12	30	43
South Carolina State	7	5	11	14
Texas Southern	7	12	34	38
West Virginia State	6	9	10	23
Winston-Salem	5	4	15	15

TABLE 6

**Staffing Levels of Libraries in Selected Private
Institutions: Actual Versus Baumol and Marcus Model**

Institution	Professional Staff *Actual Model*		Total Staff *Actual Model*	
Benedict	6	5	10	14
Fisk	9	9	19	30
Hampton	5	9	15	33
Lane	3	5	7	13
St. Augustine	4	4	8	13
Tuskegee	8	12	20	47
Virginia Union	3	6	6	18
Xavier	7	7	13	22

master's degrees, one holds the ALA (London), and five hold bachelor's degrees in library science as their highest degree.[3] Two librarians who hold the doctorate were employed by private institutions and one by a public institution.

Inquiry was made to determine which library schools were attended by library staff members in these institutions and to determine whether or not these librarians tended to study in a particular geographical area. Table 7 gives a list of library schools attended by one or more librarians, although it fails to indicate the actual number of persons from each library who attended a particular school. Responses to this section of the questionnaire do not permit meaningful interpretations and conclusions, but they do suggest that additional research in this area is needed.

TABLE 7

Library Schools Attended by Personnel in Black Colleges, September 1, 1969

Library School	Number of Colleges Represented
Atlanta	61
Berkeley	1
Case Western Reserve	12
Catholic University	2
Chicago	4
Columbia	10
Denver	6
Drexel	2
East Texas State	4
Emory	1
Florida State	4
*Hampton	11
Hawaii	1
Illinois	10
Indiana	7
Kansas State	2
Kent State	1
Kentucky	1
Louisiana State	6
Michigan	9
North Carolina, Chapel Hill	5
North Carolina Central	15
North Texas State	2
Oklahoma	7
Peabody	5
Pittsburgh	3
Pratt	2
Rosary	2

TABLE 7 (continued)

Library School	Number of Colleges Represented
Rutgers	11
Simmons	3
Syracuse	13
Texas (Univ. of)	1
Texas Women's Univ.	2
UCLA	1
Villanova	2
Wayne State	1
Western Michigan	3
Western Ontario	1
Wisconsin	4
Others	
Brighton School of Librarianship	1
Nazareth College	1

NOTE: *Figures represent the number of libraries reporting under each library school rather than the actual number of staff in attendance.*
*No longer maintains a library school

In addition to formal training, library staff members have a professional obligation to attend workshops and other training programs to promote growth and to keep pace with advances in librarianship. In this connection, types of inservice-training programs, workshops, and similar activities in which library staffs in the black colleges have participated were identified. These included MARC workshops, the Workshop on Conversion of Classification Systems and Improvement of Library Personnel Utilization for Academic Libraries, the Workshop on Computer Technology, Atlanta University workshops and internship programs for librarians in black colleges, library buildings institutes, and the Conference on Afro-American Studies. These workshops attended by library staffs were listed in a predominant number of the reports, although several other professional conferences were attended by a smaller proportion of the librarians reporting. A total of fifty-two libraries, or 80 percent of all libraries included in the study, indicated that members of their staffs participated at inservice meetings, workshops, internships, and similar activities.

The institutions have provided some support for those librarians who wished to attend workshops and other professional meetings. Table 8 shows travel support given to librarians during the period of this study.

It is evident that a large number of institutions provide no travel support for librarians.

The study revealed that the length of the work week for librarians in the black colleges varied from a minimum of thirty-five hours per week to a maximum of forty hours per week. Thirty, or 49.1 percent, of the sixty-one respondents reported that professional personnel worked forty hours. Three libraries reported data unsuitable for tabulation.

Clerical persons in these libraries worked a maximum of forty hours per week and a minimum of thirty-five hours, with an average work week of 37.5 hours. Thirty-seven, or 60.6 percent, of the sixty-one respondents reported that the work week for professional and clerical personnel was the same.

TABLE 8

Expenditures for Travel in Certain Black
College Libraries, 1964-65 Through 1968-69

Institution	1964-65	1965-66	1966-67	1967-68	1968-69
Alabama A & M*					$600
Alabama State*	$325	$250	$600	$400	450
Alcorn*					
Arkansas A M & N*	23	95	318		163
Atlanta**	223	378	564	203	624
Barber-Scotia**					
Benedict**	500	250	500	946	606
Bishop**					
Central State*					
Cheyney*					
Claflin**	235	3		61	222
Clark**					
Dillard**		350	350	350	350
Elizabeth City*					
Fayetteville*					
Fisk**	208		522	211	744
Florida A & M*	434	402	492	492	500
Florida Memorial**					
Fort Valley*					
Grambling*	400	300	475	200	200
Hampton**					
Huston-Tillotson**		50			
Jackson State*					
Jarvis Christian**			655	500	
Johnson C. Smith**	52	25	196	83	29

TABLE 8 (continued)

Institution	1964-65	1965-66	1966-67	1967-68	1968-69
Kentucky State*	335	288	300	400	400
Knoxville**	250	250	300	300	300
Lane**					
Langston*	200	400	300	500	
LeMoyne-Owen**					
Lincoln (Mo.)*	475	425	500	400	400
Lincoln (Pa.)**	1,209	989	1,332	2,088	1,695
Livingstone**	180	172	48	2	15
Miss. Valley*				134	547
Morris**					
Morris Brown**		194		150	
Norfolk*					
North Carolina A & T*					
North Carolina Central*	193				
Oakwood**					
Paine**					
Paul Quinn**					
Philander Smith**					
Prairie View*					
St. Augustine**			107	82	275
Shaw**					
Simmons**					
South Carolina State*					
Southern*					
Southern Univ. N. O.*			143		
Stillman**					
Talladega**					
Texas College**					
Texas Southern*	300	500	500	1,000	1,050
Tougaloo**					
Tuskegee**	1,200	1,200	2,400	2,400	2,400
Virginia State*					
Virginia Union**	218	21	192	183	227
Voorhees**					
West Virginia State*					
Wilberforce**					
Wiley**	300	476	777		1,209
Winston-Salem*				400	400
Xavier**	225	153	75	120	69

*public.
**private.

As the study attempted to evaluate the current adequacy of library personnel in terms of staff size, ratio of clerical to professional staff, and educational qualifications, it also sought to determine the personnel needs for the next five years as perceived by the librarians in the black college libraries. Findings showed that in terms of professional personnel, the reported maximum number needed in a single library was 26, while the minimum number was 1. A total of 318 professional staff persons was reported as being needed. Three libraries reported no additional personnel requirements.

The number of clerical personnel reported as being required during the next five years makes for an interesting comparison. The maximum number reported by a library was 58, while the minimum number reported was 1. A total of 521 such persons was reported. One library listed no additional clerical personnel requirements during the period in question. As was pointed out previously, only seventeen libraries in the survey met their expressed needs in terms of the two to one ratio of clerical to professional staff. According to the forecasts by the libraries, this ratio of clerical to professional personnel will not be achieved during the next five years.

As a means of easing their personnel requirements, the libraries responding indicated that they made heavy use of student employees. However, much of the student employment was provided in order to give financial support to needy persons who sought a means of meeting the cost of their education. Fifty-five libraries responded to the question concerning the number of hours of student assistance and reported a total of 827,555 hours, or an average of 15,046 hours per library, the equivalent of approximately eight staff positions. The highest number of student assistance hours reported totaled 56,841, while the lowest was 32.

The question of academic status and/or faculty rank has been a pressing issue in the black libraries. Of the sixty-five libraries, seventeen reported that only the head librarian received academic status. In forty-five, or 67.2 percent of the libraries, academic status was provided for all librarians. Four, or 6.1 percent, of the respondents indicated that such status was unavailable to all members of their professional staffs.

One measure of the academic status available to librarians is the privilege of voting in faculty meetings. Fifty-three, or 81.5 percent, of the libraries reported that all members of the professional staff were afforded this privilege; ten, or 15.3 percent, reported that the privilege was limited to the head librarian; and two, or 3 percent, reported that no members of the professional staff were eligible to vote in faculty meetings.

Forty-one, or 63 percent, of the libraries reported that all professional staff were entitled to tenure; ten, or 15.3 percent, reported that only the head librarian was so entitled; and fourteen, or 21.5 percent, reported that tenure was unavailable to all members of the professional staff.

The majority of the libraries—fifty-three, or 81.5 percent—reported that all of their professional staff members were eligible to sit on various faculty committees. Eight, or 12.3 percent, reported that only the head librarian served on such committees; and four, or 6.1 percent, reported that none of their librarians were eligible for such committees. Perhaps the most important committee on which the head librarian or members of the library professional staff serve is the curriculum committee. New curricular programs and long-range educational goals are generally introduced to this committee, and it is necessary that library staffs be aware of these new programs as they attempt to develop collections and services. In twenty-eight, or 43 percent of the institutions reporting, only the head librarian served on the curriculum committee. Twenty-five, or 38.4 percent, of the libraries reported that all members of the professional staff were eligible to serve on the curriculum committee, while twelve, or 18.4 percent, of the libraries reported that no members of the professional staff were eligible.

Faculty rank seemed somewhat less easily attainable than academic status in these libraries. Fifteen, or 23 percent, of the sixty-five libraries reported that faculty rank was available to the head librarian only; thirty-five, or 53.8 percent, reported that such rank was available to all librarians; and fifteen, or 23 percent, reported that faculty rank was unavailable to their professional staffs.

Salary data on professional, subprofessional, and clerical personnel were reported for both publicly and privately supported institutions; yet in most instances, publication of the data was restricted.[4]

Of primary importance in recruiting and retaining well-qualified staff is the provision of adequate salaries as well as the provision of various benefits. Tables 9 and 10 show salaries of professional, subprofessional, and clerical personnel in both publicly and privately supported institutions reporting in the study. Analysis of the tables indicates that the highest salary paid to a library director as of the fall of 1969 was $21,500

TABLE 9

Salaries of Personnel in Certain Privately
Supported Black Colleges, September 1, 1969

		SALARIES			
Direc-tor	Assistant Director	Department Head	Other Librarians	Subpro-fessional	Clerical
$ 8,000*	$ 9,600*				$4,036
9,000	8,500	$ 8,500*	$ 5,500*	$5,000	
12,000	11,000	9,000	8,000		
13,590	10,000	10,650	9,900	7,500	4,200
9,500	8,000	7,500			8,400
7,900*	7,400*				
12,083		10,500	8,000	6,000	4,233
12,000	9,000	7,875	6,600	7,100	5,700
11,700		10,250	8,200		4,750
11,300	9,600		8,400	5,400	5,400
8,600	7,000	4,500	3,600	4,500	3,600
12,300	9,000	8,000		5,000	3,800
9,000	7,000	7,000			6,800
9,200	7,600		6,500		3,000
7,600		8,600	6,000	5,800	3,600
10,800	8,500		7,200	5,400	5,200
8,000				3,600	
7,500	6,500				4,888
10,500		8,500			3,600
9,000			7,000	5,000	4,000
7,500			7,300	5,000	
		6,700	6,500	5,200	4,000
11,910	12,000	9,500*	9,000*	6,900*	4,380
11,000	8,700*	9,900*	10,000*	9,100*	5,520
1,000†	1,000†				
9,000	8,500				3,400
7,800	7,000				3,600
9,000	6,500	4,500		3,600	3,600
8,160		8,160	7,440	6,600	
13,000		9,700	8,000	6,000	5,800
10,200	9,840	8,280		5,160	4,560
10,000	8,500		8,500	6,999	4,999
16,500	10,000	8,700	8,000	6,900	4,500
10,000	9,800	7,500	7,200	5,500	3,420

*Nine or ten months.
†Part-time only.

TABLE 10

Salaries of Personnel in Certain Publicly Supported Black Institutions, September 1, 1969

| | | SALARIES | | | |
Director	Assistant Director	Department Head	Other Librarians	Subprofessional	Clerical
$14,000		$10,200	$7,800	$5,200	$3,000
12,000		8,500	9,000	6,500	3,300
12,200		8,400	8,400	6,000	4,800
8,148			7,500	6,084	4,764
12,500	$ 9,156	9,450	9,450	5,990	4,368
13,000		12,000	8,500	5,785	4,992
11,000			8,800		
13,000		9,600	8,028	5,328	4,656
21,500	17,600	14,500	12,100	8,940	8,940
14,040		10,600	8,900	7,400	4,200
16,273	12,947	9,281	7,340	6,900	4,020
12,060	10,726	9,240	8,734	5,100	4,400
13,400		9,300	7,600	7,000	4,000
13,000			7,000	8,200	5,300
16,500	10,212	9,888	9,708		4,416
	9,500	8,800	8,400	6,800	4,800
			13,600	7,680	6,432
11,000		9,400	8,100	6,408	6,708
	9,744	9,644	9,216	6,120	6,120
14,160	15,000	9,840	8,400	8,040	4,740
12,300		8,500		4,786	5,000
14,500	10,800	8,267	7,420	6,200	4,420
12,240		15,840	11,760	7,032	5,880
14,364		10,572		8,160	4,944
12,400		8,800		5,328	4,872

for eleven to twelve months, while the lowest for that period was $7,500. The highest salary for a library director employed for nine to ten months was $11,910, while the lowest was $7,500.

Salaries paid to assistant directors varied from a high of $17,600 for eleven to twelve months to a low of $6,500. The highest salary paid to assistant directors employed on a nine- to ten-month basis was $9,840, with a low of $7,000.

Department heads employed on an eleven- to twelve-month basis received a high salary of $15,840 and a low salary of $4,500. Those employed on a nine-to ten-month basis received a high salary of $9,900 and a low of $6,700.

Respondents were requested to indicate the highest salary paid to all other librarians employed on an eleven- to twelve-month basis. The findings showed a high salary of $13,640, with a low of $3,600. Those employed on a nine- to ten-month basis received a high salary of $10,000 and a low of $6,200.

Highest salary paid to subprofessional personnel employed on an eleven to twelve-month basis was $15,368, while the lowest for that period was $3,600. Those employed on a nine- to ten-month basis received a high salary of $9,100 and a low of $4,500.

Analysis of salaries paid to clerical personnel showed a high of $8,940 for eleven to twelve months, and a low of $3,000. None of these personnel were employed on a nine- to ten-month basis.

Further analysis of salaries of library personnel by the type of institution showed that, on the whole, salaries were considerably higher in publicly supported institutions than in privately supported ones. This finding was true of each position listed in the tables.

Concerning eligibility for fringe benefits and other such privileges, the study revealed that various practices are followed in the libraries in question. Nine institutions, or 13.8 percent of the total, reported that sabbatical leave was available to the head librarian only; twenty-eight, or 43 percent, reported that all of their librarians were eligible; and twenty-eight, or 43 percent, reported that none of their professional staffs were eligible.

Hospitalization benefits were available to all librarians in fifty-eight, or 89.2 percent, of the libraries, with no such benefits available in only six libraries. One library failed to respond to the question.

Fifty-eight libraries, or 89.2 percent, reported that all professional staff members were eligible for the institution's retirement plan; two, or 3 percent, reported that only the head librarian was eligible; and four, or 6.1 percent, reported that retirement benefits were unavailable to the professional staff. One library failed to respond to the question.

The Collections

The question of applying quantitative measures to determine the adequacy of a library's collection is receiving increased attention in library literature. Many authorities are convinced that there are varying elements within the academic institution itself which must be considered before attempts are made to evaluate the library, particularly the collection. They contend that the collection must be studied in terms of its relationship to the educational program and that the size of the collection itself is no yardstick for measuring quality.

As one reliable measure of their quality, library collections should be checked frequently against various standard lists, both in general and in special subjects. Among the dangers cited in using these lists, however, are that they lead to uniformity in evaluation, frequently disregarding differences in institutions; that they are soon outdated; and that they obviously omit certain titles that might be useful in a given library. Nevertheless, such lists are generally prepared by experts and can be highly useful in collection development.

Many of the respondents indicated that their collections had been at least partially checked against general and special subject bibliographies within the five years immediately preceding this study, and some libraries indicated that they were in the process of evaluating their collections. Those lists most frequently used by the libraries reporting were: "Choice Opening Day Collection," *Books for College Libraries,* and Winchell's *Guide to Reference Books.* Such older guides as the *Catalogue of the Lamont Library, Harvard College,* and Shaw's *List of Books for College Libraries* were used in a considerable number of these libraries. Some of the special subject bibliographies used were Hawkins's *Scientific, Medical and Technical Books Published in the U.S.A.* and the Mathematical Association of America's *Basic Library List.*

In determining tools commonly used for book selection in the reporting libraries, the study found that particular journals were frequently used by the majority of the libraries. These were *Choice, Library Journal, Wilson Library Bulletin, Publishers Weekly,* and *Booklist and Subscription Books Bulletin.* A handful of libraries reported that they used professional journals of the major disciplines on campus as tools for book selection.

Responsibility for book selection was evenly divided between the faculty and the library staff in twenty-seven of the institutions reporting. Twenty-three libraries reported that their staffs had responsibility for book selection, while fourteen reported that their faculty had this responsibility. The extent to which faculties in these institutions have been active in selection was reported to be especially good. Sixty libraries indicated that their faculties were active, while five reported that they were inactive.

To assist in building library collections, some libraries employ the services of a bibliographer. Three of the reporting libraries indicated that they employed a bibliographer, while sixty-one indicated that they did not.

Library staffs, working with faculty members and students, should develop acquisition policy statements which clearly define subject areas, cross departmental lines, and determine the types of materials to be collected. Such a policy helps insure development of the collection in a systematic manner and frequently avoids the neglect of subject areas. Thirty-eight of the reporting libraries indicated that they had such policy statements, twenty-five indicated that they did not, and one failed to respond to the question.

Procedures followed in acquiring library materials were heavily weighted in terms of ordering through the business office. Forty-three of the libraries reported that they followed this procedure, while twenty-two reported that orders were sent directly from the library to jobbers or publishers.

The use of duplicate exchange unions to acquire materials or to dispose of duplicate items was reported by twenty-two of these libraries, with forty-three indicating that they had no membership in such exchange programs. Of the twenty-two libraries that did participate, fifteen reported that they sent a combined total of 4,780 items and received a total of 6,720 items in exchange.

Many libraries have been able to strengthen their collections through the inclusion of significant numbers of government documents available to them through their designation as full or partial depository libraries. Sixteen of the respondents reported that they were either full or partial depositories of federal documents, while seventeen respondents reported that they received documents from their particular states.

Verner W. Clapp and Robert T. Jordan reviewed statements by the various regional accrediting agencies concerning the evaluation of library collections, studied the Standards for College Libraries adopted in 1959 by the Association of College and Research Libraries of the American Library Association, and concluded that by placing weights on various controlling conditions, "it is possible to provide a meaningful quantitative measure of adequacy in library collections."[5]

While the Clapp-Jordan formula is not being applied here, it must be pointed out that determining the size of collections in the libraries included in this study necessarily provides some measure of their adequacy. It is possible to have a small collection of carefully chosen volumes. However, given the history of neglect in these libraries, it is highly unlikely that the size of the collection immediately suggests adequacy. On the other hand, it is much more likely that the larger collections will include a greater number of titles that relate to the academic program of the institution than will the smaller ones.

Table 11 shows the total number of volumes processed and ready for use in sixty-five black institutions, gives enrollment figures and the minimum number of volumes required by the ALA standards of 1959, and indicates any deficiency in volume count.

ALA standards suggest that there is a correlation between the size of the student body and the size of the library collection and give as a convenient measure the following formula: up to 600 students, 50,000 volumes; for each additional 200 students, 10,000 volumes. Using this formula as a guide, the total number of volumes required in sixty-two of the reporting institutions was computed, and deficiencies were recorded. As Table 11 further indicates, fifty-three, or 85.4 percent, of the libraries reporting have deficiencies in the size of their collections. The aggregate number of deficiencies in these collections equaled 2,368,799 volumes.

As was stated earlier, in recent years a sizable number of institutions reporting in the survey have prepared for evaluation by the Southern Association of Colleges and Schools. In an effort to reduce the level of deficiency in the size of their collections by the time of the Association's visit, many institutions have accelerated the growth rate of their collections. Other institutions have been less vigorous in increasing their collections but have added volumes according to budgetary provisions.

Table 12 shows the number of volumes added each year by type of institution, beginning with 1964-65 and ending with 1968-69. Those institutions reporting the largest increase in collection size were Florida A & M, Norfolk State, Southern University, and Southern University at New Orleans. The table further shows the aggregate number of volumes added to library collections in these institutions during each of the years in question, showing a grand total of 5,164,673 volumes added during the five-year period.

Baumol and Marcus included "Volumes Added" as one of the variables in their study. Using their regression equation, calculations have been made for volumes added by some institutions included in the present study. These

TABLE 11

**Adequacy in Size of Collections of Certain
Black College Libraries, September 1, 1969**

Institution	Number of Volumes	Enrollment	Standard	Deficiency	Volumes Per Student
Alabama A & M*	104,641	2,091	130,000	25,359	50
Alabama State*	96,475	2,340	140,000	43,525	42
Alcorn*	65,017	2,300	140,000	74,983	28
Arkansas A M & N*	59,523	3,728	210,000	150,477	16
Atlanta**	240,000	1,407			171
Barber-Scotia**	41,119	599	50,000	8,881	69
Benedict**	49,261	1,259	90,000	40,739	39
Bethune**	52,763	1,165	80,000	27,237	45
Bishop**	72,058	1,968	120,000	47,942	37
Central State*	90,000	2,262	160,000	70,000	40
Cheyney*	86,760	2,041	130,000	43,240	43
Claflin**	38,385	709	60,000	21,615	54
Clark**†		1,168			
Dillard**	87,511	922	70,000		95
Elizabeth City*	62,658	1,039	80,000	17,342	60
Fayetteville*	64,499	1,115	80,000	15,501	58
Fisk**	163,467	1,248	90,000		131
Florida A & M*	175,169	4,300	240,000	64,831	41
Florida Memorial**	41,862	757	60,000	18,138	55
Fort Valley*	86,242	2,247	140,000	53,758	38
Grambling*	80,754	3,455	200,000	119,246	23
Hampton**	120,616	2,384	140,000	19,384	51

TABLE 11 (continued)

Institution	Number of Volumes	Enrollment	Standard	Deficiency	Volumes Per Student
Huston-Tillotson**	47,035	697	60,000	12,965	67
Jackson State*	62,151	4,385	240,000	177,849	14
Jarvis Christian**	38,522	554	50,000	11,478	70
Johnson C. Smith**	81,360	1,209	90,000	8,640	67
Kentucky State*	58,806	1,610	110,000	51,194	37
Knoxville**	46,627	918	70,000	23,373	51
Lane**	40,010	974	70,000	29,990	41
Langston*	108,218	1,225	90,000		88
LeMoyne-Owen**	50,586	703	60,000	9,414	72
Lincoln (Mo.)*	90,108	2,013	130,000	39,892	45
Lincoln (Pa.)**	117,612	1,130	80,000		104
Livingstone**	44,156	809	70,000	25,844	55
Miss. Valley*†		2,314			
Morris**	21,025	534	50,000	28,975	39
Morris Brown**	22,000	1,495	100,000	78,000	15
Norfolk*	99,625	4,411	250,000	150,375	23
North Carolina A & T*	274,584	3,714	210,000		74
North Carolina Central*	181,620	3,290	190,000	8,380	55
Oakwood**	48,000	600	50,000	2,000	80
Paine**	43,823	656	60,000	16,177	67
Paul Quinn**	25,150	621	60,000	34,850	40
Philander Smith**	55,676	596	50,000		93
Prairie View*	116,358	4,138	230,000	113,642	28
St. Augustine**	49,009	1,099	80,000	30,991	45
Shaw**	45,566	1,031	80,000	34,434	44

TABLE 11 (continued)

Institution	Number of Volumes	Enrollment	Standard	Deficiency	Volumes Per Student
Simmons**	7,000	119	50,000	43,000	59
South Carolina State*	90,000	2,025	130,000	40,000	44
Southern*	212,435	8,385	440,000	227,565	25
Southern Univ. N. O.*	65,076	1,309	90,000	24,924	47
Stillman**	39,121	678	60,000	20,879	58
Talladega**	56,013	550	50,000		102
Texas College**	48,426	468	50,000	1,574	103
Texas Southern*	179,866	3,980	220,000	40,134	45
Tougaloo**	56,400	694	60,000	3,600	81
Tuskegee**	177,500	3,000	170,000		59
Virginia State*	123,195	2,498	150,000	26,805	49
Virginia Union**	85,721	1,325	90,000	4,279	66
Voorhees**	37,227	715	60,000	22,773	52
West Virginia State*	100,779	3,063	180,000	79,221	33
Wilberforce**	37,933	1,008	80,000	42,067	38
Wiley**	27,063	468	50,000	22,937	58
Winston-Salem*	71,620	1,275	90,000	18,380	57
Xavier**	102,891	1,364	90,000		75
TOTAL	5,164,673	114,154	7,050,000	2,368,799	47

*public.
**private.
†Not included in average per student.

TABLE 12

Growth of Collections in Certain Black College
Libraries, 1964-65 Through 1968-69

Institution	1964-65	1965-66	1966-67	1967-68	1968-69
Alabama A & M*	5,000	6,064	11,000	12,000	6,648
Alabama State*	8,157	6,794	4,813	5,223	4,257
Alcorn*	5,114	6,300	5,355	6,548	4,059
Arkansas A M & N*	4,233	4,924	3,175	4,927	10,763
Atlanta**	6,869	6,988	8,072	9,259	9,000
Barber-Scotia**	2,250	3,447	6,140	5,148	4,306
Benedict**		2,026	2,712	3,121	5,541
Bethune**	291	3,454	3,688	3,947	2,786
Bishop**	4,193	5,619	14,654	9,628	4,113
Central State*	3,852	4,567	4,801	5,173	4,727
Cheyney*	5,200	4,708	5,503	8,263	9,674
Claflin**					
Clark**	756	1,462		3,360	3,316
Dillard**	3,082	3,981	3,777	4,560	6,298
Elizabeth City*	4,249	3,349	3,200	4,000	3,645
Fayetteville*	3,265	2,207	2,224	6,053	3,326
Fisk**	4,618	2,056	3,832	6,082	3,085
Florida A & M*	19,158	16,604	26,194	24,536	17,465
Florida Memorial**		3,046	5,540	2,500	3,822
Fort Valley*	4,128	3,109	5,556	10,657	10,592
Grambling*	2,509	9,682	13,824	5,047	2,508
Hampton**	3,156	3,896	4,416	5,932	5,570
Huston-Tillotson**	2,659	1,421	1,691	2,461	6,699

TABLE 12 (continued)

Institution	1964-65	1965-66	1966-67	1967-68	1968-69
Jackson State*	1,181	5,297	8,014	6,401	7,411
Jarvis Christian**		2,805	3,358	3,485	3,001
Johnson C. Smith**	4,258	4,058	3,031	4,649	8,931
Kentucky State*	1,872	2,017	2,007	11,851	3,425
Knoxville**	3,636	3,224	3,723	5,355	3,605
Lane**	3,034	2,960	3,642	3,128	3,096
Langston*	2,518	2,749	4,052	3,161	5,678
LeMoyne-Owen**	2,157	2,695	3,329	2,781	2,925
Lincoln (Mo.)*	2,927	3,322	2,979	3,998	7,644
Lincoln (Pa.)**	4,042	3,984	4,634	5,367	2,249
Livingstone**	1,286	1,296	3,961	2,874	5,998
Miss. Valley*	6,073	4,817	4,975	5,679	7,736
Morris**	678	799	1,449	1,333	2,265
Morris Brown**		2,585	1,406	1,085	13,065
Norfolk State*	16,730	11,607	11,921	7,735	15,290
North Carolina A & T*	5,460	8,374	8,933	16,855	9,866
North Carolina Central*	10,581	7,783	8,582	7,202	5,000
Oakwood**	3,000	4,000	4,000	5,000	2,380
Paine**	1,540	1,760	1,970	1,737	
Paul Quinn**					
Philander Smith**	1,856	2,048	7,556	2,403	3,994
Prairie View*	4,296	5,057	4,337	3,243	5,113
St. Augustine**	2,634	2,695	2,335	5,064	10,019
Shaw**	4,115	2,582	2,439	4,989	4,410

TABLE 12 (continued)

Institution	1964-65	1965-66	1966-67	1967-68	1968-69
South Carolina State*	3,898	3,928	5,170	5,092	9,380
Simmons**					
Southern*	10,624	10,871	11,487	12,741	8,990
Southern Univ. N. O.*	12,507	11,361	9,145	15,518	7,099
Stillman**	2,055	2,351	1,971	2,432	1,851
Talladega**		2,224	1,774	1,814	2,794
Texas College**		492	6,766	4,917	10,743
Texas Southern*	7,101	7,750	9,967	17,403	15,495
Tougaloo**	3,209	4,608	3,497	2,046	4,638
Tuskegee**	7,407	7,113	9,655	11,331	12,772
Virginia State*	6,469	6,632	7,254	5,646	7,709
Virginia Union**	5,375	6,536	7,971	7,461	6,186
Voorhees**	1,074	2,674	2,225	12,000	4,897
West Virginia State*	3,755	4,530	6,854	11,670	9,708
Wilberforce**	501	933	3,723	3,021	4,159
Wiley**	1,260	300	1,021	1,278	1,565
Winston-Salem*	2,955	2,478	5,351	7,086	6,602
Xavier**	3,176	1,866	3,107	2,771	3,841
TOTAL	248,849	300,865	329,847	388,027	374,730
GRAND TOTAL	1,642,318				

*public.
**private.

results are given in Tables 13 and 14. These results show that a substantial number of the libraries in the present study fall below the regression line in this category.

TABLE 13

Volumes Added to Libraries in Selected Public Colleges, 1967-68

Institution	Baumol-Marcus Model	Actual
Alabama A & M	8,627	12,000
Alabama State	8,208	5,223
Alcorn	7,666	6,548
Central State	11,299	5,173
Florida A & M	16,476	24,536
Fort Valley	7,616	10,657
Grambling	10,708	5,047
Kentucky State	7,447	11,851
Langston	9,100	3,161
Lincoln (Mo.)	8,502	3,998
North Carolina A & T	27,670	16,855
North Carolina Central	19,790	7,202
South Carolina State	8,117	5,092
Texas Southern	18,078	17,403
West Virginia State	11,456	11,670
Winston-Salem	7,765	7,086

TABLE 14

Volumes Added to Libraries in Selected Private Colleges, 1967-68

Institution	Baumol-Marcus Model	Actual
Benedict	5,272	3,121
Dillard	6,292	4,560
Fisk	8,365	6,082
Hampton	10,040	5,932
Lane	5,063	3,128
St. Augustine	5,181	5,064
Tuskegee	12,402	11,331
Virginia Union	6,043	7,461
Xavier	6,655	2,771

Standards of the various regional accrediting agencies as well as those of the ALA stress the importance of weeding library collections of outmoded materials, superseded editions, superfluous duplicates, badly worn items, and so forth. Therefore, libraries were asked to report the total number of volumes withdrawn over a five-year period beginning in 1964-65 and ending in 1968-69. Table 15 shows the extent to which these volumes have been withdrawn by certain institutions. Among those institutions withdrawing large amounts of materials, considering the size of their collections, were Fisk, Florida A & M, Jarvis, North Carolina Central, Voorhees, Wiley, and Xavier. The aggregate number of volumes withdrawn over a five-year period from collections in all libraries reporting totaled 146,792.

The extent to which collections in the black libraries may grow and develop has been estimated through projections for a five-year period beginning in 1969-70 and ending in 1973-74. Table 16 gives projections for the institutions reporting varying levels of expected growth. Florida A & M and Prairie View expected their collections to increase substantially during the years in question, while more conservative estimates were indicated for Barber-Scotia, Langston, LeMoyne-Owen, Livingstone, and others. A few institutions were unable to make growth projections for their library collections.

Increasingly, libraries are assuming responsibility for housing and disseminating audiovisual materials for the entire campus. Even when the full audiovisual services are maintained elsewhere, certain nonprint materials are available in the library. Tables 17 and 18 show the types of nonprint materials available in the libraries reporting and indicate that these collections contain considerably more microfilm and recordings than other types of nonprint media. With one or two exceptions, those institutions reporting holdings in the form of microcard and microfiche are publicly supported. Only one library, LeMoyne, reported holdings in the form of microprint.

Many libraries indicated that they had photographs in their collections but that these items were uncounted. Other types of materials found in these libraries were tapes, slides, filmstrips, films, and reproductions.

The library should include a well-balanced and carefully chosen collection of periodicals, as well as current newspapers which provide local, regional, and national coverage. Frequently, respondents indicated that their collections of periodicals and newspapers required strengthening. Table 19 shows the number of periodical and newspaper subscriptions

TABLE 15

Volumes Withdrawn from Collections in Certain Black
College Libraries, 1964-65 Through 1968-69

Institution	1964-65	1965-66	1966-67	1967-68	1968-69
Alabama A & M*	25	3,089		800	7
Alabama State*	80	422			547
Alcorn*	27	30	39	43	55
Arkansas A M & N*				200	
Atlanta**	339	182	67	339	514
Barber-Scotia**	256	89		55	1,086
Benedict**					
Bethune**					
Bishop**	308	602	495	501	356
Central State*					
Cheyney*					
Claflin**					
Clark**					
Dillard**	35	20	42	40	75
Elizabeth City*	85	110	112	98	105
Fayetteville*	208	339	108	207	97
Fisk**	1,320	2,770	2,523	540	4,261
Florida A & M*			3,465		555
Florida Memorial**					
Fort Valley*			790	1,077	
Grambling*	892	1,138	370		2,019
Hampton**					

TABLE 15 (continued)

Institution	1964-65	1965-66	1966-67	1967-68	1968-69
Huston-Tillotson**			104	17	130
Jackson State*	98	157	444	366	890
Jarvis Christian**	1,738	3,800	1,404	1,040	
Johnson C. Smith**	99	200	269	300	165
Kentucky State*	219	108	105	228	337
Knoxville**		147	32	57	100
Lane**	95	20	20	43	8
Langston*	58	411	235	99	146
LeMoyne-Owen**	170	104	150	136	160
Lincoln (Mo.)*	460	444	299	439	471
Lincoln (Pa.)**	81	93	123	324	319
Livingstone**					
Miss. Valley*	722	444	851	222	563
Morris**					800
Morris Brown**					
Norfolk*					
North Carolina A & T*	10	517	940	800	2,650
North Carolina Central*		1,820		2,562	
Oakwood**					
Paine**	113	33	75	225	284
Paul Quinn**				158	210
Philander Smith**					1,953
Prairie View*					
St. Augustine**	41	274	35	799	575
Shaw**		138	1,772	113	
Simmons**					

TABLE 15 (continued)

Institution	1964-65	1965-66	1966-67	1967-68	1968-69
South Carolina State*					
Southern*	251	36	460	456	
Southern Univ. N. O.*					
Stillman**		75	95	63	327
Talladega**			347	5,376	746
Texas College**					
Texas Southern*		560	235	1,105	936
Tougaloo**		88	200	112	181
Tuskegee**	550	850	2,015	2,561	2,230
Virginia State*	82	34	65	1,007	600
Virginia Union**			72	650	560
Voorhees**	8,308	6,362	7,954	8,944	
West Virginia State*	105	557	10	15	112
Wilberforce**		573	1,181	1,232	4,143
Wiley**	2,000	270	2,300	350	1,400
Winston-Salem*					
Xavier**	2,175	3,510	485	632	134
TOTAL	20,950	30,416	30,288	34,331	30,807
GRAND TOTAL	146,792				

*public.
**private.

TABLE 16

Projections in Growth of Collections in Certain
Black College Libraries, 1969-70 Through 1973-74

Institution	1969-70	1970-71	1971-72	1972-73	1973-74
Alabama A & M*	12,500	13,000	13,500	14,000	14,000
Alabama State*	7,000	8,000	8,000	8,500	8,500
Alcorn*	5,963	6,000	8,000	9,000	10,000
Arkansas A M & N*					
Atlanta**	12,000	15,000	15,000	20,000	20,000
Barber-Scotia**	1,302	1,802	2,302	2,802	3,302
Benedict**	5,000	7,000	10,000	20,000	15,000
Bethune**					
Bishop**		27,500	17,500	17,500	17,500
Central State*	8,000	12,000	27,000	27,000	47,000
Cheyney*	9,355	4,568			
Claflin**	8,000	9,000			
Clark**	3,625	4,000	4,000	5,000	5,300
Dillard**		5,000	5,000	6,000	7,000
Elizabeth City*	5,000	5,000	10,000	10,000	10,000
Fayetteville*					
Fisk**	4,000	5,000	6,000	7,000	8,000
Florida A & M*	48,000	48,000	48,000	48,000	48,000
Florida Memorial**		5,000	6,000	4,000	5,000
Fort Valley*					
Grambling*					
Hampton**	7,000	18,000	18,000	18,000	20,000

TABLE 16 (continued)

Institution	1969-70	1970-71	1971-72	1972-73	1973-74
Huston-Tillotson**		1,800	2,500	2,500	5,000
Jackson State*	8,693	15,000	25,000	30,000	50,000
Jarvis Christian**	6,285	5,687	10,162	5,872	1,383
Johnson C. Smith**	5,000	5,000	5,000	5,000	5,000
Kentucky State*	11,000	15,000	17,000	17,000	10,000
Knoxville**	6,500	8,000	8,500	10,000	10,000
Lane**	4,000	4,200	4,500	4,700	5,000
Langston*	2,500	3,000	3,000	3,000	3,000
LeMoyne-Owen**	2,000	2,500	3,000	3,500	5,000
Lincoln (Mo.)*	3,500	4,800	5,000	6,100	7,000
Lincoln (Pa.)**	7,730	8,530	9,380	10,280	11,280
Livingstone**	3,500	3,500	3,000	3,000	3,000
Miss. Valley*	8,000	10,000	12,000	15,000	19,000
Morris**	8,000	10,000	10,000	1,500	1,500
Morris Brown**		7,800	5,000	5,000	10,000
North Carolina A & T*	20,000				
North Carolina Central*					
Oakwood**		5,000	5,000	5,000	5,000
Paine**	2,500	2,700	2,900	3,000	3,000
Paul Quinn**	3,000	20,000	5,000	5,000	5,000
Philander Smith**		3,000	3,000	3,000	3,000
Prairie View*	46,000	46,000	46,000	46,000	46,000
St. Augustine**		5,000	3,000	5,000	5,000
Shaw**		5,000	5,000	5,000	5,000
Simmons**	5,000				

TABLE 16 (continued)

Institution	1969-70	1970-71	1971-72	1972-73	1973-74
South Carolina State*	1,000	12,000	14,000	16,000	18,000
Southern*					
Southern Univ. N. O.*	5,000	3,000	7,000	8,500	10,000
Stillman**	6,000	5,000	5,000	5,000	5,000
Talladega**	2,473	3,000	3,000	3,500	4,000
Texas College**		5,000	5,500	4,500	5,000
Texas Southern*		18,500	19,000	21,000	20,200
Tougaloo**					
Tuskegee**					
Virginia State*	8,000	9,000			
Virginia Union**	5,000	5,000	5,000	5,000	5,000
Voorhees**	7,000	7,500	8,000	9,000	10,000
West Virginia State*	2,000	5,000	5,000	5,000	5,000
Wilberforce**	3,650	3,650	3,650	3,650	3,650
Wiley**	8,000	12,000	12,000	12,000	12,000
Winston-Salem*	3,000	3,000	3,000	3,000	3,000
Xavier**					
TOTAL	341,076	477,037	481,394	507,404	557,615
GRAND TOTAL	2,364,526				

*public.
**private.

TABLE 17

Holdings in Nonprint Media in Certain Black
College Libraries, September 1, 1969

Institution	Microfilm	Microcard	Microfiche	Records	Photographs
Alabama A & M*	2,749				50
Alabama State*	2,945	542		170	
Alcorn*	1,029	1,151	49	1,520	
Arkansas A M & N*	452				
Atlanta**	39			73	
Barber-Scotia**	777				
Benedict**				339	
Bethune**	458			230	
Bishop**	1,500			20	
Central State*	2,263			700	50
Cheyney*	3,224	1,890	2,165	1,435	
Claflin**	570			261	
Clark**					
Dillard**	1,600	2,000		731	
Elizabeth City*	227			496	
Fayetteville*	2,963		346	454	170
Fisk**	3,301			500	
Florida A & M*	4,505		2,058	985	
Florida Memorial**	433				
Fort Valley*	842	50			100
Grambling*	3,189			397	
Hampton**	1,529			331	2,000
Huston-Tillotson**	116			1,152	

TABLE 17 (continued)

Institution	Microfilm	Microcard	Microfiche	Records	Photographs
Jackson State*	1,481		1,187	190	
Jarvis Christian**	415			555	
Johnson C. Smith**	512			61	100
Kentucky State*	465			1,285	60
Knoxville**	400			600	200
Lane**	107			395	47
Langston*	539			150	
LeMoyne-Owen**	14			500	150
Lincoln (Mo.)*	672		17	515	681
Lincoln (Pa.)**	1,965	162		1,500	
Livingstone**	412	1,490		424	
Miss. Valley*	433			247	
Morris**	504			134	13
Morris Brown**					
Norfolk*	2,253			660	
North Carolina A & T*	4,485		50	349	
North Carolina Central*	9,474				
Oakwood**	370			200	
Paine**	1,750			707	
Paul Quinn**					
Philander Smith**	171				
Prairie View*	2,321	175	3,400	204	2,547
St. Augustine**	8			115	
Shaw**	625		800	750	
Simmons**				10	

TABLE 17 (continued)

Institution	Microfilm	Microcard	Microfiche	Records	Photographs
South Carolina State*	4,320	747			200
Southern*	5,001				
Southern Univ. N. O.*	8,116	871		513	
Stillman**	227				
Talladega**	1,512			1,253	
Texas College**	199			570	
Texas Southern*	2,363	2,202		993	40
Tougaloo**	797			1,233	250
Tuskegee**	2,500			400	
Virginia State*	2,057	3,262		800	
Virginia Union**	5,368	695		1,841	
Voorhees**	532			186	35
West Virginia State*	1,304			643	
Wilberforce**	660	11		334	350
Wiley**	370			468	75
Winston-Salem*	214			221	2,773
Xavier**	978		7	359	

*public.
**private.

TABLE 18

Holdings in Nonprint Media in Certain Black College
Libraries, September 1, 1969

Institution	Tapes	Slides	Film-strips	Films	Repro-ductions
Alabama A & M*	374	2,173	57	150	160
Alabama State*	40		3,007	220	
Alcorn*		312	126	3	
Arkansas A M & N*	50	200	371		
Central State*	10			5	
Cheyney*	235	4,000	1,960	431	
Claflin**	30		41		
Dillard**	12				
Elizabeth City*	15	73	272	1	40
Florida Memorial**			316		
Grambling*	25		164		
Hampton**		1,000			2,000
Huston-Tillotson**	10	15	66	6	
Jackson State*	48	600	23		25
Jarvis Christian**	10		208	28	
Johnson C. Smith**	35	690	221	25	300
Kentucky State*	183	500	585	212	175
Knoxville**	29	500	400	55	
Lane**	10	37	311	58	
LeMoyne-Owen**					
Lincoln (Mo.)*	9	26	605	24	31
Livingstone**	8		165	6	5

TABLE 18 (continued)

Institution	Tapes	Slides	Film-strips	Films	Repro-ductions
Miss. Valley*	49	156	790	739	
Morris**			190		1
North Carolina A & T*	55		612	466	99
Paine**	5		57		
Prairie View*		1,569	1,275	648	
St. Augustine**	28		225	5	101
Shaw**	408		191	25	
Simmons**			24		
Southern Univ. N. O.*	12				
Stillman**	56				
Talladega**		1,628	312		511
Texas College**	55		60		
Texas Southern*	25		6		
Tougaloo**			343		
Virginia Union**	219	590	434	192	
Voorhees**	60	3,000	36	33	
West Virginia State*	42	124	465		
Wilberforce**	152	908	106	5	
Wiley**			107	2	
Xavier**	25	300	423	19	25

*public.
**private.

TABLE 19

Number of Periodical and Newspaper Subscriptions in
Certain Black College
Libraries, September 1, 1969

Institution	Subscriptions		Newspapers on Microfilm
	Periodicals	Newspapers	
Alabama A & M*	981	66	16
Alabama State*	597	38	5
Alcorn*	931	50	3
Arkansas A M & N*	408	42	2
Atlanta**	663	64	5
Barber-Scotia**	274	32	50
Benedict**	417	28	
Bethune**	330	44	2
Bishop**	550	30	4
Central State*	937	48	185
Cheyney*	896	18	1
Claflin**	379	11	4
Clark**	269	16	
Dillard**	435	25	1
Elizabeth City*	550		2
Fayetteville*	452	31	2
Fisk**	807	47	5
Florida A & M*	2,038	90	2
Florida Memorial**	346	21	2
Fort Valley*	627	20	3
Grambling*	1,290	60	2
Hampton**	662	39	5
Huston-Tillotson**	265	14	1
Jackson State*	812	30	4
Jarvis Christian**			
Johnson C. Smith**	315	12	1
Kentucky State*	610	22	2
Knoxville**	380	16	2
Lane**	390	15	1
Langston*	738	36	
LeMoyne-Owen**	190	7	
Lincoln (Mo.)*	700	40	128
Lincoln (Pa.)**	801	31	2
Livingstone**	144	19	1
Miss. Valley*	536	30	15
Morris**	221	50	1
Morris Brown**	126	25	

TABLE 19 (continued)

| Institution | Subscriptions | | Newspapers on Microfilm |
	Periodicals	Newspapers	
Norfolk*	1,016	20	3
North Carolina A & T*	1,048	76	8
North Carolina Central*	1,260	45	15
Oakwood**	350	10	
Paine**	199		2
Paul Quinn**	257	23	
Philander Smith**	335	20	1
Prairie View*	1,322	42	
St. Augustine**	317	10	1
Shaw**	308	15	4
Simmons**	20	2	
South Carolina State*	467	30	5
Southern *	191		
Southern Univ. N. O.*	933	64	25
Stillman**	302	19	1
Talladega**	289	14	1
Texas College**	379	18	1
Texas Southern*	1,509	58	6
Tougaloo**		7	2
Tuskegee**	1,523	75	4
Virginia State*	1,129	40	5
Virginia Union**	584	18	5
Voorhees**	285	12	1
West Virginia State*	700	35	2
Wilberforce**	257	23	3
Wiley**	399	47	1
Winston-Salem*	578	34	35
Xavier**	501	30	1

*public.
**private.

received and further indicates the number of newspapers that were also available on film. Analysis of the tables shows that the larger publicly supported institutions—including Florida A & M, Grambling, North Carolina A & T, North Carolina Central, Texas Southern, and Virginia State—received the largest number of periodical subscriptions. Of the privately supported institutions, only Tuskegee received 1,000 or more periodical subscriptions.

Cataloging and Classification

While libraries are bound by high standards of collection development, they are also bound by equally high standards of classification and cataloging in order to provide maximum accessibility of subject matter and materials. ALA standards require the full organization of collections for use according to generally acceptable schemes. Inquiring into the cataloging and classification practices in these libraries, the survey revealed that twenty-four libraries make use of the Library of Congress Classification system, while forty-one employ the Dewey Decimal Classification system. Eleven libraries that used LC Classification and one that used Dewey were in the process of reclassifying their collections by LC Classification. Twelve libraries that used LC Classification and four that used Dewey were further converting their collections to LC Classification rather than recataloging their entire collections. Some of the recataloging and conversion activities were under way as a result of certain libraries' affiliation with the Cooperative College Library Center, which required members to adopt LC Classification.

Facilities

Efficient and effective library service depends as much on an adequate library facility as it does on a well-qualified staff and a well-balanced collection of materials. Attention must be given to the general condition of the building, its size, provisions for study, space for housing materials, quarters for processing and other staff activities, lighting, heating and ventilation, and general atmosphere.

In terms of the age of library facilities, the respondents in the survey indicated that seventeen, or 28.3 percent of the sixty libraries reporting, were constructed in 1970, two in 1969, six in 1968, five in 1967, two in 1966, and one in 1965. Twenty-six, or 43.3 percent of the sixty libraries reporting, indicated that their buildings were erected between 1960 and 1970. Twelve, or 20 percent, were erected between 1950 and 1960; seven, or 11.7 percent, between 1940 and 1950; and fourteen, or 23.3 percent, were constructed prior to 1940 or were thirty or more years old. Four institutions had new facilities under construction, and one institution occupied a new structure during the course of the study.[6] The oldest building in the group was erected in 1896 but was renovated in 1967. With two exceptions, those libraries that were constructed between 1896 and 1947 had undergone renovation. Even so, some of these renovations took place in earlier years. For example, one building was erected in 1907 and renovated in 1938.

In rating the physical condition and general appearance of their library buildings, librarians generally indicated that they were good. Thirteen rated their buildings as excellent, four rated them as very good, seven rated them as fair, and eight rated them as poor. Fifty, or 83.3 percent of the sixty libraries responding to this section of the questionnaire, indicated that their libraries were air-conditioned. Librarians generally rated furnishings in their buildings as good, although in some instances furnishings were rated as excellent, very good, and fair. Five libraries indicated that their library furnishings were poor.

Provisions for study were generally made at tables, and some seating was available in lounge areas as well as at carrels. Table 20 indicates the types of seating provided in the libraries reporting. A few libraries—including Alabama A & M, Hampton, LeMoyne-Owen, Lincoln (Pa.), South Carolina State, and Texas Southern—provided significant amounts of their seating at carrels. Further comparison of the total number of seats available to the student body shows that sixteen, or 26.7 percent of the institutions reporting, were able to seat one-third of their total enrollment at a given time. Thirty-four, or 56.7 percent of these libraries, failed to meet ALA standards requiring this proportion of seating for the student body, while five libraries failed to report seating provisions.

The amount of staff work space available in these libraries was much more difficult to ascertain, for statistics on office and work quarters were generally unavailable. Site visits to the libraries, however, showed that the space for technical services was inadequate even in some of the newer facilities.

An analysis of the shelf capacity of the library buildings revealed that ten had nearly exhausted their space. If current acquisition rates continue, within a year or two the shelves will be filled. Eight libraries had already exceeded their shelf capacity at the time of the study.

Standards of the ALA and the various regional accrediting agencies require that students have easy access to library materials. Physical barriers separating users from materials are discouraged. Fifty-seven, or 89 percent, of the sixty-four libraries responding to this question reported that open stacks were available to their students.

TABLE 20

Seating Capacity of Certain Black College Libraries,
September 1, 1969

| Institution | Number of Seats | | Total Seating | |
	Number of Carrels	Tables and Lounge Area	Students	Faculty
Alabama A & M*	274	626	901	12
Alabama State*				
Alcorn*	128	791	919	47
Arkansas A M & N*		550	550	
Atlanta**	74		74	
Barber-Scotia**				
Benedict**				
Bethune**				
Bishop**	39	600	639	
Central State*	72	500	572	5
Cheyney*	28	181	209	3
Claflin**	100	197	297	3
Clark**	15		15	
Dillard**	45	350	395	
Elizabeth City*	79	138	217	16
Fayetteville*	64	383	447	
Fisk**	61	312	373	10
Florida A & M*	30	515	545	
Florida Memorial**	10	450	460	
Fort Valley*	104	328	432	8
Grambling*	77	70	147	18

TABLE 20 (continued)

Institution	Number of Carrels	Number of Seats Tables and Lounge Area	Total Seating Students	Faculty
Hampton**	321	500	821	7
Huston-Tillotson**	6	164	170	7
Jackson State*	76	544	620	
Jarvis Christian**				
Johnson C. Smith**	175		175	7
Kentucky State*				
Knoxville**	84	216	300	
Lane**	4	176	180	
Langston*		255	255	
LeMoyne-Owen**	250		250	10
Lincoln (Mo.)*	42	6	48	
Lincoln (Pa.)**	75	140	215	
Livingstone**	58	217	275	
Miss. Valley*	31	12	43	
Morris**		84	84	
Morris Brown**	25	225	250	
Norfolk*		350	350	
North Carolina A & T*	122	688	810	
North Carolina Central*	34	534	568	12
Oakwood**	6		6	6
Paine**	13	209	222	
Paul Quinn**	14	142	156	7
Philander Smith**	18	6	24	

TABLE 20 (continued)

Institution	Number of Seats		Total Seating	
	Number of Carrels	Tables and Lounge Area	Students	Faculty
Prairie View*	33		33	
St. Augustine**	25	225	250	
Shaw**	180	150	330	
Simmons**		16	16	
South Carolina State*	311	179	490	10
Southern*	52	850	902	
Southern Univ. N. O.*	10	600	610	
Stillman**	6	187	193	
Talladega**	21	292	313	
Texas College**	6	252	258	
Texas Southern*	560	1,150	1,710	
Tougaloo**	9	115	124	
Tuskegee**	36	596	632	
Virginia State*	88	556	644	
Virginia Union**	2	250	252	
Voorhees**	15	160	175	
West Virginia State*		300	300	7
Wilberforce**		125	125	
Wiley**	32	344	376	3
Winston-Salem*	75	285	360	
Xavier**	4	218	222	

*public.
**private.

Service

The intangible factors involved in library services make the evaluation of these services difficult. Some measure of service can be made, however, if attention is given to the hours of service that the library provides each week, the extent of faculty and student use of the library, and the various tasks performed by library staffs which attempt to promote library use.

Hours of service in these institutions varied from a high of ninety-four to a low of thirty hours per week. Standards of the Southern Association of Colleges and Schools, which accredits most of these institutions, require that college libraries be open for service a minimum of sixty hours per week and call for eighty hours of service per week at universities. On the whole, the institutions tend to meet this standard, although a few far exceed it and a few fall below it.

Fifty-six, or 87.5 percent, of the sixty-four respondents to this section stated that they prepared bibliographies for faculty, student, or community use. Sixty-one, or 95.3 percent, engage in forms of orientation for faculty and students. Forty, or 62.5 percent, reported that they provided bibliographic services as needed. Library publications were issued by fifty, or 78.1 percent, of the libraries reporting. For the most part, these publications were in the form of library handbooks, special subject bibliographies, or acquisition lists.

Table 21 shows faculty use of libraries between 1964-65 and 1968-69 in certain institutions responding. While per capita circulation figures were unavailable, the table indicates fluctuation in use of materials in the various libraries. It must be considered that statistics on use may be suspect, for they generally disregard items used from open shelves. Nevertheless, these statistics do provide some measure of the extent to which library materials are used.

Table 22 shows student use of libraries between 1964-65 and 1968-69 in those institutions responding. As was the case with faculty use, a more realistic picture would be possible if per capita circulation figures were examined. In view of this limitation, however, the table can be analyzed to show the extent to which circulation statistics increased or decreased during the years in question. Furthermore, student use of library materials tended to fluctuate at most of the institutions reporting.

Circulation figures for reserve books at the reporting institutions between 1964-65 and 1968-69 can be seen in Table 23. If one compares these fig-

TABLE 21

Faculty Use of Collections in Certain Black College
Libraries, 1964-65 Through 1968-69

Institution	1964-65	1965-66	1966-67	1967-68	1968-69
Alabama A & M*		160	194	300	651
Alabama State*	839	539			314
Alcorn*	844	678	681	860	1,340
Arkansas A M & N*	381	1,462	1,770	604	956
Atlanta**	1,882	2,169	2,028	2,784	2,534
Barber-Scotia**		300	500	495	164
Benedict**					
Bishop**		666	760	593	720
Central State*	1,574	1,496	1,887	1,344	1,076
Cheyney*					
Claflin**	89	92	98	120	132
Clark**					
Dillard**	899	898	825	943	1,191
Elizabeth City*	2,091	1,302	33	733	487
Fayetteville*			445	552	732
Fisk**	252	636	789	853	148
Florida A & M*	3,056	2,926	3,095	2,322	5,074
Florida Memorial**					
Fort Valley*	1,458	1,499	1,713	2,069	1,132
Grambling*					
Hampton**					
Huston-Tillotson**	625	259	482	448	520
Jackson State*		435	568	510	574

TABLE 21 (continued)

Institution	1964-65	1965-66	1966-67	1967-68	1968-69
Jarvis Christian**					
Johnson C. Smith**	734	1,069	906	1,359	309
Kentucky State*	569	503	482	511	645
Knoxville**	527	379	417	644	1,196
Lane**	873	349	235	373	395
Langston*	1,059	583	731	1,362	1,728
LeMoyne-Owen**					
Lincoln (Mo.)*	591	707	681	785	728
Lincoln (Pa.)**	1,289	1,494	1,767	2,227	2,456
Livingstone**	124	366	231	237	297
Miss. Valley*					
Morris**					
Morris Brown**	177	225	210	203	357
Norfolk*	967	1,446	2,162	1,653	831
North Carolina A & T*	4,531	5,729	6,977	5,781	6,313
North Carolina Central*	6,234	6,665	4,397	5,159	5,261
Oakwood**	500	600	700	800	900
Paine**	1,290	903	649	775	1,082
Paul Quinn**					
Philander Smith**					
Prairie View*					
St. Augustine**	1,347	955	745	989	577
Shaw**	141	239	204	362	322
Simmons**					
South Carolina State*	1,786	2,073	1,611	892	703

TABLE 21 (continued)

Institution	1964-65	1965-66	1966-67	1967-68	1968-69
Southern*					
Southern Univ. N. O.*	628	653	798	801	873
Stillman**	1,193		253	204	216
Talladega**		624			
Texas College**	131	519	64	268	168
Texas Southern*				1,032	1,774
Tougaloo**	1,103	1,079	594	546	
Tuskegee**					
Virginia State*					
Virginia Union**	798	2,244	1,729	974	943
Voorhees**	63	42	58	65	85
West Virginia State*	658	795	1,915	1,094	888
Wilberforce**					
Wiley**	261	217	521	569	375
Winston-Salem*					
Xavier**	2,601	2,477	1,042	1,143	1,475

*public.
**private

TABLE 22

Student Use of Collections in Certain Black College Libraries, 1964-65 Through 1968-69

Institution	1964-65	1965-66	1966-67	1967-68	1968-69
Alabama A & M*		30,667	31,152	39,580	39,138
Alabama State*	58,238	57,297			55,795
Alcorn*	53,958	40,087	31,835	25,957	33,392
Arkansas A M & N*	34,118	57,546	41,685	22,762	49,017
Atlanta**	51,242	67,829	66,043	58,356	53,879
Barber-Scotia**		2,093	1,045	1,200	2,343
Benedict**	31,089	44,086	55,956	34,483	40,081
Bishop**		23,109	14,481	15,815	16,986
Central State*	66,627	65,403	58,291	49,205	38,764
Cheyney*	27,548	22,279	25,256	24,803	26,066
Claflin**	8,037	9,751	12,234	6,638	7,070
Clark**	42,977	36,250	21,031	22,041	14,302
Dillard**	14,141	16,764	17,781	18,622	21,838
Elizabeth City*	20,593	18,664	12,086	11,093	7,718
Fayetteville*			22,980	20,773	20,376
Fisk**	12,413	14,527	14,835	13,343	16,020
Florida A & M*	54,864	77,284	86,060	61,106	52,240
Florida Memorial**					
Fort Valley*	87,407	106,620	110,776	119,089	128,914
Grambling*					
Hampton**	91,805	81,107	88,924	96,657	74,873
Huston-Tillotson**	16,655	10,287	9,336	10,237	7,514
Jackson State*		128,452	135,673	134,511	168,711

TABLE 22 (continued)

Institution	1964-65	1965-66	1966-67	1967-68	1968-69
Jarvis Christian**					
Johnson C. Smith**	26,958	29,090	24,778	25,633	27,000
Kentucky State*	20,957	20,003	18,885	17,164	21,406
Knoxville**	33,608	31,664	35,475	50,579	45,745
Lane**	40,948	39,482	43,588	51,463	53,070
Langston*	13,343	18,968	19,791	41,203	41,416
LeMoyne-Owen**					
Lincoln (Mo.)*	19,028	19,222	20,426	21,682	15,141
Lincoln (Pa.)**	14,529	17,834	19,784	20,804	19,931
Livingstone**	8,622	13,721	8,365	10,975	15,051
Miss. Valley*	81,808	82,037	93,034	79,802	69,121
Morris**					
Morris Brown**	9,099	10,815	11,750	11,358	14,095
Norfolk*	84,077	107,288	101,728	95,853	17,436
North Carolina A & T*	106,985	120,792	115,184	115,021	108,705
North Carolina Central*	182,212	187,010	187,076	161,802	168,078
Oakwood**	24,200	31,000	40,000	45,000	50,000
Paine**	15,444	17,798	21,802	16,259	16,949
Paul Quinn**					
Philander Smith**					11,464
Prairie View*					
St. Augustine**	37,975	34,703	43,737	31,486	33,989
Shaw**	14,709	15,039	13,825	12,675	26,645
Simmons**					
South Carolina State*	55,960	50,050	53,577	50,503	48,964

TABLE 22 (continued)

Institution	1964-65	1965-66	1966-67	1967-68	1968-69
Southern*					147,941
Southern Univ. N. O.*	32,879	40,681	60,676	63,186	65,076
Stillman**	14,721	17,875	11,806	8,979	8,061
Talladega**		21,003	11,231	12,625	12,188
Texas College**	13,373	16,246	13,125	13,788	9,442
Texas Southern*				53,989	74,360
Tougaloo**	52,685	50,519	50,708	36,509	
Tuskegee**					
Virginia State*	61,820	63,250	63,533	59,187	58,518
Virginia Union**	26,154	28,211	29,837	24,573	21,646
West Virginia State*	52,440	51,036	51,228	49,269	48,017
Wilberforce**	3,806	7,838	11,597	14,103	8,397
Wiley**	10,277	9,465	6,903	35,410	16,612
Winston-Salem*	54,221	56,377	58,287	49,614	41,579
Xavier**	28,718	21,024	23,404	25,444	27,853

*public.
**private.

TABLE 23

Use of Reserve Books in Certain Black College
Libraries, 1964-65 Through 1968-69

Institution	1964-65	1965-66	1966-67	1967-68	1968-69
Alabama A & M*		9,420	10,141	15,611	13,560
Alabama State*	5,795	3,182			
Alcorn*					
Arkansas A M & N*					
Atlanta**	13,687	13,290	16,012	8,631	2,914
Barber-Scotia**		502	122	350	463
Benedict**					
Bishop**		10,758	12,756	6,548	6,235
Central State*	22,608	19,792	19,368	12,499	8,721
Cheyney*	11,978	9,861	7,806	6,184	5,464
Claflin**	612	522	435	650	1,297
Clark**					
Dillard**	12,521	11,619	7,946	7,118	5,699
Elizabeth City*	23,167	12,971	5,427	9,791	12,415
Fayetteville*			12,873	13,778	7,220
Fisk**	1,449	2,773	2,254	1,400	1,577
Florida A & M*	29,241	21,054	23,478	59,717	120,745
Florida Memorial**					
Fort Valley*	7,988	8,495	6,109	6,262	6,265
Grambling*					
Hampton**	27,340	31,195	20,289	17,157	8,281
Huston-Tillotson**	3,995	2,322	2,387	2,387	2,771
Jackson State*		3,439	2,928	4,110	1,102

TABLE 23 (continued)

Institution	1964-65	1965-66	1966-67	1967-68	1968-69
Jarvis Christian**	936	950	899	1,246	1,333
Johnson C. Smith**	13,241	8,774	7,116	6,488	6,856
Kentucky State*	21,070	14,490	4,803	6,260	7,027
Knoxville**	12,534	8,106	5,378	9,286	7,685
Lane**					
Langston*					
LeMoyne-Owen**	33,841	32,022	30,318	27,861	24,441
Lincoln (Mo.)*	11,102	16,642	13,803	17,153	13,256
Lincoln (Pa.)**	1,313	1,622	617	366	561
Livingstone**					
Miss. Valley*					
Morris**	4,746	6,828	8,501	7,561	3,780
Morris Brown**	17,436	21,350	25,002	29,658	30,842
Norfolk*				23,083	19,890
North Carolina A & T*	38,226	72,727	61,266	53,510	20,400
North Carolina Central*					
Oakwood**	17,736	18,184	17,120	15,639	9,541
Paine**					
Paul Quinn**					
Philander Smith**					
Prairie View*	70,295	37,895	14,631	3,167	12,446
St. Augustine**	6,738	4,451	2,341	2,538	2,591
Shaw**					
Simmons**					

TABLE 23 (continued)

Institution	1964-65	1965-66	1966-67	1967-68	1968-69
South Carolina State*	6,254	6,043	6,150	4,450	3,735
Southern*					
Southern Univ. N. O.*	10,891	11,315	16,928	17,116	17,825
Stillman**	16,389	13,775	12,529	11,262	10,071
Talladega**			5,224	5,522	5,452
Texas College**	6,139	6,875	2,306	1,281	2,079
Texas Southern*				15,458	13,486
Tougaloo**	4,503	15,234	10,045	4,670	
Tuskegee**					
Virginia State*	29,583	37,138	32,187	36,747	45,295
Virginia Union**	3,861	3,777	5,786	3,011	4,839
Voorhees**	2,848	2,403	3,551	1,113	2,254
West Virginia State*	5,192	6,355	7,309	7,802	6,719
Wilberforce**	500	1,000	1,500	2,736	2,038
Wiley**	420	381	357	795	463
Winston-Salem*	19,948	19,688	14,975	6,954	9,560
Xavier**	9,425	10,437	11,652	10,799	13,312

*public.
**private.

ures to student use of libraries, the results suggest that these libraries have
had generous circulation of reserve items and that students and faculty tend
to rely heavily on reserve materials.

Library Cooperation

The use of interlibrary loan to provide convenient access to certain
materials not housed in the borrowing library is a popular practice long
observed in libraries. It is perhaps the oldest example of library cooperative programs in existence. Table 24 shows the number of items bor-
rowed on interlibrary loan by the reporting institutions between 1964-
65 and 1968-69.

In recent years, membership in library consortia has mushroomed as
libraries seek means of strengthening their resources and services through
cooperative programs with other libraries. The study revealed that thirty-
three, or 50.7 percent, of these libraries contributed to local or regional
union lists of library materials. Thirty-five, or 53.8 percent, of the libraries reporting held membership in one or more consortia. Cooperative acquisitions programs involved twenty-two, or 33.8 percent, of the libraries;
while thirty-seven, or 56.9 percent, of the libraries were involved in various types of special agreements with other libraries.

Some of the cooperative programs in which these libraries were engaged
were restricted to local libraries, as was the case with Lane College and two
additional area colleges. Some were statewide, as was the Alabama Center
for Higher Education. Still others transcended local and state boundaries,
as was the case with the Cooperative College Library Center in Atlanta
and the Tri-State Library Cooperative, in which Lincoln (Pennsylvania)
participates.

Automated Services

As educators have placed increased attention on the use of the computer in the academic institution, their attention has also been extended
to library operations and services.[7] The survey pointed out that certain
of the libraries reporting had already automated some of their services
or had made plans to do so. Sixteen, or 24.6 percent, planned to automate cataloging practices, while two had already automated these services. Fourteen, or 21.5 percent, planned to automate book selection
routines. Twenty-eight, or 43 percent, planned to automate acquisition
practices, while two libraries had already done so. Fifteen, or 23 percent,
planned to automate processing activities; and one had already converted.
Automated circulation systems were planned in twenty-nine, or 44.6 per-

TABLE 24

Materials Circulated Through Interlibrary Loan in Certain Black College Libraries, 1964-65 Through 1968-69

Institution	1964-65	1965-66	1966-67	1967-68	1968-69
Alabama A & M*				150	85
Alabama State*				13	15
Alcorn*					
Arkansas A M & N*				17	15
Atlanta**	77	79	28	51	63
Barber-Scotia**		15	12	20	35
Benedict**					
Bishop**	20	17	25	33	41
Central State*	48	36	74	94	152
Cheyney*		17	20	23	22
Claflin**		4	4	10	16
Clark**					
Dillard**	6	10	23	4	27
Elizabeth City*					
Fayetteville*	26	32	29	28	51
Fisk**	156	95	75	73	60
Florida A & M*	82	20	104	63	6
Florida Memorial**					
Fort Valley*	27	25	34	75	98
Grambling*					
Hampton**	277	231	120	138	141
Huston-Tillotson**					
Jackson State*		79	70	112	96

TABLE 24 (continued)

Institution	1964-65	1965-66	1966-67	1967-68	1968-69
Jarvis Christian**					
Johnson C. Smith**	3	2	5	12	10
Kentucky State*	106	191	155	168	173
Knoxville**	112	92	84	116	112
Lane**	12	3	11	25	19
Langston*					
LeMoyne-Owen**	107	215	387	281	189
Lincoln (Mo.)*	45	7	23	89	237
Lincoln (Pa.)**					
Livingstone**					
Miss. Valley*	10	16	29	31	19
Morris**					
Morris Brown**					
Norfolk*	60	48	40	65	21
North Carolina A & T*	22	10	60	72	56
North Carolina Central*			159	150	255
Oakwood**					
Paine**			7	3	3
Paul Quinn**					
Philander Smith**					2
Prairie View*	99	97	115	146	638
St. Augustine**					
Shaw**	30	30	25	20	15
Simmons**					
South Carolina State*	18	56	21	62	58

TABLE 24 (continued)

Institution	1964-65	1965-66	1966-67	1967-68	1968-69
Southern*					
Southern Univ. N. O.*	20	32	49	72	53
Stillman**	27		37	17	19
Talladega**					
Texas College**					
Texas Southern*				387	285
Tougaloo**	1	1	17	43	30
Tuskegee**					
Virginia State*	109	251	218	242	264
Virginia Union**	11	3	2	6	
Voorhees**	12				
West Virginia State*				209	252
Wilberforce**	19	42	163	405	191
Wiley**					
Winston-Salem*		2	57		21
Xavier**	34	47	42	39	54

*public.
**private.

cent, of the libraries, while six had already automated. Library fines systems were planned for automation in twenty, or 30.7 percent, of the libraries. Twelve, or 18.4 percent, of the libraries planned to automate their inventory systems, while four had already done so. A system of automated budgeting was planned in twelve, or 18.4 percent, of the libraries; four had already initiated an automated system; and another had a system which was partially automated.

Audiovisual Equipment

ALA standards suggest that libraries provide audiovisual services on campus if no other department has assumed that responsibility. Many of these libraries have made some provisions for housing and servicing various media and have, to some extent, provided equipment for utilization. Fifty-one, or 78.4 percent, provided record players; twenty-four, or 36.9 percent, had overhead projectors; thirty-six, or 55.3 percent, provided tape recorders; thirty-two, or 49.2 percent, provided movie projectors; and twenty-two, or 33.8 percent, provided other types of audiovisual equipment. Fourteen, or 21.5 percent, reported that their libraries were equipped with wet carrels.[8]

Budgets

Of primary importance in determining the quality of library services, resources, and facilities is the extent to which funds are provided for their support. In small, developing institutions such as those included in this study, where years of neglect have taken their toll, the library budget must necessarily come under careful scrutiny in an attempt to determine whether or not adequate funds have been placed at the librarian's disposal.

Table 25 shows total library expenditures for the reporting institutions between 1964-65 and 1968-69. In 1964-65, only thirteen, or 23.6 percent, of the fifty-five institutions reporting expended $100,000 or more for all library purposes. By 1968-69, nineteen, or 34.5 percent, had expended $100,000 or more; ten, or 18.1 percent, had exceeded $200,000; one, or 1.8 percent, had expended over $300,000; and two, or 3.6 percent, had exceeded $400,000. At the other extreme for 1968-69, one library reported a total budget of $5,697, while another claimed $61,193. These low expenditures no doubt lead to the inadequate staff salaries, meager book budgets, and other inadequacies found in some of these libraries.

TABLE 25

Total Library Expenditures in Certain Black Colleges,
1964-65 Through 1968-69

Institution	1964-65	1965-66	1966-67	1967-68	1968-69
Alabama A & M*	$80,220	$94,700	$158,247	$181,168	$187,764
Alabama State*	88,350	81,125	87,824	71,247	82,325
Alcorn*	85,595	79,807	122,714	160,419	165,822
Arkansas A M & N*					
Atlanta**	167,095	210,599	251,327	225,684	244,995
Barber-Scotia**	4,883	11,262	4,244	4,517	5,697
Benedict**	39,561	73,098	74,964	100,228	105,509
Bishop**	61,810	116,258	127,666	223,327	246,130
Central State*	101,678	115,387	126,668	172,970	180,177
Cheyney*	171,635	217,281	290,936	218,250	314,715
Claflin*	32,833	44,475	51,910	74,944	94,517
Clark**	26,680	17,797	26,833	35,392	38,965
Dillard**	43,549	64,275	70,562	68,483	109,326
Elizabeth City*	42,740		48,718	63,401	70,283
Fayetteville*	63,109	56,919	55,280	101,555	147,613
Fisk**	63,531	102,489	143,792	166,119	163,833
Florida A & M*	187,064	245,017	249,493	462,004	454,297
Florida Memorial**		25,062	31,334	37,226	49,636
Fort Valley*	102,024	135,272	143,910	176,600	208,991
Grambling*	139,871	192,753	265,380	232,827	230,836
Hampton**	93,320	98,784	135,247	157,351	165,588
Huston-Tillotson**	30,484	32,132	45,030	52,505	62,869
Jackson State*					

TABLE 25 (continued)

Institution	1964-65	1965-66	1966-67	1967-68	1968-69
Jarvis Christian**	57,124		52,538	94,570	103,831
Johnson C. Smith**					
Kentucky State*	49,883	63,203	77,819	127,956	157,508
Knoxville**	47,246	58,050	70,367	92,954	90,211
Lane**	51,418	54,579	67,998	66,980	90,280
Langston*	58,169	63,096	67,790	79,117	87,439
LeMoyne-Owen**	34,281	38,593	44,314	44,515	57,646
Lincoln (Mo.)*	74,562	85,077	118,914	128,103	134,301
Lincoln (Pa.)**	65,531	72,665	103,911	140,948	202,309
Livingstone**	29,215	37,684	54,631	56,310	56,879
Miss. Valley*	68,706	77,461	105,642	144,827	198,176
Morris**	12,317	19,919	35,571	31,212	37,221
Morris Brown**	23,031	35,687	40,872	36,317	94,053
Norfolk*					
North Carolina A & T*	175,294	224,315	310,508	195,452	298,507
North Carolina Central*	167,709	174,395	197,775	246,457	268,691
Oakwood**	25,482	25,904	28,894	40,264	39,542
Paine**	20,190	40,493	54,731	56,306	68,577
Paul Quinn**	15,626			31,204	43,670
Philander Smith**	21,119	27,368	31,254	56,834	68,621
Prairie View*	83,836	100,108			
St. Augustine**	14,200	32,000	60,179	81,623	83,475
Shaw**			54,529	70,161	136,519
Simmons**					

TABLE 25 (continued)

Institution	1964-65	1965-66	1966-67	1967-68	1968-69
South Carolina State*	81,158	65,647	99,142	92,720	195,022
Southern*	193,579	227,589	302,358	250,175	
Southern Univ. N. O.*	113,922	115,421	121,193	179,457	175,501
Stillman**	32,220	42,080	56,503	51,809	61,193
Talladega**					
Texas College**	24,891	23,764	40,178	61,981	77,925
Texas Southern*	131,677	186,339	230,073	314,269	419,962
Tougaloo**	48,280	53,616	67,452	82,438	86,267
Tuskegee**	176,940	232,196	259,965	273,107	270,463
Virginia State*	162,610	160,059	178,064	187,670	223,303
Virginia Union**	76,111	91,656	121,167	137,126	112,754
Voorhees**	12,511	12,668	19,125	112,700	74,299
West Virginia State*	79,918	102,570	123,933	152,610	153,376
Wilberforce**	19,661	34,702	43,390	78,682	77,657
Wiley**	29,212	28,683	29,145	69,817	102,523
Winston-Salem*	43,877	47,755	78,300	104,886	112,580
Xavier**	49,523	45,549	51,862	63,049	68,683

*public.
**private.

Tables 26 and 27 give a comparison of the actual operating costs of the libraries included in this study to the corresponding operating costs calculated for them by using the Baumol and Marcus regression equations.

TABLE 26

Total Operating Costs for Selected
Public Colleges, 1967-68

Institution	Baumol-Marcus Model	Actual
Alabama A & M	$156,314	$181,168
Alabama State	122,318	71,247
Alcorn	83,477	160,419
Central State	129,290	172,970
Florida A & M	449,763	462,004
Fort Valley	111,343	176,600
Grambling	147,032	232,827
Kentucky State	138,597	127,956
Langston	76,996	79,117
Lincoln (Mo.)	123,139	128,103
North Carolina A & T	224,885	195,452
North Carolina Central	247,144	246,457
South Carolina State	146,129	192,720
Texas Southern	307,398	314,269
West Virginia State	210,749	152,610
Winston-Salem	134,351	104,886

TABLE 27

Total Operating Costs For Selected
Private Colleges, 1967-68

Institution	Baumol-Marcus Model	Actual
Benedict	$ 60,543	$100,228
Dillard	81,955	68,483
Fisk	144,267	166,119
Hampton	127,324	157,351
Lane	53,039	66,980
St. Augustine	72,251	81,623
Tuskegee	218,120	273,107
Virginia Union	109,419	137,126
Xavier	84,601	63,049

A comparison of library budgets for salaries appears in Table 28. A wide variance in the figures reported appears for each year between 1964-65 and 1968-69. For example, in 1964-65, a high of $88,411 was reported, with a low of $5,583. This wide range continued through 1968-69, when a high of $243,634 was reported, with a low of $16,812. On the whole, salary figures were higher at the publicly supported institutions than at the privately supported ones.

A comparison of library expenditures for wages between 1964-65 and 1968-69 appears in Table 29. As the table indicates, there was a wide variation in these expenditures beginning in 1964-65, when a high of $9,322 was reported, with a low of $722. In 1968-69, a high of $67,000 was reported, with a low of $1,900.

ALA standards suggest that usually at least twice as much should be expended for salaries as for books. When expenditures for salaries and wages in the reporting institutions are combined, one finds an incidence of libraries that do not meet this standard. This fact does not necessarily indicate that the institutions are spending too much for materials but rather that they may be spending too little for salaries and wages.

Table 30 shows a comparison of book budgets in fifty-one reporting institutions between 1964-65 and 1968-69. As the table indicates, there was a wide range in expenditures for books at various institutions during each year in question. In 1964-65, for example, the highest amount allocated was $99,504, while the lowest was $1,101; and by 1968-69, the highest was $200,950 and the lowest $3,304. In each of the years, expenditures were considerably greater at the publicly supported institutions than at the privately supported ones, although it must be kept in mind that higher enrollments are also found at the publicly supported institutions.

Tables 31 and 32 compare the actual costs of volumes added in 1967-68 to the corresponding costs calculated by using the Baumol-Marcus regression equations.

An examination of the expenditures for periodicals in these institutions, as shown in Table 33, reveals wide variations among institutions between 1964-65 and 1968-69. In 1964-65, for example, the highest amount expended for periodicals was $43,081, while the lowest was $1,002. By 1968-69, the highest amount allocated was $35,000, while the lowest was $954. It is unsound to make comparisons between expenditures at the publicly and privately supported institutions because much of the data is lacking for several of the publicly supported schools. One can see, however, that when

TABLE 28

Expenditures for Salaries in Certain Black College
Libraries, 1964-65 Through 1968-69

Institution	1964-65	1965-66	1966-67	1967-68	1968-69
Alabama A & M*				$ 84,596	$ 92,000
Alabama State*					
Alcorn*					
Arkansas A M & N*	$30,382	$ 38,800	$ 48,337	57,263	85,055
Atlanta**	83,325	94,484	101,628	107,523	111,956
Barber-Scotia**					
Benedict**	22,075	34,339	33,780	45,131	47,650
Bishop**					
Central State*	66,224	73,595	93,464	99,400	118,113
Cheyney*	63,996	68,575	75,328	92,353	105,265
Claflin**	18,034	25,013	31,523	36,789	44,620
Clark**					
Dillard**	17,285	29,245	23,224	28,866	34,124
Elizabeth City*	25,539				
Fayetteville*	33,133	35,657	36,265	48,371	61,570
Fisk**	46,775	74,005	94,518	110,764	127,912
Florida A & M*		111,855	143,990	203,404	243,634
Florida Memorial**					
Fort Valley*	67,715	70,955	99,000	102,500	111,960
Grambling*		128,735	123,621	113,537	130,136
Hampton**	62,794	70,436	83,338	89,889	94,695
Huston-Tillotson**	14,050	15,017	25,680	23,535	37,689
Jackson State*					

TABLE 28 (continued)

Institution	1964-65	1965-66	1966-67	1967-68	1968-69
Jarvis Christian**	14,875	28,966		31,224	32,610
Johnson C. Smith**	26,800	38,900	44,000	51,770	57,970
Kentucky State*	28,134	35,742	31,300	52,070	73,868
Knoxville**	27,229	39,379	49,807	68,954	61,797
Lane**	23,721	24,635	34,271	35,427	40,138
Langston*	31,620	34,910	38,890	42,400	45,000
LeMoyne-Owen**					
Lincoln (Mo.)*	49,244	53,267	68,840	75,840	74,230
Lincoln (Pa.)**	42,889	44,380	58,104	71,479	109,646
Livingstone**	20,763	24,136	29,093	28,831	32,046
Miss. Valley*	52,068	61,149	75,988	82,971	119,561
Morris**					
Morris Brown**	12,433	19,881	20,470	22,550	34,959
Norfolk*					
North Carolina A & T*	85,151	108,411	125,524	133,000	138,136
North Carolina Central*		112,872	133,944	156,416	171,457
Oakwood**	5,583	5,804	9,844	11,952	16,812
Paine**	12,923	17,331	28,555	30,683	38,685
Paul Quinn**					
Philander Smith**	11,405	16,009	15,454	17,222	242,298
Prairie View*					
St. Augustine**			28,194	30,541	40,000
Shaw**			27,000	32,528	63,349
Simmons**					
South Carolina State*					

TABLE 28 (continued)

Institution	1964-65	1965-66	1966-67	1967-68	1968-69
Southern*		115,022	134,648	144,324	
Southern Univ. N. O.*	62,041	72,843	68,265	85,190	98,840
Stillman**	18,385	18,249	20,797	28,350	27,747
Talladega**					
Texas College**	12,837	12,990	17,661	23,874	23,868
Texas Southern*	88,411	127,335	128,329	172,650	211,113
Tougaloo**	26,861	35,566	40,897	47,537	51,004
Tuskegee**	80,000	94,000	100,000	116,344	119,200
Virginia State*	86,390	88,962	106,214	108,408	88,773
Virginia Union**	34,388	28,800	30,568	42,147	46,892
Voorhees**	8,943	7,623	5,609	20,387	33,201
West Virginia State*	53,886	67,530	76,111	78,113	80,541
Wilberforce**					
Wiley**	17,575	15,300	16,433	43,303	52,115
Winston-Salem*	24,853	28,066	25,766	40,288	39,558
Xavier**	19,636	19,682	28,179	34,000	35,300

*public.
**private.

TABLE 29

Expenditures for Wages in Certain Black College
Libraries, 1964-65 Through 1968-69

Institution	1964-65	1965-66	1966-67	1967-68	1968-69
Alabama A & M*				$ 8,500	$10,239
Alabama State*	$6,500	$10,125	$ 2,849	2,962	
Alcorn*					
Arkansas A M & N*	6,982	8,171	2,088	10,934	8,619
Atlanta**	8,818	10,466	12,416	16,707	24,993
Barber-Scotia**					
Benedict**	2,000	19,136	17,830	18,720	20,418
Bishop**					
Central State*		8,865	7,836	3,000	5,000
Cheyney*	3,200	2,800	2,600	3,500	5,000
Claflin**	1,292			1,155	3,098
Clark**					
Dillard**	6,475	5,943	8,435	4,151	18,902
Elizabeth City*					
Fayetteville*	1,907	1,824	1,898	3,335	1,900
Fisk**					
Florida A & M*	9,140	12,207	18,000	14,400	21,825
Florida Memorial**					
Fort Valley*	3,000	7,700			4,800
Grambling*	7,879		34,054	55,312	55,550
Hampton**	8,022	5,017	6,744	8,809	9,457
Huston-Tillotson**	2,565	6,322	9,466	8,908	3,282
Jackson State*					

TABLE 29 (continued)

Institution	1964-65	1965-66	1966-67	1967-68	1968-69
Jarvis Christian**	1,825		17,000	29,220	
Johnson C. Smith**	722	1,928	1,225	3,598	4,347
Kentucky State*	2,664	5,242	5,138	5,079	6,200
Knoxville**					
Lane**	9,322				
Langston*	8,000	9,000	10,000	14,000	14,000
LeMoyne-Owen**					
Lincoln (Mo.)*	3,000	3,500	4,000	7,600	5,865
Lincoln (Pa.)**					
Livingstone**	869	1,940	2,077	2,001	3,954
Miss. Valley*	3,362	1,664	1,662	8,865	6,448
Morris**					
Morris Brown**	1,903	5,787	7,546	5,309	14,024
Norfolk*					
North Carolina A & T*	8,043	29,770	88,600	38,400	42,215
North Carolina Central*		13,116	6,543	8,690	8,952
Oakwood**	3,403	2,492	4,245	6,299	5,420
Paine**		2,660	6,499	5,130	8,354
Paul Quinn**					
Philander Smith**				14,415	20,753
Prairie View*					
St. Augustine**					
Shaw**					
Simmons*					

TABLE 29 (continued)

Institution	1964-65	1965-66	1966-67	1967-68	1968-69
South Carolina State*					
Southern*	4,120	17,343	33,322	16,904	
Southern Univ. N. O.*	3,955		2,369	9,059	7,721
Stillman**	3,744			9,800	12,048
Texas College**		2,400	15,809	16,000	16,000
Texas Southern*					
Tougaloo**	1,467	896	3,573	3,873	13,586
Tuskegee**		45,120	58,505	64,466	67,000
Virginia State*		18,940	19,500	23,287	31,544
Virginia Union**		8,947	13,924	17,255	8,043
Voorhees**	6,194				
West Virginia State*		16,471	24,053	11,978	11,218
Wilberforce**				50,741	60,000
Wiley**	1,532	1,041	3,627	4,567	13,842
Winston-Salem*	2,549	2,988	3,029	5,224	4,980
Xavier**	5,922	5,958	5,614	22,000	24,214

*public.
**private.

TABLE 30

Expenditures for Books in Certain Black College
Libraries, 1964-65 Through 1968-69

Institution	1964-65	1965-66	1966-67	1967-68	1968-69
Alabama A & M*	$28,500	$ 35,979	$ 70,864	$ 85,000	$ 82,000
Alabama State*	54,000	42,000	45,000	35,000	40,000
Alcorn*					
Arkansas A M & N*	15,748	22,930	35,238	26,660	54,344
Atlanta**	31,341	46,957	63,091	59,005	52,174
Barber-Scotia**	2,641	5,588	463	2,282	3,304
Benedict**	7,072	11,903	17,320	28,758	26,049
Bishop**					
Central State*	17,066	29,786	35,935	40,000	50,000
Cheyney*	99,504	144,106	205,308	118,897	200,950
Claflin**	8,412	10,275	10,871	16,240	16,109
Clark**					
Dillard**	11,494	18,287	28,358	24,440	46,357
Elizabeth City*	14,046				
Fayetteville*	25,120	16,502	14,697	44,300	80,408
Fisk**	12,318	8,544	11,302	22,500	28,824
Florida A & M*	41,018	72,000	49,456	166,000	144,794
Florida Memorial**					
Fort Valley*	14,339	28,044	27,186	51,652	64,636
Grambling*	7,258	36,171	54,066	37,898	18,812
Hampton**	12,198	12,572	30,526	43,531	37,129
Huston-Tillotson**	11,352	7,752	14,749	15,438	16,581

TABLE 30 (continued)

Institution	1964-65	1965-66	1966-67	1967-68	1968-69
Jackson State*	8,846	11,200	20,367		15,000
Jarvis Christian**	21,298	18,930	23,816	14,919	12,846
Johnson C. Smith**	11,750	12,888	29,000	50,166	54,450
Kentucky State*	6,339	13,000	13,647	23,824	15,000
Knoxville**	8,827	21,612	23,404	25,874	31,718
Lane**	12,866	7,100	10,900	14,062	17,139
Langston*					
LeMoyne-Owen**	10,296	11,068	23,671	24,000	30,760
Lincoln (Mo.)*	10,847	9,759	24,394	29,782	39,123
Lincoln (Pa.)**	3,730	7,060	17,366	19,035	12,103
Livingstone**	2,653	3,711	15,498	34,232	40,492
Miss. Valley*					
Morris**					
Morris Brown**	6,351	5,003	10,000	6,163	39,658
Norfolk*					
North Carolina A & T*	73,946	77,886	83,785	115,313	109,085
North Carolina Central*	47,821	42,483	47,498	69,699	76,065
Oakwood**	10,802	12,734	12,163	19,268	13,058
Paine**	5,341	12,259	16,777	15,873	17,098
Paul Quinn**					
Philander Smith**	7,314	7,447	14,666	17,489	17,616
Prairie View*	35,713	54,461			46,965
St. Augustine**			26,480	47,683	31,500
Shaw**			16,157	17,962	35,036
Simmons**					

TABLE 30 (continued)

Institution	1964-65	1965-66	1966-67	1967-68	1968-69
South Carolina State*					
Southern*					
Southern Univ. N. O.*	29,364	32,011	31,340	60,868	56,630
Stillman**	5,925	7,431	11,612	6,821	12,547
Talladega**					
Texas College**	2,881	4,432	1,892	16,238	25,746
Texas Southern*	27,000	33,382	60,922	107,266	157,266
Tougaloo**	14,389	11,835	18,045	24,939	10,695
Tuskegee**	40,000	47,000	48,300	48,250	47,900
Virginia State*	46,718	26,080	23,443	44,628	74,658
Virginia Union**	20,692	26,344	49,630	50,755	35,266
Voorhees**	1,101	2,534	12,742	73,906	33,508
West Virginia State*	15,791	21,532	33,288	46,297	49,762
Wilberforce**	4,180	14,145	13,380	18,863	11,289
Wiley**	8,854	6,470	3,545	14,852	18,000
Winston-Salem*	11,869	11,783	45,260	50,267	61,544
Xavier**	7,219	9,460	7,132	8,200	13,286

*public.
**private.

TABLE 31

Cost of Volumes Added in 1967-68 to the Library
Collections of Selected Public Colleges

Institution	Baumol-Marcus Model	Actual
Alabama A & M	$ 70,130	$ 85,000
Alabama State	43,220	35,000
Alcorn		
Central State	46,284	40,000
Florida A & M	202,552	166,000
Fort Valley	67,429	51,652
Grambling	45,936	37,898
Kentucky State	75,491	50,166
Langston	33,205	14,062
Lincoln (Mo.)	38,243	24,000
North Carolina A & T	187,280	115,313
North Carolina Central	54,612	69,699
South Carolina State		
Texas Southern	141,584	107,266
West Virginia State	100,606	46,297
Winston-Salem	54,184	50,267

TABLE 32

Cost of Volumes Added in 1967-68 to the Library
Collections of Selected Private Colleges

Institution	Baumol-Marcus Model	Actual
Benedict	$18,421	$28,758
Dillard	30,045	24,440
Fisk	47,279	22,500
Hampton	40,456	43,531
Lane	17,541	25,874
St. Augustine	27,197	47,683
Tuskegee	91,679	48,250
Virginia Union	43,821	50,755
Xavier	23,650	8,200

TABLE 33

Expenditures for Periodicals in Certain Black College
Libraries, 1964-65 Through 1968-69

Institution	1964-65	1965-66	1966-67	1967-68	1968-69
Alabama A & M*					
Alabama State*	$12,000	$14,000	$15,000	$11,600	$14,000
Alcorn*					
Arkansas A M & N*	189	1,740	3,049	4,568	954
Atlanta**	9,922	17,113	12,751	13,828	11,770
Barber-Scotia**	1,002	2,534	2,094	982	2,426
Benedict**	3,000	2,589	2,858	1,604	4,674
Bishop**					
Central State*				10,000	15,000
Cheyney*					
Claflin**	2,733	4,033	4,421	4,776	4,689
Clark**					
Dillard**	5,785	6,349	7,235	8,060	6,781
Elizabeth City*					
Fayetteville*					
Fisk**					
Florida A & M*	13,016	16,064	8,782	16,000	19,000
Florida Memorial**					
Fort Valley*	10,000	11,000	10,897	11,831	14,223
Grambling*	11,219	13,471	55,882	16,533	19,120
Hampton**	5,804	5,730	9,111	8,505	11,551
Huston-Tillotson**	3,135	2,553	3,800	3,893	4,020
Jackson State*					

TABLE 33 (continued)

Institution	1964-65	1965-66	1966-67	1967-68	1968-69
Jarvis Christian**	1,048	2,107	2,877	4,235	5,432
Johnson C. Smith**	2,496	4,311	3,750	3,636	6,500
Kentucky State*	2,875	3,265	2,700	4,800	3,500
Knoxville**	2,000	2,500	1,974	2,441	2,667
Lane**	2,003	2,448	3,100	2,639	5,300
Langston*	2,178	2,630		4,855	
LeMoyne-Owen**					
Lincoln (Mo.)*	5,000	6,943	10,061	5,000	6,012
Lincoln (Pa.)**	4,311	6,663	3,946	7,511	13,473
Livingstone**	1,292	1,249	1,106	2,600	1,988
Miss. Valley*	4,137	3,032	1,269	7,125	12,851
Morris**		2,695	6,288	3,119	
Morris Brown**	1,209	851	820	155	1,227
Norfolk*					
North Carolina A & T*					
North Carolina Central*					
Oakwood**	793	1,316	1,062	735	1,475
Paine**	664	847	1,019	965	1,844
Paul Quinn**		1,700			
Philander Smith**	1,600	9,968		2,139	15,230
Prairie View*	8,259		3,765		5,250
St. Augustine**			3,158	3,664	5,036
Shaw**					
Simmons**					
South Carolina State*					

TABLE 33 (continued)

Institution	1964-65	1965-66	1966-67	1967-68	1968-69
Southern*	43,081	86,496	19,076	84,705	
Southern Univ. N. O.*					
Stillman**	1,468	1,531	1,628	1,985	3,331
Talladega**					
Texas College**	1,603	1,561	1,820	2,361	2,297
Texas Southern*	8,000	12,200	26,000	29,000	35,000
Tougaloo**	1,824	2,296	2,649	2,750	3,519
Tuskegee**	20,000	22,000	22,000	25,000	26,000
Virginia State*		9,416	10,734	5,117	7,863
Virginia Union**	3,487	4,662	5,649	3,990	3,655
Voorhees**		867			
West Virginia State*	6,346	7,013	6,834	8,247	8,359
Wilberforce**	1,340	2,977	2,374	3,000	3,000
Wiley**			1,807	2,331	3,613
Winston-Salem*	2,129	464	991	1,690	1,960
Xavier**	2,843	3,734	5,240	4,200	3,010

*public.
**private.

low expenditures have appeared, they have almost always been at the privately supported institutions.

A different appraisal of the library expenditures in those institutions reporting may be made upon examination of Table 34, which shows the percentage of the institutions' educational and general expenditures allocated for library purposes. ALA standards require a minimum of 5 percent and suggest that this percentage be higher if the library's collection is seriously deficient, as has been the case with many of the institutions reporting in this survey. Analysis of this table shows that in 1964-65, thirty-nine institutions met the minimum standard, while twenty-four fell below it. In that year, a few institutions far exceeded the minimum standard, with two expending over 8 percent, one expending over 9 percent, and two expending 10 percent. During the next year, only twenty-eight institutions met the minimum standards. In 1966-67, thirty-five met the standard, while forty-nine had met it by 1967-68, and thirty-six had met it by 1968-69. At certain periods, some libraries were operating below the subsistence level, receiving even less than 3 percent of the educational and general budgets of their institutions.

It is necessary to underscore that a significant number of institutions fall below minimum standards in terms of the percentage of educational and general funds expended for library purposes, particularly in light of the many deficient collections. On the other hand, many libraries have exceeded minimum standards in terms of the percentage of educational and general budgets expended; yet their collections have not reached even minimum requirements in terms of size for their enrollments. A question might also be raised concerning the adequacy of the institution's educational and general budget, which itself might still be too low. Looking at the institutions as a whole, Table 34 further shows that these institutions spent slightly more than the recommended 5 percent of the educational and general budgets for total library purposes.

Libraries in the study were asked to make projections for financial support between 1969-70 and 1973-74, estimating the percentage of the institution's educational and general expenditures that might be allocated for library purposes. Table 35 shows that, with six exceptions, the libraries expected to receive 5 percent or more of their institutions' expenditures for educational and general purposes in each of the years in question. While these projections give no assurance that such appropriations will be granted, they suggest that the librarians have faith in the institutions' concern for proper development of the libraries.

TABLE 34

Percentages of Educational and General Budgets Expended
for Library Purposes in Certain Black Colleges,
1964-65 Through 1968-69

Institution	1964-65	1965-66	1966-67	1967-68	1968-69
Alabama A & M*	5.1	4.6	6.1	6.2	6.7
Alabama State*	8.7	8.2	7.8	7.0	8.1
Alcorn*	5.8	4.9	6.1	6.6	6.1
Arkansas A M & N*	3.4	2.3	2.5	3.3	2.4
Atlanta**		8.0			
Barber-Scotia**	6.5	7.1	4.1	5.9	3.0
Benedict**			7.1	7.6	5.4
Bishop**	6.2	9.3	8.0	9.1	8.1
Central State*	7.4	5.1	4.7	3.8	4.6
Cheyney*	10.0	11.0	12.0	7.5	8.2
Claflin**	3.3	6.4	6.0	7.0	7.2
Clark**	3.4	3.1	2.3		
Dillard**	4.0	4.3	4.0	3.8	3.0
Elizabeth City*		4.0		3.2	5.0
Fisk**	3.2	4.3	4.8		
Florida A & M*	4.5	4.7	5.3	5.7	6.0
Florida Memorial**		7.3	6.5	5.7	5.9
Fort Valley*	8.8	8.2	8.3	9.5	6.6
Grambling*	3.2	3.4	5.5	4.0	3.8
Hampton**	3.6	2.5	4.3	4.1	3.5
Huston-Tillotson**	6.1	4.8	4.9	4.8	5.3
Jackson State*	3.8	4.2	5.2	4.7	4.3

TABLE 34 (continued)

Institution	1964-65	1965-66	1966-67	1967-68	1968-69
Johnson C. Smith**	6.4	7.5	5.3	6.1	3.7
Kentucky State*	4.5	3.9	3.7	4.6	5.8
Knoxville**	5.0	4.8	6.0	5.9	5.4
Lane**	10.0	6.0	7.1	6.4	5.5
Langston*	5.5	4.3	5.6	4.2	4.7
LeMoyne-Owen**	7.4	6.0	5.8	5.0	5.5
Lincoln (Mo.)*	5.0	5.0	5.0	5.0	5.0
Lincoln (Pa.)**	6.6	8.8	8.8	6.4	7.1
Livingstone**	3.0	4.0	5.0	6.0	4.0
Miss. Valley*	5.8	5.7	6.0	7.3	7.9
Morris**	4.0	6.0	8.0	5.0	4.0
Morris Brown**	3.3	3.6	3.2		
Norfolk*	5.5	6.5	6.1	7.9	7.1
North Carolina A & T*	4.8	5.6	7.0	6.6	6.0
North Carolina Central*	6.1	5.0	5.7	6.1	5.5
Oakwood**	5.0	4.0	4.0	5.0	4.0
Paine**	4.5	6.3	6.3	6.4	4.8
Philander Smith**	4.3	4.6	4.6	8.2	8.0
Prairie View*	5.0	5.0	4.0	5.0	5.0
St. Augustine**	5.0	6.0	5.0	6.0	6.0
Simmons**		1.0	2.0	3.0	5.0
South Carolina State*	4.7	5.4	5.5	7.2	5.8
Southern*	4.0	3.5	4.0	3.1	
Southern Univ. N. O.*	9.8	9.6	10.2	9.5	12.7
Stillman**	7.1	6.9	5.8	4.2	3.8

TABLE 34 (continued)

Institution	1964-65	1965-66	1966-67	1967-68	1968-69
Texas College**	5.7	5.0	4.6	8.1	6.7
Texas Southern*	3.6	5.6	4.2	5.8	7.0
Tougaloo**	7.5	7.0	7.4	7.9	6.4
Tuskegee**	4.6	4.8	4.9	4.3	3.6
Virginia State*	5.0	4.5	3.6	4.0	3.8
Virginia Union**	7.8	7.9	8.2	7.2	9.0
Voorhees**	4.2	3.7	4.4	14.1	5.5
West Virginia State*	5.2	4.9	6.1	5.2	
Wilberforce**	3.0	3.2	4.8	5.9	5.2
Wiley**	5.0	5.0	5.0	10.1	
Winston-Salem*	4.1	4.0	6.4	7.3	6.3
Xavier**	3.3	3.3	3.3	3.3	5.0

*public.
**private.

TABLE 35

Percentages of Educational and General Budgets Projected for Library Purposes in Certain Black Colleges, 1969-70 Through 1973-74

Institution	1969-70	1970-71	1971-72	1972-73	1973-74
Alabama A & M*	7.0				
Alabama State*	6.1	6.0	6.0	6.0	6.0
Alcorn*	7.4				
Arkansas A M & N*					
Atlanta**	2.3	6.0	7.0	7.0	7.0
Barber-Scotia**					
Benedict**	8.0	8.0	8.0	8.0	8.0
Bishop**	5.0	7.0	10.0	10.0	10.0
Central State*	10.0	10.0	10.0	10.0	10.0
Cheyney*	7.5	7.7	8.0	8.2	8.4
Claflin**					
Clark**	4.0	4.2	4.3	5.0	5.2
Dillard**		8.0	8.0	8.0	8.0
Elizabeth City*					
Fayetteville*	5.0	5.5	6.0	6.5	7.0
Fisk**	6.5	7.0	7.5	7.5	8.0
Florida A & M*					
Florida Memorial**	7.0	7.2	7.5	8.0	8.0
Fort Valley*			5.0	5.5	5.5
Grambling*	4.0	4.2	4.5	4.7	5.0
Hampton**	5.3	5.4	5.8	6.1	6.6
Huston-Tillotson**					

TABLE 35 (continued)

Institution	1969-70	1970-71	1971-72	1972-73	1973-74
Jackson State*	4.4	6.3	6.5	6.5	6.5
Jarvis Christian**					
Johnson C. Smith**					
Kentucky State*	5.9	6.3	7.0	6.0	6.0
Knoxville**	6.0	7.0	7.0	7.0	7.5
Lane**	5.0	5.0	5.0	5.0	5.0
Langston*	5.0	5.0	5.5	6.0	6.5
LeMoyne-Owen**					
Lincoln (Mo.)*					
Lincoln (Pa.)**					
Livingstone**					
Miss. Valley*					
Morris**	6.0				
Morris Brown**	8.0	8.0	9.0	9.0	10.0
Norfolk*	8.0	8.5	9.0	9.5	10.0
North Carolina A & T*					
North Carolina Central*	7.0	7.0	6.0	6.0	6.0
Oakwood**	5.0	5.0	5.0	5.0	5.0
Paine**	6.0	6.0	6.0	6.0	6.0
Paul Quinn**					
Philander Smith**	8.0	8.0	8.5	8.5	8.5
Prairie View*					
St. Augustine**	6.0	7.0	8.0	9.0	10.0
Shaw**	5.0	6.0	6.0	6.0	6.0
Simmons**					

TABLE 35 (continued)

Institution	1969-70	1970-71	1971-72	1972-73	1973-74
South Carolina State*					
Southern*					
Southern Univ. N. O.*					
Stillman**	7.2	12.8	12.4	13.2	13.3
Talladega**					
Texas College**	5.0	5.1	5.0	5.1	5.2
Texas Southern*					
Tougaloo**	7.1	7.5	7.8	8.1	7.5
Tuskegee**					
Virginia State*					
Virginia Union**					
Voorhees**	4.1	5.0	5.0	5.0	5.0
West Virginia State*	5.5	5.7	5.9	6.2	6.5
Wilberforce**	6.0	6.5	7.0	7.5	8.0
Wiley**	10.0	9.3	8.2	8.0	7.2
Winston-Salem*					
Xavier**	5.0	5.0	5.0	5.0	5.0

*public.
**private.

The extent to which grants and gifts have been awarded to these libraries may be seen in Table 36. With only a few institutions reporting that grants and gifts had been received, it is difficult to draw conclusions.[9] Whether or not these libraries took advantage of federal grants available to them for library resources is undeterminable in some cases. One institution, Voorhees College, received sizable funds from outside sources between 1964-65 and 1968-69.

Projections in Library Development

Realizing their strengths as well as their inadequacies, librarians who participated in the study generally gave brief descriptions of plans that their institutions had made for the proper development of the library. For the most part, projections in development were centered around expansion of the collection, construction of new facilities, expansion of present facilities, addition of staff persons, and expansion of holdings of microforms and other nonprint media. Three librarians reported that plans had been made to build new learning resource centers. Two librarians planned to expand their collections of black materials, while one librarian planned to establish a department of archives in the library. The three institutions in the Atlanta Center—Atlanta, Clark, and Morris Brown—planned to join two additional institutions in the Center who did not participate in the survey, Morehouse and Spelman, in constructing and administering a central library facility to serve the needs of the member institutions.

Library Education Programs

Analysis of library education programs in the black colleges showed that three of the institutions—Alabama A & M, Atlanta, and North Carolina Central—maintained graduate programs of library science which led to the master's degree. The program at Alabama A & M focused on library media.

In studying programs at the remaining black colleges, it was found that the administration of these educational units varied. Nine programs were administered by schools or departments of education, seven were administered by the library, five were administered by departments of library education or library science, one was administered by the department of English, and one by the department of social studies. In one instance, the program was not assigned to a particular department. Five of these pro-

TABLE 36

Grants and Gifts Received in Certain Black College
Libraries, 1964-65 Through 1968-69

Institution	1964-65	1965-66	1966-67	1967-68	1968-69
Alabama A & M*	$ 5,000			$ 5,300	
Barber-Scotia**		$ 5,000			$ 2,278
Benedict**		15,000			700
Claflin**					
Clark**	3,000	5,000			
Dillard**	11,494	18,286			
Fayetteville*				850	700
Fisk**		16,238	$31,016	34,200	
Hampton**	600	125,300		2,000	1,953
Huston-Tillotson**	3,333	3,333		1,666	3,067
Jarvis Christian**		25,000		5,000	
Johnson C. Smith**		15,000		40,000	
Knoxville**	2,339	5,000			
Lane**		16,400		845	1,000
Langston*	625	875		3,200	6,500
LeMoyne-Owen**	10,000	5,000			
Lincoln (Pa.)**			6,806	6,278	5,373
Morris Brown**	4,000				
Oakwood**		1,000		5,000	7,000
Paine**	1,000	5,000		5,612	
Prairie View*		5,000		17,849	11,272

TABLE 36 (continued)

Institution	1964-65	1965-66	1966-67	1967-68	1968-69
St. Augustine**					1,500
Simmons**					2,000
Stillman**	5,000	2,500			2,000
Tougaloo**		7,559		11,171	
Virginia Union**	5,025	12,500			
Voorhees**	126,016	145,079		362,074	310,553
Wilberforce**	8,250	8,250		659	1,800
Wiley**	25,000			5,000	5,000
Winston-Salem*					25,000
Xavier**	10,000	5,000			500

*public.
**private.

grams offered a major in library science, five offered a minor, and the remaining programs led to state certification as either school librarians or teacher-librarians.

Thirteen institutions offered one or two courses in library science either to orient freshmen and new students or to meet requirements for courses in children's literature by departments of English and/or education. Eighteen institutions offered no library education programs, while four other institutions failed to respond to the question.

SUMMARY OF FINDINGS AND RECOMMENDATIONS

The present status of libraries in black colleges, as determined through evaluative reports by accrediting agencies and through this study, reflects the years of neglect and deprivation which they have suffered. In recent years, as many institutions prepared themselves for evaluation by the Southern Association of Colleges and Schools, great thrusts were made through the crash programs which they initiated in order to upgrade their libraries. Crash programs were no doubt required, though not merely on a temporary basis, for many of these libraries have not yet overcome their deficiencies. It is reasonable to conclude that the libraries included in this study have consistent deficiencies in facilities, resources, services, or personnel.

On the basis of findings presented in this report, each library included in the study will be able to compare its status to those of other black college libraries. By applying median and mean figures included in *Library Statistics of Colleges and Universities, Fall 1969, Analytic Report,* the library also can compare itself to libraries in institutions of similar size, with or without graduate students, and to those that are either publicly or privately supported.

Recommendation 1. Institutions should immediately reassess their libraries in terms of the academic program of the college, with student, faculty, library staff, and administrative involvement. Rigorous and serious attention should be given to the library in order to upgrade it as rapidly and as systematically as possible and to provide for its continuous development once it has reached the level desired by the accrediting agencies and required by the institution's academic program.

The pattern of governance varies widely among the reporting institutions. All head librarians report to a senior administrator, but this person is not necessarily the chief academic officer. Many of the institutions have library committees, but one finds a wide range of responsibilities and involvement. Many of the libraries have no stated policies or operational handbooks or manuals.

Whether or not the head librarians report directly to the president, vice-president, or academic dean is a matter to be dealt with in the institutions themselves. It is necessary, however, that library administration continue to be centralized; that library committees of the faculty, which involve librarians, students, and possibly a member of the administration, be active; and that firm policies be prepared to govern library administration.

Recommendation 2. All institutions should review the assignment of the library in the reporting structure. Assignment to a senior officer other than the chief academic officer should be continued only for clear and justifiable reasons, and the documentation in support of those reasons should be made a part of the permanent records of the institution.

Recommendation 3. Every institution should include the library committee among the standing committees of the institution, and the manner of determining its membership and the responsibilities of the committee should be clearly stated and included among the permanent records of the institution. It is further recommended that the responsibilities include: *(a)* the establishment and review of policies related to the quality scope, and size of the collection and to the quality and extent of service; *(b)* the evaluation of the library; and *(c)* self-evaluation of the committee.

Recommendation 4. All libraries should develop a policy and operations handbook.

The writer infers from the information provided for this study that librarians in these institutions do not enjoy a clear professional status. Faculty rank and tenure are not consistently available, and funds for professional development are limited.

Recommendation 5. Each institution should establish a mechanism for a thorough review of the professional status of its librarians. Such a review should include matters of level and diversity of training, faculty rank and tenure, participation in professional development programs, and salary structure.

In many institutions the library staff—professional and other—appears to be below the level required for the delivery of satisfactory service to the institution's constituencies. Further, the ratio of subprofessional to professional staff is often unfavorable. If filled, the staff vacancies reported in these libraries in 1968-69 would reduce the ratio of clerical to professional persons. Libraries, in their projections, have made little provision for correcting the present trend toward too few clerical persons on their staffs.

Heavy use of student employees was seen in most of the libraries included in the study. Many students in black colleges are required to help finance their educations through work-study or work-aid. Black institutions have the responsibility of providing as much financial assistance to these students as possible, especially through federal assistance programs. They also have the responsibility of providing a sufficient number of full-time library personnel to meet requirements for library service. In many instances, hourly rates for students are equal to those for certain clerical personnel.

Recommendation 6. Libraries should alter their staffing patterns to provide a more favorable ratio of clerical to professional persons and should avoid relying too heavily upon student employees. Further, each library should develop a staffing pattern based on the programs which the library conducts; and working with and through the chief academic officer and the budget officer, it should develop a plan to implement an acceptable staffing pattern.

Library staffs in the reporting institutions appear to be adequate in terms of background and experience; yet the need for continuing education is paramount. However, it appears that there is too high a concentration of librarians who have received their training in the South, particularly at one institution. The reasons for this concentration may be varied, and this study failed to explore accurately the impact of the situation on individual libraries. Even so, there appears to be a need for more staff members trained in a wider variety of library schools. Some of these staff members hold a second master's degree, while in a few cases head librarians and/or one or two staff persons hold the doctorate. Attendance at workshops and inservice meetings has, on the whole, been good, as librarians and staff members sought to update competencies. Their attendance at the annual meeting of the American Library Association has been relatively poor because of budgetary constraints.

Recommendation 7. Provisions should be made to recruit promising black
students for the library profession and to upgrade library staffs in the
black colleges through scholarship and fellowship programs, workshop
and internship programs, and travel programs.

Scholarship and fellowship programs for black students, many
of whom are in the black colleges, should permit them to pursue
degrees in librarianship at the library schools of their choice. Such a
program should be extended to clerical staff persons in the library.

Workshop and internship programs for library administrators, supportive librarians, and library technical assistants should be launched.
Special consideration should be given to administrators and library
technical assistants. In particular, a one-year internship program should
be developed for new library administrators or for those who will be
elevated to that position.[10]

Librarians and their staffs should be further encouraged to participate in professional meetings, especially the annual meeting of the
American Library Association. This goal is best met through adequate
budgetary provisions.

Of primary importance in the recruiting and retention of qualified professional personnel are the salary level provided, the availability of faculty
rank, and the availability of certain fringe benefits normally given to the
regular teaching faculty. Of equal importance in recruiting and retaining
good professional staff members is the careful selection and retention of
a strong supportive staff. Salaries and fringe benefits afforded library staffs
in the black institutions indicate that these provisions have hardly been
attractive, especially when training and experience are considered. In the
privately supported institutions in particular, salaries have been low. In addition, findings show that too little attention has been given to developing
strong supportive staffs.

Recommendation 8. Salaries of all library personnel should be reviewed
to insure that they are more in line with those offered in other institutions of similar size and purpose. When staff persons have certain
competencies as well as higher degrees, their salaries should be equal
to those of comparable administrative officers, department heads,
or teaching faculty, even though this amount may exceed that normally paid in an institution of comparable size.

Library collections in sixty-three black institutions total 5,164,673 volumes, or 47 volumes per student. The publicly supported institutions reported 2,806,179 volumes, or 24 volumes per student, as compared to 2,358,494 volumes in the privately supported institutions, which averaged 20 volumes per student. While the picture is somewhat brighter for the public colleges, findings show a deficiency of 2,368,799 volumes in these institutions as a whole. Using the figure of $16 as the average cost of purchasing and processing a library book today (as determined from *The Bowker Annual of Library and Book Trade Information,* 1971), these libraries would require a combined total of $37,900,784 to remove volume deficiencies in their collections.

In an effort to correct deficiencies, these libraries added a combined total of 1,876,055 volumes to their collections between 1964-65 and 1968-69. Despite these efforts, a significant volume deficiency remains.

With few exceptions, a limited amount of weeding has been done in the black college library collections. Many librarians reported a reluctance to remove volumes from the collection simply because of pressures to meet greater volume counts as required by the accrediting agency. Examination of many of these collections showed a high incidence of duplicate titles or multiple copies of titles and a prevalence of outdated ones. It is reasonable to estimate that one-fourth of the collections in black college libraries should be weeded and replaced with newer editions or newer titles which are more directly related to the academic programs. Reference collections in these libraries bear the same limitations.

After examining collections in libraries in Texas, Edward G. Holley and Donald D. Hendricks stated that "many of the colleges with small enrollments whose existence goes back quite a number of years can easily meet the ALA standard."[11] This statement is untrue where the black college libraries are concerned. While most of these institutions were established prior to 1900, even with their small enrollments they have been unable to overcome size and content deficiencies in their collections.

Recommendation 9. Granting agencies should consider awarding special and sustained funds to black academic libraries. Such funds should be earmarked solely for removing size and content deficiencies in their collections, including those that exist as a result of increased enrollments, those that exist as a result of new degree programs (especially the master's and the doctorate), and those that would exist if obsolete materials were weeded, thereby reducing volume count.

In view of the fact that such grants to remove deficiencies and to support model institutions would necessitate additional staff for processing, the Cooperative College Library Center, located in Atlanta, Georgia, should be approached concerning its ability to process immediately the materials necessary for the black academic libraries.

Each library should be required to submit a plan for systematically removing deficiencies in its collection, making judicious use of standard guides in order to evaluate the collections and involving faculty and students in the selection process.

Nontraditional forms of library media have been provided in these libraries, although more attention has been given to the selection of microfilmed and recorded materials than to materials in other forms. The learning resource center is generally missing in these libraries. However, such emphasis is apparent at Shaw; and a few institutions, including Fisk, Alabama A & M, and Florida A & M, tend to be moving in this direction.

Recommendation 10. Funds should be provided to enable at least a portion of these libraries to become learning resource centers and to enable others to purchase the newer forms of library media and equipment necessary for their use.[12]

On the whole, subscriptions to periodicals in black college libraries are low. While the survey made no attempt to identify the actual volume coun of periodicals, it tried to show the extent to which these libraries include periodical titles in their collections. Although complete back runs of certain periodical titles are not always required in institutions where no graduate work is offered, libraries must provide back numbers in sufficient depth to meet the requirements of the current instructional program.

Recommendation 11. Black academic libraries should carefully examine their periodical collections, both in terms of subscriptions received and in terms of back runs required. Funds should be provided to enable these libraries to remove deficiencies in their periodical collections through the addition of new subscriptions, which are needed in most of these libraries, as well as some retrospective volumes as required. Attention should be given to purchasing the back volumes in microform.

Clearly defined acquisition policy statements are useful in guiding the systematic development of the library collection. These libraries, which have suffered too long from budgetary constraints, should have careful plans for expending the funds that they do have as well as for expending funds that may be granted. Collections should develop systematically rather than in a haphazard manner, as can happen when policies and practices are undefined. Such policies should govern all gift collections that are available to the library. Histories of the black academic libraries and examinations of their collections show that they have been plagued with far too many gift collections, most of which have been of doubtful value to the collections. At best, they only served to swell volume count and to occupy shelf space needed for other purposes. Not infrequently, administrators in these institutions encouraged and/or accepted gifts for the library.

Recommendation 12. Each library in the black colleges should develop well-defined acquisition policy statements, working closely with the faculty, representatives of the student body, and the administration. The policy statement should be geared closely to the provision of materials to support the curricular, research, and cultural programs of the college. Any provisions for gift books must meet the criteria set forth in the policy statement.

Procedures followed in the acquisition of library materials are of particular importance. Far too many libraries in these institutions make use of outmoded systems of acquisition, with some requisitions requiring the signature of the dean or president and others being controlled too tightly by the business office. It is not uncommon to find methods of bookkeeping that are time consuming and costly.

Recommendation 13. Working closely with the business office, libraries in these institutions should develop modern methods for keeping records and acquiring materials. Ideally, orders should be sent directly from libraries to jobbers, thereby eliminating as much repetition of work as possible in view of the limited number of staff in these institutions.

Some libraries have become members of duplicate exchange programs as a means of acquiring needed materials free of charge or for disposing of broken sets and other items no longer needed. Obviously, such a program can be meaningful, particularly when budgets are limited.

Recommendation 14. Libraries in the black academic institutions should join duplicate exchange unions and take advantage of the benefits such programs offer.

Libraries in the black institutions are generally bound by high standards of cataloging and classifying their collections. Some are either reclassifying or converting their collections from the Dewey Decimal Classification to the Library of Congress system, either to meet a requirement for joining the Cooperative College Library Center or to remedy other problems that they had in classification and cataloging. As is the case with most libraries, many of these libraries have cataloging arrearages, filing arrearages, older problems in classification, and so forth.

Recommendation 15. Funds should be provided to support a study of the classification and cataloging problems and requirements of the libraries in black institutions, with some provision for helping them to meet these needs.

To some extent, the findings of McGrath and Jordan are reinforced by this study. Generally, library facilities in these institutions are adequate, with a few bordering on excellent. McGrath and Jordan concluded that, on the whole, library buildings in the black institutions were more adequate than their collections. While this statement may be generally true, as the present study substantiates, one must not overlook the fact that some of the buildings in these institutions were hardly as adequate as their collections, while others were extremely inadequate in terms of buildings as well as collections.

Site visits to the libraries revealed that many which were rated as "good" or "adequate" were indeed entitled to their rating; but the buildings were lacking in modern concepts of design, aesthetics, and function. While some had been planned with the assistance of a building consultant, there was evidence that the consultant was unaware of the requirements for service in small academic libraries. A splendid example of a building designed for function, aesthetics, and minimum staff supervision may be seen at LeMoyr

Seating space in some of these libraries, particularly the older ones, is inadequate; and far too little provision has been made for individual seating. Quarters for processing are, on the whole, inadequate. In terms of shelf spac for materials, some libraries have already exceeded their capacity, while oth ers have nearly done so.

While almost all of these libraries have opened their stacks to students, a few still have not. Barriers between students and study materials in such institutions must be removed.

Recommendation 16. The writer is fully aware of the serious financial condition of higher education generally and therefore cannot recommend that inadequate structures be replaced at this time. However, any institution having a library building which impedes the improvement of library services should consider placing a new structure very high on its list of building priorities. Other institutions, utilizing available consulting services, should explore innovative ways of increasing the user's access to library materials.

As funds become available for building construction, a team of consultants should be selected to work with these institutions. Such a team should include representatives of black college libraries who have already experienced building programs or who are fully aware of the requirements of black institutions. New or renovated facilities should provide for modern concepts of function, aesthetics, and innovation.

Services of these libraries include those traditionally found in libraries; bibliographies are prepared, bibliographic services are offered, and materials are made available for faculty and student use. While circulation statistics as reported in this study tend to fluctuate, per capita circulation statistics are required in order to provide more meaningful data on student and faculty use of the library and to determine whether actual use is increasing or decreasing.

Libraries in black institutions are charged with initiating ways of bringing more students and faculty into the library, fostering better study and reading habits, and stimulating independent work. Generally lacking in these institutions are innovative programs which would relate the library more closely to the academic program and which would attempt to establish the library as an integral part of the student's intellectual environment. Examples of such programs may be seen at Dillard, Howard, and Jackson State, where special grants have been provided under a joint program of the Council on Library Resources and the National Endowment for the Humanities.[13]

Recommendation 17. Libraries in these institutions should make per capita use studies of library circulation over the past five years to determine the extent to which actual use is increasing or decreasing (as far as can be determined when open access to materials is provided). Innovative programs which closely relate the library to the instructional programs should be developed in each of these institutions, even if on modified bases. Innovative instructional programs which foster greater use of the library must be initiated.

Library consortia and various types of cooperative programs are participated in by many of the black college libraries. Services and resources in these institutions can be strengthened through cooperative programs with other libraries, and such programs can be supported through federal grants earmarked for this purpose. When libraries are located in close proximity, consortia become necessary and natural; and the building of duplicate collections in the same geographical area is discouraged.

Recommendation 18. Libraries in these institutions should look toward consortia or cooperative programs as a means of strengthening resources and services. These consortia should seek external funds for library resources.

Examples of automated services can be seen in some of the libraries in the black colleges. For the past several years, Mississippi Valley has made use of computers in its acquisition program and has met with relative success. A number of other institutions plan to automate certain functions as funds and space permit. Computer services and automated functions can be costly, and libraries will need to reexamine their budgets and their requirements for library services prior to embarking on such programs.

Recommendation 19. Computer services and automated activities should be initiated in these libraries according to the needs of the institutions and the funds available for the support of such new programs.

The detailed analysis which has been made of budgets in these libraries during the period from 1964-65 through 1968-69 suggests that efforts are being made to remove the deficiences that exist in facilities, resources, staff, and services. Analysis of the book budget alone suggests that rigorous efforts were being made to improve the collections in some institutions. Far too many libraries still neglect their periodical collections, for meager funds are often provided for their support. In terms of binding, some libraries have been consistent in their efforts to keep up their stock, while others have scarcely had funds to preserve materials in this manner. Budgets for travel have been fairly generous at some institutions; yet a mere pittance was provided at others. Certainly this situation would discourage staff attendance at professional meetings and workshops.

An examination of budgets for supplies shows that some of the libraries have been impoverished and hardly able to exist. In some cases, it has been a miracle that they survived in view of the meager funds provided for their support. Budgets for salaries and wages varied widely. The larger libraries obviously provided larger numbers of staff and, in many instances, paid higher salary rates. A few institutions reported budgets for audiovisual materials and equipment; yet these figures were generally at a minimum level, and some were exceedingly low. Statistics for other operating expenses were given; but because data were generally lacking in this area, few conclusions could be drawn.

Total library budgets were generally higher in the publicly supported institutions than in the privately supported ones, although it must be kept in mind that enrollments were generally much higher in the publicly supported institutions. Whether or not these libraries are taking full advantage of grants and gifts is questionable, judging from the data reported. In one instance, however, a rather generous amount was shown.

Substantial improvement was observed in the allocation of financial resources to the libraries under study. However, in general the library expenditures per student still fall below the averages of the libraries included in the Baumol-Marcus study. Nearly half of those reporting were also expending amounts below the minimum ALA requirements of 5 percent. It must be remembered that 84.1 percent of the reporting libraries are deficient in volume count while, as reported previously, clearly one-fourth of the collections in each of these libraries should be weeded.

Recommendation 20. In view of a long history of inadequate support for libraries included in this study, support well beyond the typical 5 to 8 percent of the E and G budget is required. Support for the current operation of the library, particularly for building the collection, should be given a high priority in each institution's developmental effort.

Recommendation 21. A percentage of certain grants and gifts to the university for educational purposes—including training programs, institutes, and the creation and/or development of specific departments —should be allocated for library development.

Programs in library education are offered in the black colleges and, for the most part, are designed to prepare students as teacher-librarians or as school librarians. Five programs lead to a minor in library science, five lead to a major, and three offer the master's degree. Atlanta University is the leading producer of black librarians in this country, having graduated far more black students than any other library school. Together, the three library schools offering the master's degree have the potential for playing an increasingly important role in providing graduate library education in the South, particularly for the black students who tend to study there but also for other students who are beginning to seek their degrees in black schools.

Recommendation 22. Careful study should be made of the graduate library education programs at Atlanta, Alabama A & M, and North Carolina Central, which are training the preponderance of black students. Increased and sustained financial assistance should be provided for their support.

NOTES

1. At the time of this study, the ALA Standards of 1969 were in effect.

2. William J. Baumol and Matityahu Marcus, *Economics of Academic Libraries* (Washington, D.C.: American Council on Education, 1973). The Baumol-Marcus work is used to examine several aspects of the black academic library in this study.

3. Increasing numbers of librarians in black colleges now hold the doctorate.

4. Because this data was considered confidential, institutions are not identified in the salary tables.

5. Verner W. Clapp and Robert T. Jordan, "Quantitative Criteria for Adequacy of Academic Library Collections," *College and Research Libraries* 26 (September 1965), p. 371-80.

6. The incidence of new library facilities in these colleges has increased substantially since the study was completed.

7. Many black college libraries are now members of the Southeastern Interlibrary Network (SOLINET) and of a similar network known as AMIGOS.

8. Many of these libraries have now established learning resource centers or have expanded significantly their media holdings and equipment for their use.

9. Many black academic institutions have received sizable grants through Title III, United States Office of Education, under particular components known as Basic Institutional Development program and Advanced Institutional Development program. Portions of these grants have been provided for such library projects as the development of learning resource centers, support of SOLINET and other automated programs, library-based tutorial programs, and other activities. The Office of Institutional Research, Fayetteville State University, is conducting a study of the impact of Title III grants on black academic institutions. It is likely that the study will report on various library activities supported through Title III funds.

10. To some extent, the ACRL and CLR internships address this issue (cf. Chapter 2, note 38).

11. Edward G. Holley and Donald D. Hendricks, *Resources of Texas Libraries* (Austin: Texas State Library, Field Services Division, 1968), p. 96.

12. This conclusion requires further study, in view of the previously cited trend toward establishing the LRC (cf. note 8).

` 13. Council on Library Resources, "Recent Developments," no. 17 (Washington, D.C.: November 5, 1971), p. 1.

In 1975, the CLR announced the beginning of its Library Service Enhancement Program, which aims at assisting academic libraries in becoming full partners in the teaching/learning process on campus. Council on Library Resources, "Recent Developments" (Washington, D.C.: November 15, 1975). The only black institution which was awarded a grant under the initial funding in 1976-77 was A and T State University.

5

Special Collections of Black Literature in Black Colleges

As we view it today, black librarianship, like black education, is between two worlds. The full entrance of black librarianship into the mainstream of librarianship is yet to be achieved. Rather, it continues to lie in the outer realm of those institutions which were created to serve a purely segregated society. The high level of mechanization, massive collections, and generous budgets that characterize many of the prestigious libraries in America are unknown to black libraries. Black institutions and their libraries were born and have survived against great odds; those imposed by the society in which these libraries were created and those imposed as a result of chronic underfinancing.

McGrath's contention that black colleges as a group "lack their share of distinctive or exceptional libraries" is challenged when critical attention is given to the primary and secondary resource materials collected by some of these libraries.[1] Almost immediately, the incompleteness of scholarship is clearly visible as the untapped sources of black studies materials are identified in the black libraries. While, as a whole, these libraries may be indistinctive and unexceptional, elements of some of them are both distinctive and exceptional.

Libraries in black institutions have been neither self-sufficient nor self-contained. Despite the fact that there are unique elements among them, the development of these libraries and their collections has been hampered by a number of factors which will be identified in this chapter. The richness of some of their collections in black studies materials points out their potential for contributing to the development of scholarship. The depth that these collections have achieved may be directly attributed to the fore-sight of early librarians, or sometimes faculty members, who were en-dowed with the determination, dedication, and interest necessary to pre-serve black history and culture in records.

HISTORICAL BACKGROUND

Patterns vary in the development of special collections of black litera-ture in black colleges. In one case, materials on this subject were in the collection which was established when the college was founded; while in other cases, collections were established through the generosity of bene-factors, either in gifts of money or in materials. As was seen in the histor-ies of black libraries in general, full records of the development of these collections are lacking. From bits and pieces found in some records, how-ever, a sketchy history can be drawn.

Special collections of black culture can be found in various types of libraries throughout the United States. One group of these comprises the black institutions—libraries in black colleges and universities, black branch-es of public libraries, special black research centers, black museums, and black associations and organizations. Other groups include college libraries in the predominantly white institutions, university libraries, private or uni-versity-related research libraries, larger public libraries, state libraries, librar-ies of associations and learned societies (including groups that have religious affiliations), historical societies (including state, city, and county organiza-tions), general museums, and governmental libraries (including the National Archives, presidential libraries, and the Library of Congress).

Libraries in various types of black institutions—whether public or pri-vate, academic, political, or social—provide rich and valuable collections of manuscript and archival materials for research in black culture. Unlike the special collections that are found in the predominantly white colleges and universities, ones found in black colleges and universities tend to be limited to subjects on blacks or subjects that are black related. For ex-ample, such collections are likely to contain the papers of black authors, black religious leaders, black educators, or black organizations. However,

they may also contain the papers of white sympathizers of the black struggle whose works are represented through educational, political, or religious
organizations or through their private libraries.

Historically, libraries in the black colleges have included materials on
black subjects in their general collection development as they met the
needs of curricular programs in black history or black literature or as they
attempted to provide black students with materials which reflected their
black heritage. It may be said that black studies were founded in the early
curricular programs offered in the black colleges. Not infrequently,
these few courses were offered as a requirement for all students. For the
most part, materials supporting these courses were added to the general
collection. An examination of collections in many of these institutions
during this study revealed that first editions of important works now long
out of print were located on the shelves, attesting to the fact that librarians
or faculty members in these institutions had an early interest in gathering black materials.

Collecting practices also resulted in the purchase of black newspapers
and periodicals. The *National Survey of Higher Education of Negroes* reported in 1942 that

> in their holdings of Negro periodicals and newspapers . . .
> the collections of the Negro institutions are more substan-
> tial than their holdings in other newspaper and periodical
> titles. Twenty-five colleges were checked for their holdings
> of 5 Negro periodicals: *The Crisis, Journal of Negro Educa-
> tion, Journal of Negro History, Opportunity,* and *Quarterly
> Review of Higher Education Among Negroes.* With but two
> exceptions they hold all or all but one of the 5 Negro period-
> icals mentioned. These same institutions were asked also to
> report on their holdings of Negro newspapers. The returns
> to the questionnaire show that their holdings of Negro news-
> papers are fairly strong.[2]

Libraries in eight of the black colleges examined for the current study
maintain exceptionally rich resources in black studies. While only seven
of these libraries participated in the study, the eighth, Howard University,
is being included because of its significance to the purpose of the study.
Howard was also visited in connection with the project.

At Atlanta University, the history of the Negro Collection as a separate department dates back to 1946, when the university purchased the famous Henry P. Slaughter Collection. Represented in this collection were materials from many countries by and about black people. In 1932, Anson Phelps presented to the Trevor Arnett Library at Atlanta University the papers of Thomas Clarkson, an English abolitionist who lived from 1760 to 1846.

The larger Negro Collection also contains a Countee Cullen Memorial Collection of black materials, founded at the university in 1942 by Harold Jackman, a friend of the late Countee Cullen. The founder moved in artistically creative circles in America and in Europe and was associated with the brilliance of the Harlem Renaissance during the 1920s and 1930s. An authority on arts and letters, he was also consistently devoted to the major artistic movements in Harlem and in Greater New York. He met such notable participants in the Harlem Renaissance as Langston Hughes, Rose McClendon, Claude McKay, and Countee Cullen. The Harold Jackman Memorial Committee continues the efforts of Jackman by presenting additions to the collection periodically.

The Thayer Lincoln Collection was opened in the Atlanta library in 1953. Items there form perhaps the most important collection on the Great Emancipator that is located in the South. The collection was a gift of Anna Chittendon Thayer of New York, who maintained a lifelong interest in Lincoln.

Recent additions to the collections are the papers of Irwin McDuffie, Clark Foreman, the Chautauqua Circle, and C. Eric Lincoln, who has written on the Black Muslims in America and who served on the Atlanta faculty.

In 1969, when the Amistad Research Center moved from Fisk to Dillard, it took an unusual collection of research items to a campus where few materials of that nature had been maintained. Although not properly a part of the Dillard library or of the university, it may be counted among the collections on the black campuses. The American Missionary Association Archives, which form the major portion of the collection, were formerly at the Fisk University library, where they were deposited in 1947.

Other materials in the Amistad Center include the Countee Cullen Collection, the American Home Missionary Society Archives, the Mary McLeod Bethune Papers, and Archives of the Race Relations Department of the United Church Board for Homeland Ministries.

One of the oldest, most exhaustive, and most distinguished collections of black studies materials is housed in the Fisk library. The university was founded in 1866; and the library, which was already established, contained some materials about black people at that time. When a new building was erected in 1908 to serve as a library and as a center for other activities, provisions were made to house special black materials.

Fisk made its first systematic effort to assemble materials by and about black people in 1929-30, when it made special provisions for housing these items in a separate collection forming a part of the library's resources. Foreign dealers were consulted in an effort to obtain materials. Some of the outstanding purchases of the day included manuscripts which dealt with the early history of the black domestic servant in Europe.

Arthur A. Schomburg, a Puerto Rican of African descent, was appointed curator of the collection in 1929. Later curator of the Schomburg Collection of the New York Public Library, Schomburg provided the impetus for maintaining a collection which was similar to his own distinguished one.

In 1936, the Fisk library received its first big boost, both in financial support and in materials acquired. In that year, Fisk purchased the entire library of the Southern YMCA College located in Nashville, Tennessee. The YMCA College library was headed by W. D. Weatherford, an author who was also a local pioneer in collecting materials in the field of race problems. The library specialized in securing materials relating to black people after 1865. As this collection merged with the Fisk collection, which specialized in black materials prior to 1865, an outstanding group of research materials was formed.

The Fisk collection has been greatly augmented by periodic gifts and purchases. The E. R. Alexander Collection, founded at Fisk in 1945, is an example. Established by Mrs. Alexander in honor of her husband, the intention was to provide Fisk with the opportunity to acquire items that might otherwise be too costly for the university to purchase. Of particular importance among these materials were the more than two hundred published minstrel sketches.

A small yet valuable group of manuscripts, photographs, programs, sheet music, and other items was presented to Fisk in 1948, forming the Scott Joplin Collection. The Langston Hughes Collection, established at Fisk in the 1940s by the author himself and increased periodically by small additions, also helped to enrich the history and resources of the library. Upon the author's death in 1967, and under terms specified in his will, a large collection of tape and disc recordings was added to the existing Langston Hughes materials. The Charles Waddell Chesnutt Collection, acquired by Fisk in 1952, includes important research materials relating to this popular literary figure.

In 1962, Marjorie Content Toomer presented to the Fisk library the papers of her husband, Jean Toomer, one of the most significant writers of the Harlem Renaissance. An additional group of papers was added in 1967, after Toomer's death. Among other groups of materials which the Fisk library has acquired are the papers of Charles Spurgeon Johnson (1967), the Julius Rosenwald Fund Archives (1948), and a considerable number of W. E. B. DuBois items (1961).

Although not dealing exclusively with black subjects, the George Gershwin Memorial Collection of Music and Musical Literature is a valuable source of materials relating to black people. The collection was presented to Fisk in 1944 by Carl Van Vechten in honor of his close friend.

An unusual part of the Fisk collection is a group of paintings which form the Baldridge Collection. These works were presented to the library in 1931 by Samuel Insull of Chicago.

More recent additions to the Fisk collection include a group of 1,334 notable titles on black people in Africa and America and such smaller manuscript collections as those of Naomi Long Madgett, Slater King, John W. Work, Louise Meriwether, William Lloyd Imes, and Robert Burgette Johnson, the son of Charles Spurgeon Johnson.

Of particular significance to the development of the research materials at Fisk was approval of the Archives Charter by the Board of Trustees in 1945. This document paved the way for the library to collect, preserve, and administer the university's archives. Thus papers of former Fisk administrators and other records are housed in the archives division of Special Collections.

The Hampton Institute collection was established in 1905, when George Foster Peabody purchased 1,004 books, pamphlets, and other documents from Tucker A. Malone and loaned them to the library. The loan was changed to a gift in 1908.

In 1914, the private collection of Phil B. Brooks of Washington, D.C., was purchased. This collection of ten thousand books, pamphlets, and documents dealt with slavery and Reconstruction in the United States. Included were original bills of sale and inventories of slaves on plantations.

Among the archival materials in the collection, some of which date back to 1868, are items on the *Proceedings of the Lake Mohonk Negro Conference,* slavery documents, records and correspondence relating to the American Missionary Association, materials from the Hampton Negro Conference, three thousand photographs of persons and events in the history of Hampton Institute, and papers relating to Hollis Burke Frissell, Samuel C. Armstrong, Booker T. Washington, Alexander Crummell, Frederick Douglass, James Weldon Johnson, and Mary McLeod Bethune. Also included in the collection are transcripts of interviews with former slaves in Virginia.

Hampton's early emphasis on education for black as well as Indian students is represented in the archives. Letters to Indians and materials on the Indian Rights Association are included. Hampton is the only known black college which made special provisions for educating American Indians and which provided research materials on the subject. These materials may prove useful in studying the relationships that existed between blacks and American Indians, as has been suggested in primary as well as secondary sources and as has been substantiated through the black oral tradition.

Beginning in 1970, rigorous efforts were made to expand and to update substantially the collection of black titles in the Hampton collection. This collection is perhaps the foremost untapped source for research in black studies. Unlike the collections at Howard, Fisk, and Tuskegee, the Hampton collection has been overlooked by scholars writing on black subjects.

In 1914, the Moorland Foundation, the Library of Negro Life and History, was established by the Board of Trustees of Howard University. At that time, one of the trustees, Jesse E. Moorland, gave the university his private library of more than three thousand items relating to black subjects, including many engravings, portraits, manuscripts, curios, pictures, and clippings. By combining the Moorland materials with those of Lewis Tappan, which were donated to the library in 1873, one of the most valuable collections on anti-slavery literature was formed.

Through the years, numerous collections have gravitated to the Moorland-Spingarn Research Center, as it is now known, and have thus made possible a constantly growing and highly significant collection. The Spingarn Collection of books by black authors is especially noteworthy and serves an important function in identifying black authors and in making it possible to study their works.[3] Continuing his interest in supporting the development of black collections, Carl Van Vechten presented to Howard an extensive photograph collection of blacks in the theater.

The manner in which the Moorland-Spingarn Research Center developed during the years is not unlike the notable black collections assembled in such black institutions as Hampton, Tuskegee, and Fisk. Although the collection was originally built around two private libraries, the distinguishing feature of its development has been in its relationship to the curriculum. Its focus and expansion were basically conditioned by courses which Howard offered in black life and culture as well as by traditional courses which also included a study of black subjects.

The information that was made available on Moorland-Spingarn was sketchy and failed to do justice to the vast quantity of research materials which it contains. However, it can be reported that the collection now houses over one hundred thousand cataloged and indexed items. Manuscript materials in the collection include the papers of Blanche Kelso Bruce, Thomas Clarkson, Frederick Douglass, E. Franklin Frazier, the Grimke' family, Oliver Otis Howard, Alain Leroy Locke, Kelly Miller, P. B. S. Pinchback, Rosey Pool, Joel E. Spingarn, Arthur E. Spingarn, Mary Church Terrell, U.S. Colored Troops, Booker T. Washington, Daniel Hale Williams, and the Washington, D.C., branch of the NAACP.

The Heartman Negro Collection of Texas Southern University was purchased in 1948 from Charles Frederick Heartman, a book dealer and author who spent from forty to fifty years gathering the materials for his private collection. Most of the collection was developed near Biloxi, Mississippi. For many years, the Heartman Collection had an historical emphasis; but in recent years, the emphasis of the black literature collection has centered on more contemporary items.

The private collection of another individual, whose identity is undetermined, also helped form the basis for the development of the black collection at Texas Southern. Together, these two collections constitute perhaps the largest and most important one of this type in the Southwest. The library also houses the university's archives, which date from the founding of Texas Southern in 1947.

While the exact origin of the Negro Collection at Lincoln (Pennsylvania) is unknown, the collection was established between 1935 and 1940. Holdings include over six thousand volumes, numerous periodicals, pamphlets, and other items. Books on Africa, which are included, emphasize the area south of the Sahara. University archives, dating back to 1845, are also housed in the library. In addition, the library contains the minutes of the Pennsylvania Colonization Society, covering the period from 1838 to 1913. Of particular importance is the Langston Hughes Collection, which contains the personal library and certain literary effects of this noted Harlem Renaissance writer. Special gifts which the library received in recent years include the Langston Hughes Collection of 3,000 items; the Reid Collection, which consists of 500 books on Africa and the Negro; and the Scott Collection, which consists of 375 general titles on black subjects. In 1968-69, the Negro Collection was greatly augmented through the purchase of the entire holdings of a local book store.

The Washington Collection and Archives of Tuskegee Institute is internationally known for its rare primary and secondary resources on black subjects. These include books, manuscripts, correspondence, photographs, phonograph discs, tapes, newspaper clippings, microfilm, and other items.

The nucleus of the Washington Collection consisted of first editions and rare items by and about blacks which were collected after the founding of Tuskegee Institute in 1881. In 1932, these items were moved from the old Carnegie Library Building to the Hollis Burke Frissell Library, where they were housed in a separate room and named for the founder and first president of the school, Booker T. Washington.

On invitation from President Washington, Monroe Nathan Work went to Tuskegee in 1904 and established the Department of Records and Research to collect, analyze, and disseminate materials pertaining to black people in America. Among its other activities, this department gathered all lynching statistics since 1881 and published the *Lynching Reports* (1913-1953), which are available at Tuskegee. From 1954 until the final issue in 1963, the *Race Relations Reports* replaced the *Lynching Reports.* Also published by this department were eleven editions of *The Negro Year Book* (1912-1951) and the *Bibliography of the Negro in Africa and America*, issued in 1928 and reprinted in 1965. This work is still the definitive and authoritative source for bibliographical research on black subjects before 1928.

After Work's retirement in 1946, the Department of Records and Research was continued until 1966 under the leadership of Ralph N. Davis and Jessie Parkhurst Guzman. In its history, the department amassed one of the largest and most comprehensive newspaper clippings files available, consisting of more than 350,000 items relating to all aspects of the black experience.

In 1968, all materials formerly housed in the Department of Records and Research became a part of the Washington Collection and Archives. An inventory of all the manuscripts, correspondence, newspaper clippings, rare books, memorabilia, and related archival materials was completed under a project financed by the Ford Foundation and the Robert Moton Memorial Institute.

The collection now contains over twenty-five thousand titles on blacks in Africa, America, and the Caribbean; subscriptions to ten black newspapers and over fifty periodical titles; seven hundred phonograph records; and seventy-five pieces of sheet music. More than 300 speeches, articles, theses and dissertations, newspapers, and magazines are contained in the microfilm collection. Included in the manuscript collections of the archives are papers of Booker T. Washington, Robert Russa Moton, Frederick D. Patterson, George Washington Carver, Albon L. Holsey, Thomas Monroe Campbell, Isaac Fisher, the files of the Southern Conference Educational Fund, and the *Southern Courier* and other papers. Tapes and transcripts of the Oral History Project, sponsored by the Alabama Center for Higher Education (ACHE), are also included in the collection.

Although not associated with a black college, the Schomburg Center for Research in Black Culture of the New York Public Library, popularly known as the Schomburg Collection, should be recorded among the significant collections of black materials available for research. The collection is considered one of the most important centers in the world for research and study in black culture.

The Schomburg Center has three histories, each playing a central part in its development. In the infancy of the New York Public Library itself, some interest was shown in collecting black materials. Documents relating to the American Colonization Society and items on slavery were collected by the library in this early period.

The Harlem community, in which the Schomburg Center is located, is equally significant in its history. In 1905, the 135th Street Branch of the New York Public Library was established to serve a neighborhood of affluent American-Jewish people. An influx of black people changed the ethnic composition of the community; and by 1920, it was half black. Ernestine Rose was appointed librarian and was charged with the responsibility of adapting the collection to serve an altered public.

By 1924, the Harlem Renaissance—a cultural revolution in which black writers, musicians, artists, and scholars began to express their talents—was in bloom. The Renaissance leaders and their works attracted talent and leadership from black people all over the United States and the Caribbean, and they joined the 150,000 black people who had migrated to Harlem by 1924. Harlem was thus the acknowledged capital of black America.

The rigorous efforts of Ernestine Rose and such leaders as Arthur A. Schomburg, Louis Latimer, J. E. Bruce, James Weldon Johnson, and John B. Nail culminated in the founding of the new Division of Negro Literature, History, and Prints on May 8, 1925, at the 135th Street Branch.

In 1926, the Carnegie Corporation of New York purchased the private library of Arthur A. Schomburg and presented it to the 135th Street Branch. This acquisition of between five and six thousand volumes, three thousand manuscripts, two thousand etchings, and thousands of pamphlets formed the nucleus of the materials in the Division of Negro Literature, History, and Prints. Schomburg was retained as curator of the collection in 1932, through a financial gift from the Carnegie Corporation.

The Schomburg Center for Research in Black Culture now represents a reference and research library which provides various types of manuscript and archival items relating to black authorship, history and historical works, photographs, broadsides, and other materials. Papers of such notable black persons as Ira Aldridge, William Stanley Braithwaite, Alexander Crummell, Countee Cullen, Jupiter Hammon, Langston Hughes, Alain Leroy Locke, Rose McClendon, Claude McKay, Hiram Rhoades Revels, Arthur A. Schomburg, Harriet Tubman, Booker T. Washington, and Richard Wright are included in the collection.

In addition to the black colleges, notable collections of black materials can also be found in such institutions as the Library of Congress, Yale University (which houses the James Weldon Johnson Memorial Collection), the Boston Public Library (which houses a sizable portion of the papers of Martin Luther King, Jr.), the Detroit Public Library, the Hall Branch of the Chicago Public Library, Oberlin College, and the University of California at Los Angeles.

Over the years, black collections in libraries including the Schomburg Center, Howard, Fisk, Yale, UCLA, and others have felt the influence of such persons as Arthur A. Schomburg, Carl Van Vechten, Langston Hughes and Arthur Spingarn, either through materials which they presented to these libraries to enrich their collections or through the purchase of collections which they assembled. Such persons have therefore had a marked effect on the development of notable collections of black literature.

In addition to their focus on black materials, the common element in the history of the black libraries just described, including the Schomburg Center, is the lack of proper financial support, staff, and quarters for processing and preserving the rich materials and for making them more readily available to scholars. While they have relied heavily upon gifts of notable materials to help build the collections, these libraries have been handicapped by a shortage of funds required to maintain the collections. At the other extreme are the rewards that these collections can bring to scholars by the mere fact that they have survived in spite of undue hardships.

ADMINISTRATION, ORGANIZATION, AND PERSONNEL

A study of the administrative organization of black libraries housing materials in black studies indicates that twenty-seven, or 41.5 percent, of sixty-five libraries reporting have established separate collections of black studies materials or special collections. Thirty, or 46.2 percent of the total, reported that black materials in their libraries were distributed among items in the general collection. Eight libraries failed to return this portion of the questionnaire.

Patterns in the administration of special collections of black materials vary. Five of the libraries reported that their special collections departments were administered by full-time librarians whose primary responsibility lay in that area. Seven reported that the collections were administered by librarians with shared responsibilities who devoted a part of their services to directing activities in special collections. The remaining collections were directly supervised by head librarians.

Reports on the assignment of professional and/or semiprofessional staff members to special collections departments show that thirteen libraries followed this practice, with five reporting that their services to the collections were full time. One of these libraries assigned two professionals to the collection on a full-time basis. Ten libraries employed semiprofessional staff members in the collections, with two libraries reporting that their services in the collections were full time. The number of hours of student assistance to the collections was generally unavailable.

In each instance where the collection was administered separately by persons other than the head librarian, these persons held the master's degree. Subprofessional and clerical persons assigned to the collections held at least the bachelor's degree.

Thirteen libraries indicated that staff persons serving these collections continued their professional development through attendance at inservice meetings, workshops, and conferences of professional organizations. These included annual meetings of the Association for the Study of Negro Life and History (now the Association for the study of Afro-American Life and History); an institute in the Selection, Organization, and Use of Materials by and about Negroes held at Fisk University; conferences on the administration of archives; a conference on Materials by and about American Negroes held at Atlanta University; institutes on archival preservation; an institute on Bibliographic Sources for a Study of the Negro held at Howard University; and short-term conferences and institutes at the local level. Also, seven libraries reported that their staffs had received additional formal education beyond their last degree.

Conferences with staff persons indicated that each of the twenty-seven libraries housing separate and special collections of black literature is seriously understaffed in these areas. Such libraries as Atlanta, Fisk, and Tuskegee, which are used heavily by researchers from various parts of the country, are especially burdened. They are required to serve the increasing needs of students and faculty as well as to lend research assistance to visiting scholars from throughout the United States and certain foreign countries, each demanding more time than present staff members can provide. Some of the visiting scholars spent several months in research at these institutions. Such libraries as Hampton, Lincoln (Pennsylvania), and Florida A & M are anxious to broaden their services but are handicapped in their activities by staffing shortages.

It would appear that while the staff persons serving these collections are limited in number, they are well trained and continue their education through workshops, institutes, and other activities. In order to overcome their difficulties, however, all of the libraries that plan to improve their services will need to increase their staffs. In projecting staffing needs for the next five years, eighteen libraries indicated that they will require an additional seventy persons, most of which will be in professional positions. Only three libraries indicated that they need to add archivists to their staffs, even though most of these libraries were collecting the archives of their institutions. Few of these libraries currently employed archivists.

Written policies governing the administration and use of these collections were available in nine libraries, with the remaining eighteen reporting that no such policies had been prepared.

PROFILES OF THE COLLECTIONS

If maximum benefits are to be reaped from special collections of black materials, the collections must be organized and indexed in an appropriate manner. When the collections involve books, this necessarily means that an accepted scheme of classification must be adopted. In terms of classification schemes used, findings show that eleven of the twenty-seven libraries used the Dewey Decimal Classification for processing materials in special collections. Three libraries reported that they used the Library of Congress Classification, while ten reported that they used both LC and DDC but were either converting or reclassifying their collections to LC. Three libraries failed to respond to the question. The reporting libraries had no substantial cataloging arrearages in monographic works.

Visits to the libraries showed that the processing of archival materials was incomplete. For the most part, these materials had been collected and were housed either in the library building or in other buildings on campus. Little had been done to index them. Collections at Hampton, Howard, Fisk, Lincoln (Pennsylvania), and Tuskegee, which included vast amounts of original research materials, were partially indexed and were preserved either through microfilming or through storage in acid-free folders and manuscript boxes. Equally large amounts of materials were unprocessed and, consequently, unavailable for use. In addition, some of these materials were deteriorating rapidly. Many of these materials were collected years ago but remained unprocessed because funds were unavailable to provide enough staff members with sufficient expertise to handle them.

Analysis of the scope and content of materials on black subjects housed in the black college libraries revealed that for the most part, and with the exception of the few research collections, increasing amounts of materials were gathered to support the epidemic of black studies programs. When extensive research collections were unassembled in these libraries, few of the institutions planned to develop them. Archival materials that were in many of these collections previously had been housed in administrative offices and recently had been added to the libraries. The primary interest of such materials lay in the collection and preservation of the institution's history.

Thirty-five of the institutions reported curricular programs in black studies, with degrees given in four of the schools and a minor offered in three. Fourteen offered programs in African studies, with degrees offered in two institutions and a minor offered in two. These new emphases, or a reemphasis on black subjects already offered in these institutions over the years, stress the need for enriching collections of black materials to support the black studies programs.

The list which follows briefly describes the nature of black materials housed in the responding libraries, whether or not such materials form a separate Negro collection. This inventory helps to determine where black materials are located, but it also reflects the need for a more thorough analysis of the content of these collections.[4]

Alabama A & M. The black resources consist primarily of books and vertical file collections of clippings, pamphlets, pictures, and photographs.

Alabama State. The collection covers all subject areas, even though sparingl with the heaviest concentration in literature (including fiction), followe by race relations. Papers on the Alabama State Teachers Association, th Montgomery Bus Boycott, and the Montgomery March are included.

Alcorn. Miscellaneous subject areas are represented in the collection.

Arkansas A M & N. The John Watson Brown Memorial Collection includes approximately 1,700 volumes as well as numerous serial publications, manuscripts, clippings, and limited college archives.

Atlanta University. The collection includes papers of the abolitionist John Brown (with his drawing of the Haymaker Plot), Thomas Clarkson, C. Eric Lincoln, Owen Dodson, Langston Hughes, Paul Laurence Dunbar, W. E. B. DuBois, William Christopher Handy, Henry Ossawa Tanner, Maude Cuney Hare, and the Association of Southern Women for the Prevention of Lynching. Other materials include the Henry Slaughter Collection, the Countee Cullen Collection, and the Atlanta University Archives. The book collection numbers approximately twenty-one thousand volumes, including many first editions.

Barber-Scotia. Included in the collection are books on general subjects and college archives which date from 1867.

Benedict. The collection contains approximately six thousand volumes representing all subject areas. Some of the volumes are both old and valuable and have been in the collection for many years. Benedict archives, dating from 1870, and archives of the Mather School, 1868 to 1968, are included.

Bethune-Cookman. Included in the collection are materials by and about Africans and black Americans.

Bishop. The collection is general in nature.

Central State. The collection was established in 1947 through gifts from educators in the community. The entire collection of writings and personal books from the Hallie Q. Brown estate was given to the library. Other titles are often received from persons in the community. Included in the collection are materials on local and school history and the college archives, dating from 1887 (which relate the history of the parent institution, Wilberforce University).

Cheyney. The collection was started in 1968 at the librarian's initiative. Materials relating to general subjects and the college archives are included.

Claflin. Materials of a general nature are included. The book collection numbers approximately two thousand volumes. College archives, dating from 1869, have been collected.

Clark. In addition to black materials on general subjects, the library contains the archives of the college.

Dillard. The book collection of the library contains titles of historical, general, and popular nature. Most of the volumes are concentrated in the social sciences, literature, and history. The Amistad Research Center contains the American Missionary Association Archives, the Countee Cullen Collection, the American Home Missionary Society Archives, the Mary McLeod Bethune Papers, Archives of the Race Relations Department of the United Church Board for Homeland Ministries, and other papers.

Elizabeth City. The collection consists of books, pamphlets, and periodicals in all fields, especially literature and the arts. A few titles on Africa, the West Indies, and Latin America are included. Rapid additions are being made of catalogs of other collections, including Moorland-Spingarn and Schomburg, which will be used to make selections for strengthening the collection. The library will become a center for Afro-American studies and materials, serving a function not provided elsewhere in the area.

Fayetteville. Materials on all aspects of black life and culture are included. Books, periodicals, some audiovisual materials, art prints, and college archives dating from 1937 are collected.

Fisk. Subjects included in the book collection are broad, with an emphasis on black subjects in America, Africa, and the Caribbean, including rare items. Materials are collected in several languages. The manuscript collections include Fisk archives and the papers of Charles Waddell Chesnutt, E. R. Alexander, John Mercer Langston, James C. Napier,

Jean Toomer, Scott Joplin, Langston Hughes, Charles Spurgeon John-
son, W. E. B. DuBois, James Weldon Johnson, the Julius Rosenwald
Fund, Robert Ezra Park, Edwin R. Embree, George Edmund Haynes,
Dorothy L. Brown, Naomi Long Madgett, John W. Work, Stephen J.
Wright, Slater King, Louise Meriwether, the Fisk Jubilee Singers, Arna
Bontemps, Robert Burgette Johnson, William L. Imes, and others. The
George Gershwin Memorial Collection and the Cyrus Leroy Baldridge
Collection also form a part of the special collections. Tapes and tran-
scripts of the Fisk Black Oral History Project are included.

Florida A & M. The Negro Collection began its embryonic development
during the period from 1936 to 1938, under the administration of
the librarian, Joseph H. Reason. Broad subject areas are represented.
College archives and materials on blacks in Florida are being collected.

Florida Memorial. In 1966, the collection was culled from the general library collection. At that time, 343 volumes were gathered. Included
in the collection are broad subject areas and a few materials dating
from as early as 1620.

Fort Valley. The library has a small collection of books dealing with the
period from slavery to the present time. Although the coverage is inade
quate, each subject area is touched.

Grambling. Black materials have been in the Grambling library since the
library was founded in organized form in 1936. Since that time, books
by and about black people have been added, with some attention given
to Africa. Increased emphasis has been placed on emerging African na-
tions. In May 1969, black materials were drawn from the general collection to form a special collection. A limited number of materials on
blacks in Louisiana are included.

Hampton. The collection, numbering 11,314 volumes, is exceptionally
strong in materials on the Civil War and Reconstruction. The collection of clippings is unusually strong on lynchings and other race problems. Archival materials include the proceedings of the Lake Mohonk
Negro Conference and the Hampton Negro Conference; papers of Holli
Burke Frissell, Samuel C. Armstrong, Alexander Crummell, Booker T.
Washington, James Weldon Johnson, and Mary McLeod Bethune; trans
cripts of interviews with former slaves in Virginia; and other items.

Huston-Tillotson. Materials by and about black people range from fiction
through all areas of the social sciences, history, and biography. College
archives, dating from 1876, are included.

Jackson State. The scope of this collection includes the history of black people in Africa and America, contemporary materials, race relations, bibliographies, literature, civil rights, slavery, and other areas. Portraits of early black leaders are included.

Jarvis Christian. Broad subject areas are represented in the collection.

Johnson C. Smith. The collection is broad in coverage. College archives, dating from 1867, are included.

Kentucky State. In 1955, a collection of 400 volumes was purchased to strengthen the existing resources. A number of first editions are included in this total of 4,305 volumes.

Knoxville. Broad subject areas are represented in the collection. College archives, dating from 1875, are included.

Lane. The collection is broad in coverage, numbering approximately 1,400 titles. Also included are college archives, dating from 1882, and papers of James E. Lane.

Langston. The collection is being developed in five major areas— blacks in the United States since 1933, the humanities and arts since 1900, business and education from the beginning to the present time, Africa, and great black authors. Included in the collection are the artifacts and personal effects of Melvin B. Tolson, donated by his widow. University archives, dating from 1897, are included.

LeMoyne-Owen. The collection was established around 1937 and includes approximately 3,000 volumes. General subjects are represented, with some first editions of earlier works. College archives, dating from 1870, include some materials which relate to LeMoyne and Owen colleges prior to their merger.

Lincoln University (Missouri). Broad subjects are represented, including materials on slavery and anti-slavery. Among the rare and unique items is a volume bearing the signature of Harriet Tubman (*X* mark).

Lincoln University (Pennsylvania). The collection includes over 6,000 volumes, numerous periodicals, pamphlets, university archives dating back to 1845, minutes of the Pennsylvania Colonization Society from 1838 to 1913, the Langston Hughes Collection of 3,000 items, the Reid Collection on Africana and Negroana, and the Scott Collection of 375 general titles on black subjects.

Livingstone. In 1895, impetus for establishing a black collection occurred when George Henry, an influential black citizen of Providence, Rhode Island, gave his entire library of black materials to Livingstone. The collection now includes histories, biographies, materials on slavery and anti-slavery, black organizations, and professions, and other subjects. The library was formerly a depository for the African Methodist Episcopal Zion Church, with some items still being received. The collection is particularly strong in early AMEZ materials, especially in scarce journals. Included also is the John Dancy Collection of books autographed by the author, materials on the Ecumenical Methodist Conference, and college archives dating from 1879.

Mississippi Valley. The collection covers those areas in support of the college curriculum as well as other areas of interest to the faculty and staff in an effort to provide for the complete study of black culture.

Morris. The collection includes materials supporting the general curriculum as well as those providing cultural enrichment. College archives dating from 1908 are included.

Morris Brown. The collection is small and general in nature; it contains a group of materials on human relations.

Norfolk State. History, religion, art, music, politics, and other broad subjects are included.

North Carolina A & T. All materials on black people that can be acquired are collected, particularly contemporary items.

North Carolina Central. The library has a special collection of materials by and about black people—the Martin Collection. All other materials on this subject area are incorporated in the general collection. The Martin Collection, purchased in 1950, was assembled by the late Charles D. Martin, a West Indian Moravian minister who pastored the Beth Pphillah Moravian Church in New York. The scope of the collection is Africana and Negroana, relating to the black people in the United States, Africa, and the Caribbean. The collection contains more than 3,500 books as well as numerous pamphlets, serials, pictures, and some miscelaneous items.

Oakwood. The collection includes materials on general subjects. College archives, dating from 1896, are included.

Paine. Materials on black subjects deal with all aspects of history, life, and culture from the middle of the nineteenth century to the present time.

Paul Quinn. The collection is small and is in its infancy as a special collection. Miscellaneous subjects are represented, including college archives which date from 1872.

Philander Smith. In 1968, all materials on black subjects were pulled together in a special collection. Prior to that time, such materials (which were few in nature) were housed with the general collection.

Prairie View. The collection was established in 1945-46, through the courtesy of T. K. Lawless, a noted dermatologist who wished to establish a memorial to his friend and fellow physician, C. Leon Wilson. General subject areas are represented. College archives, dating from 1912, are included.

St. Augustine. Materials on general subjects are represented in this collection of about 4,000 volumes.

Shaw. The collection contains materials on various subjects, including university archives which date from 1868.

Simmons. The scope is limited. For the most part, reference items and biographies form the book collection. College archives, dating from 1879, are included.

South Carolina State. Materials of a general nature are included. College archives, dating from 1896, are collected.

Southern University. During the early history of the library, black materials were kept in a separate collection. This practice was abandoned in the 1950s but was reestablished in 1969, when the Black Heritage Collection was formed. It consists of materials on black people in America, with some attention given to Africana. College archives are also collected.

Southern University, New Orleans. Materials in general subject areas are included.

Stillman. Materials of a general nature are included. Some college archives are now being collected.

Talladega. The collection consists of books on general subjects; the papers of Congregational ministers and missionaries, educators, churches, and the Alabama State Teachers Association (1882-1912); and college archives (1867-1954). A unique feature of the library building is a group of murals by Hale Woodruff which depict the Amistad slave revolt. The murals are painted on the walls of the library lobby.

Texas College. General subject areas are represented.

Texas Southern. The collection consists of 18,000 volumes, numerous periodicals, documents, musical scores, cartoons, various curios, and other items dating from 1600 to the present time. College archives, dating from 1947, are included.

Tougaloo. The collection contains basic items on black life and culture and includes many first editions. A supplementary collection on Africa has been made available as a gift from Emory Ross.

Tuskegee. The collection of books and periodicals is broad in scope, covering a variety of subjects. Many first editions and scarce items are included. The manuscript collection consists of several different parts with a combined total of countless items. Both personal and organizational papers are included. Among the various materials is a vast photograph collection which numbers 3,500 items and which depicts the early and contemporary life of black people and of Tuskegee Institute.

Among the notable collections are papers of Booker T. Washington, Robert Russa Moton, Frederick D. Patterson, George Washington Carver, William Taylor Burwell Williams, R. S. Darnaby, the Southern Conference for Human Welfare, Monroe Nathan Work (consisting of thousands of items on Africa and black people in America which he used in compiling his *Bibliography of the Negro in Africa and America,* and other materials relating to the *Negro Yearbook*), lynching reports dating from 1882 (giving information on all known lynchings), Tuskegee archives, and other materials. A special George Washington Carver Museum, located on the Tuskegee campus, complements the Carver materials in the library.

Virginia State. Selections are made on the basis of faculty requests. Generally, all subject areas are included. Of particular importance are the papers of Luther P. Jackson, John M. Gandy, Congressman Arthur Mitchell, James H. Johnston, the Prince Edward County (Virginia) Free Schools, and the Virginia Teachers Association, as well as college archives which date from 1882. There are also papers of free black persons who lived around Petersburg, Virginia, some of which are handwritten.

Virginia Union. The collection was established as a memorial to the late William J. Howard and his grandson. Broad subject areas are represented, with many first editions and scarce items included. College archives are also collected.

Voorhees. All subject areas are represented in the collection. College archives, dating from 1897, are included.

West Virginia. Subject coverage is broad. Included are archives of the college, dating from 1891.

Wilberforce. Books in the collection are limited in number and in subject coverage. Among the manuscript and archival materials included are the papers of several leaders of the African Methodist Episcopal Church in its mission work in Africa. Papers of Benjamin William Arnett, Levi Jenkins Coppin, Bishop Reverdy Cassius Ransom, Daniel L. Payne, Charles Leander Hill, and William Sanders Scarborough have been collected.

Wiley. A general collection of materials on broad subjects has been gathered. College archives, dating from 1873, are included.

Winston-Salem. A variety of subjects is represented in the collection. College archives, dating from 1892, are included.

Xavier. The collection numbers approximately 4,500 volumes on various subjects, including blacks in Louisiana. In addition, there are 300 rare books. The manuscript collection includes papers of Albert G. Brice, Charles E. A. Gayarre, Negro slave manumission reports, and miscellaneous records of the birth, baptism, and burial of free people of color (1733-1808).

In general, the scope of the collections in black studies in the historically black college libraries is geared to the curricular programs. Several of these libraries, most of them privately supported, have gathered other valuable research items along with their collections of books and periodicals. Such collections, therefore, serve curricular as well as research requirements in black studies.

Descriptions of the larger, richer collections (particularly manuscript materials)—including those at Hampton, Atlanta, Fisk, Lincoln (Pennsylvania), and Tuskegee—have been reported in various published guides. These include the *National Union Catalog of Manuscript Collections, Directory of Afro-American Resources* by Schatz, *Guide to Manuscript Collections* by Hamer, and *Subject Collections* by Ash. In addition to these sources, many of the black libraries have published handbooks, guides, acquisition lists, and other items which record and/or describe the contents of the collections. Examples of these are "Guide to Manuscripts and Archives in the Negro Collection of Trevor Arnett Library" and "Special Collections in the Fisk University Library." A more complete list of these publications is given in the bibliography for this study.

Six of the libraries included in the study have published book catalogs of their collections. These are Hampton, Fisk, Florida A & M, Jackson

State, Lincoln (Pennsylvania), and Texas Southern. Libraries not reporting in the study but which have issued notable book catalogs are Howard
and the Schomburg Center. A more complete description of these catalogs may be found in the bibliography for this study.

Statistics on the number of volumes in black studies were available from
nineteen libraries, each maintaining separate special collections. Table 37
shows, as of September 1969, a total of 157,578 volumes in black studies
in these libraries, with the largest collection reported at 30,000 volumes
and the smallest at 50. Collections housing sizable amounts of black studies materials were Atlanta (21,000 volumes), Fisk (30,000), Tuskegee
(25,000), Hampton (11,314), and Texas Southern (18,000). The table
also shows the percentage of total library materials identified as being
in black studies. It must be pointed out that certain libraries—including
those at Southern, Grambling, and Prairie View—have other black studies
materials in their general collections, and these items were not reported.

Table 38 shows that between 1964-65 and 1968-69, these collections
gained 23,771 volumes. Because statistics were not reported by the majority of these institutions, it is difficult to make an evaluation.

In projecting the growth of these collections to 1973-74, ten libraries
expect to add a total of 126,350 volumes during the five-year span. As
is shown in Table 39, the largest number of volumes projected was 11,000,
while the smallest was 200.

A report of the number of periodical subscriptions related to black
studies in the black libraries, as shown in Table 40, revealed that a high
of 120 titles was received in one library, as compared to a low of 3 in
another. A number of these were in microform. The table shows further
that most of these libraries subscribed to newspapers in the area of black
studies, with a high of twenty reported in one institution, as compared to
a low of two subscriptions in another.

Materials in forms other than books, periodicals, and newspapers were
found in a number of these libraries, particularly in the special collections
of black materials. The types of materials reported in the various libraries
are shown in Table 41. This table indicates that, as a group, libraries included in the study reported holdings in black studies materials in the form of
microfilm, microcard, microprint, and other forms. Thirty-five libraries reported that college archives are collected. Other types of materials are
generally less well represented in these collections.

A number of manuscript collections are among the special gifts of ma-

TABLE 37

Volumes of Black Studies Materials in Certain Black
College Libraries, September 1, 1969

Institution	Volumes in Black Studies	Total Volumes in Library	Percent in Black Studies
Alabama A & M*	2,103	104,641	2.0
Arkansas A M & N*	1,700	59,523	2.8
Atlanta**	21,000	240,000	8.7
Benedict**	6,000	49,261	12.1
Central State*	2,000	90,000	2.2
Cheyney*	2,000	86,760	2.3
Claflin**	767	38,385	1.9
Fisk**	30,000	163,467	18.3
Florida Memorial**	2,000	41,862	4.7
Grambling*	1,250	80,754	1.5
Hampton**	11,314	120,616	9.3
Jarvis Christian**	910	38,522	2.3
Kentucky State*	4,305	58,806	7.3
Langston*	1,714	108,218	1.5
LeMoyne-Owen**	3,000	50,586	5.9
Lincoln (Pa.)**	6,893	117,612	5.8
Livingstone**	2,476	44,156	5.6
Morris**	1,900	21,025	9.0
Paul Quinn**	2,000	25,150	7.9
Prairie View*	1,696	116,358	1.4
St. Augustine**	4,000	49,009	8.1
Southern University*	700	212,435	.3
Stillman**	850	39,121	2.1
Texas Southern*	18,000	179,866	10.0
Tuskegee**	25,000	177,500	14.0
Xavier**	4,000	102,891	3.8
TOTAL	157,578	2,416,524	14.1

*public.
**private.

terials that have been added during the past five years to such libraries as
Atlanta, Hampton, Fisk, Lincoln (Pennsylvania), Tuskegee, Virginia State,
Kentucky State, and Livingstone. Some of these collections also included
books. In 1969, the Southern Association of Colleges and Schools presented collections of paperback books in black studies to each of the black college libraries. The purpose of the gift was to enrich holdings in this area
and to make the materials easily accessible to students, particularly in libraries where few materials of this type had been collected. An examination of the collections in these libraries revealed that these books greatly

TABLE 38

Volumes in Black Studies Materials Added to Collections in Certain Black Colleges, 1964-65 Through 1968-69

Institution	1964-65	1965-66	Volumes Added 1966-67	1967-68	1968-69
Fisk**	210	124	96	146	114
Florida A & M*	322	323	200	402	353
Florida Memorial**		343	500	550	606
Hampton**	26	254	82	252	400
Jarvis Christian**		200	500	210	200
Kentucky State*	75	208	325	1,559	1,000
Langston*			300	450	100
Lincoln (Pa.)**	325	450	680	800	1,770
Paul Quinn**					2,000
Prairie View*			74	42	5,000
Xavier**				4,000	
TOTAL	958	1,902	2,757	8,411	9,743
GRAND TOTAL	23,771				

*public.
**private.

TABLE 39

**Projections in Growth of Black Studies Materials
in Certain Black College Libraries,
1969-70 Through 1973-74**

Institution	1969-70	1970-71	1971-72	1972-73	1973-74
Alabama A & M*	3,200	4,300	6,100	8,500	9,600
Fisk**		3,000	3,500	4,000	4,500
Florida Memorial**	2,500	3,000	3,500	4,000	4,500
Hampton	400	450	500	500	500
Jarvis Christian**	200	200	200	200	200
Kentucky State*	1,000	1,000	1,000	1,000	1,000
Langston*	100	200	300	300	300
Lincoln (Pa.)**	1,500				
Paul Quinn**	200	500	700	700	1,000
Prairie View*	5,000	6,000	7,000	9,000	11,000
TOTAL	14,100	18,650	22,800	28,200	32,600
GRAND TOTAL	126,350				

*public.
**private.

TABLE 40

Number of Periodical and Newspaper Subscriptions in
Black Studies Held by Certain Black College
Libraries, September 1, 1969

Institution	Periodicals		Newspapers	
	Subscription	Microform	Subscription	Microform
Alabama A & M*	15	1	9	3
Alabama State*	14	2	10	2
Benedict**	26		6	1
Cheyney*	47	5	2	
Claflin**	13	1	2	1
Dillard**		1		2
Elizabeth City*	27		8	3
Fayetteville*	16	4	9	1
Fisk**	20	2	20	2
Florida Memorial**			14	
Fort Valley*	13		3	1
Grambling*	12	3	11	1
Hampton**	115	11	16	10
Huston-Tillotson*	10		4	
Jarvis Christian**	13	1	8	
Kentucky State*	22	2	8	
Lane**	10		10	1
Langston*	14	1	7	1
Lincoln (Mo.)*	30	5	13	3

TABLE 40 (continued)

Institution	Periodicals		Newspapers	
	Subscription	Microform	Subscription	Microform
Lincoln (Pa.)**	120		8	
Livingstone**	23	2	9	1
Miss. Valley*	16	2	7	1
Morris**	10	3	10	3
Norfolk*	15		8	2
North Carolina A & T*	15		11	
Paine**	13	4	5	1
Paul Quinn**	3		4	
St. Augustine**	30		5	
Shaw**	20	5	5	2
Simmons**	12		3	
South Carolina State*	10	1	5	
Southern Univ. N. O.*		560		25
Stillman**	9		6	2
Talladega**	11		3	

*public.
**private.

TABLE 41

**Types of Black Studies Materials Held by Libraries
in Certain Black Colleges, September 1, 1969**

Type of Material	Libraries Reporting
Manuscripts	10
Microfilm	23
Microfiche	0
Microcard	20
Microprint	21
Recordings	14
Tapes (audio)	4
Tapes (video)	9
College archives	35
Other archives	6
Films	6
Filmstrips	16
Reproductions	4
Photographs	17
Slides	7
Scrapbooks	14
Uncataloged pamphlets	18
Art objects	8
Paintings	9

enriched black studies materials already gathered, frequently forming the nucleus of newer collections in that area.

Particularly significant to those colleges which were members of the United Negro College Fund in 1969 was the 3M Company's gift to each college of microfilm materials and two reader-printers. This donation helped to supplement and enrich both special collections and general collections on black studies. The microfilm collection consisted primarily of black studies materials filmed in the Schomburg Center of the New York Public Library, and it was designed for use in curriculum enrichment.

Frequently, the development of collections along desirable lines is more easily assured when acquisition policy statements are prepared and observed. Ten libraries reported that such policies had been developed for collecting black materials, with eight of these reported in libraries where separate black collections were established.

Materials used for book selection in these libraries generally included such sources as *Bibliographic Survey, Ebony, Black World, Journal of Negro History, Negro History Bulletin, Publishers Weekly, Choice, Freedomways, Phylon, Journal of Negro Education, Bibliography of the Negro in Africa and America,* and catalogs of various reprint companies. Atlanta and Fisk reported use of Library of Congress cards, which have been sent to them continuously over the years expressly for the purpose of selection in this area. A few libraries used the *Dictionary Catalog of the Schomburg Collection of Negro Literature and History* for building collections.

Responsibility for selection of materials was generally placed with the library staff, with the faculty assuming much less responsibility in this area. In some instances, however, the faculty and the library staff shared in the selection process.

The physical condition of materials on black subjects in these libraries was generally good. Four reported that the materials were in fair condition, while two reported that their condition was poor. Some of the manuscript and archival materials in the larger research collections were brittle and fragile as a result of extreme conditions of heat, humidity, and dust suffered over the years, sometimes before they were collected by the libraries and sometimes after.

FACILITIES, SERVICES, AND PROGRAMS

Standards of the American Library Association suggest that the success of a library's services presupposes an adequate library building with ample quarters for processing and similar activities. Ideally, services which the library undertakes must be provided for in areas that are well planned. These standards are immediately applicable when special collections are provided. Building layouts must take into consideration the functions that special collections are to serve, particularly when these functions involve service to the students and faculty as well as research, as is the case with several of the black colleges.

In studying the facilities for housing and servicing special black collections in the twenty-six libraries reporting, it was found that quarters in three libraries were excellent, those in fourteen were good, those in four were fair, and those in four were poor. Two responses were not given. Nineteen of the libraries reported that quarters for special collections were air-conditioned. The condition of furniture in these libraries ranged from excellent to poor, and the libraries were about evenly divided in the various categories.

The size of quarters varied from a capacity of 30,000 volumes to a capacity of 166 volumes, as is shown in Table 42. Two libraries had exceeded their capacities, while ten had room for expanding the collections. Further analysis of the facilities may be seen in Table 43, which indicates seating and study space in the libraries reporting. The table shows that most seating was provided at tables, with fewer provisions made for individual or informal seating.

Access to stack areas housing these materials was provided for undergraduate students in seventeen libraries, with ten reporting that stacks

TABLE 42

**Shelf Capacity of Quarters Housing Special Black
Collections in Certain Black College
Libraries, September 1, 1969**

Institution	Shelf Capacity	Size of Collection
Alabama A & M*	5,000	2,103
Atlanta**	15,000	21,000
Central State*	3,000	2,000
Fisk**	30.000	30,000
Grambling*	5,000	1,250
Jarvis Christian**		
Kentucky State*		
Langston*	10,000	1,714
Lincoln (Pa.)**	10,000	6,893
Morris**	4,000	1,900
Paul Quinn**	2,358	2,000
Prairie View*	166	1,696
Stillman**	1,000	850
Texas Southern*	20,000	18,000
Tuskegee**	4,500	
Xavier**	4,434	4,000

*public.
**private.

TABLE 43

Seating Capacity of Quarters Housing Special Black Collections in Certain Black College Libraries, September 1, 1969

Institution	Number of Seats		Informal Seating	Study Rooms	Total Seating
	Carrels	Tables			
Alabama A & M*		8	2	9	19
Atlanta**	32	52			84
Central State*		10			10
Cheyney*		10	7	1	18
Claflin**		8			8
Fisk**	3	13	36		52
Florida A & M*	10				10
Florida Memorial**	4	8	2		14
Grambling*			14		14
Hampton**				2	
Jarvis Christian**	18				18
Kentucky State*	4	4	4	3	15
Langston*		10	2	1	13
Lincoln (Pa.)**		6	1		6
Livingstone**			6	1	2
Paul Quinn**	7		2	1	14
Prairie View*		16	2		18
Southern*		48	11	1	60
Texas Southern*		12	5		17
Tuskegee**		32			32
Xavier**	4		10	1	
TOTAL					424

*public.
**private.

were closed. Graduate students were provided direct access to stacks housing black studies materials in seven libraries, although some of the reporting libraries had no graduate students. Faculty access to the stacks was
provided in seventeen libraries. Eight libraries reported that stacks were
closed to all patrons.

As in libraries generally, the loss of materials through theft was a common problem. Frequently, such losses reached serious proportions and de-
prived students and faculty members of items needed almost daily for
class work. Such popular and classic works as *Soul on Ice, The Negro in
American Culture, Manchild in the Promised Land,* and *From Slavery to
Freedom* were nearly always lost. New materials placed on the shelves
frequently disappeared immediately when they met the current interests
of patrons.

Equipment available in the special collections areas generally included
microfilm readers, microfilm reader-printers, record players, filmstrip projectors, and slide projectors.

Table 44 indicates that hours of service varied from a high of ninety
per week to a low of forty-four. Service at night was provided in twenty
libraries, with the highest number of night hours reported as twenty-nine
and the lowest as four. Sunday hours were provided in nineteen libraries,
with a high of eight hours provided in one library as compared to a low
of three in another.

Statistics on use of the collections, including interlibrary loan, were
generally unavailable because many libraries counted use of the collections with use of the general circulating collections. Materials in the majority of these libraries were available for use outside of the library, with
twelve libraries reporting that materials were restricted to room use only.

Thirty-one libraries reported that they provided special services such
as preparation of bibliographies. Common practices among the libraries
were assistance to faculty, students, and members of the community in
compiling bibliographies; presentation of special book reviews, lectures,
and programs during Negro History Week; and lending other assistance
as needed. Libraries housing sizable amounts of original research materials reported that they provided research assistance to visiting scholars and
assisted in the use of these materials.

Of those collections housed separately, six libraries reported that they
contributed to union lists of materials; nine participated in cooperative

TABLE 44

Hours of Service in Collections of Black Materials, September, 1, 1969

Institution	Hours Per Week	Hours Night	Sunday
Alabama A & M*	76	16	5
Atlanta**	82	26	4
Central State*	82	20	4
Cheyney*	70	24	6
Claflin**	70	22	4
Clark**	90	26	8
Fisk**	44		
Florida A & M*	81	25	5
Florida Memorial**	73	16	3
Grambling*	57	10	3
Hampton**	75	29	7
Jarvis Christian**	70	14	4
Kentucky State*	82	5	4
Langston*	28		
Lincoln (Pa.)**	45.5	8	
Livingstone**	71	20	3
Paul Quinn**	73	20	
Prairie View*	87	24	8
Southern*	85	22	6
Stillman**	73	14	4
Texas Southern*	66	15	4
Tougaloo**	76	4	5
Tuskegee**	66		
Xavier**	86	26	8

*public.
**private.

acquisition programs with other libraries in the region; and seven were involved in special agreements concerning use of materials with other libraries. Of those libraries incorporating black materials in their general collections, six were engaged in consortia activities which involved the collection and/or use of black materials.

Plans for automating various activities in special collections were reported as being under consideration in three libraries. These included information retrieval and preparation of bibliographies.

FINANCIAL ASPECTS

As is true with general library collections, adequate financial support must be provided to permit proper development of the collection. When special collections are provided, it follows that increased budgets will be needed to support the development of services for which these collections are maintained. Special collections can be costly. They may require additional staff persons, depending on the administrative organization and service requirements of this part of the library; items needed may be scarce and expensive; some items housed in the general collection may need to be duplicated here; and quarters will require special temperature and humidity control.

Separate budgets for the support of special collections were generally not provided in the libraries reporting. In only two instances were separate budgets established. Libraries indicated that funds from the regular library budget were used for this purpose.

In attempting to determine whether or not special financial grants had been provided to support these collections during the years 1964-65 throug 1968-69, it was found that six libraries received a total of $83,961 during the years in question. Grants varied from a high of $32,000 to a low of $1,200. None of the collections was endowed. A full appraisal of the expenditures for library materials in black studies in the reporting institutions, including grants and gifts as well as funds from the general library budget, cannot be made.

Selection of materials in black studies was generally done by the library staff, with a few instances of allocations to departments. Such departmental allocations were made in connection with total library development rather than with a view toward exclusive development of special collections. Proper development of the collections was attempted by strengthening weak areas as well as by gearing selection practices to fit the needs of the curricular and research programs.

PROJECTIONS FOR THE FUTURE

Libraries were asked to report any special problems which affected the development or use of their special collections. Responses may be grouped in terms of spatial, staffing, and financial needs. Many of the quarters were crowded, with little provision for staff work. A number of the libraries were understaffed, particularly in terms of librarians with the expertise needed to administer the collections. All libraries reported inadequacies in the financial support received, asserting that their unfulfilled financial needs were the primary reasons for their problems.

Projections for the future included strengthening and greatly expanding the book collections, gathering college archives, expanding collecting practices to gather other materials in the region, enlarging quarters, moving into new quarters, adding new staff members, and developing black oral history programs.

ANATOMY OF A SPECIAL COLLECTION OF BLACK LITERATURE

When judged by present measures of excellence, the outstanding libraries in American institutions are those that offer extraordinary resources and services in support of the particular role or function which they claim to serve. For example, the library in a major university may be considered outstanding when it offers its students and the larger educational community an extensive range of materials covering nearly all subjects, when these resources encourage and support research, and when the professional assistance required to maximize use of these resources is provided. The library in a small college may be considered outstanding when it offers its students and faculty a wide range of materials which are geared more to the curricular programs of the institution. The college library may also view its purpose as providing research collections in a limited number of subject areas, whether or not research activities are conducted on campus. Sometimes the resources in these research collections are so strong and complete that they help the college library achieve an outstanding reputation. It may not be unusual to find that where both the college and the university library are concerned, specialized research collections may be developed to the detriment of those areas serving the curricular programs on campus.

With few exceptions, black institutions may be regarded more as colleges than as universities. As was seen in Chapter 4, libraries in many of the institutions examined in this study are seeking to enhance their position and to move toward meeting minimum standards of the American Library Association and the regional accrediting agencies. Often regarded as poor and inadequate in nearly every respect, regardless of whether they deserve such a rating, black colleges are struggling to come into their own as important educational institutions by upgrading their facilities, resources, and curricular programs, and especially by collecting those materials that help to preserve the black heritage.

Preservation of the black heritage may be achieved quite successfully through the approach that most black libraries are taking; that is, through gathering secondary resources in limited quantity and range to support only those courses or programs which the institutions offer, and through gathering archives of the college. Bona fide research collections are thus maintained in a limited number of black college libraries.

Special collections are costly and difficult to maintain. They require professional and clerical staff with expertise in those areas which the collections offer; they require considerable funds for collection development and maintenance; they demand suitable quarters and equipment apart from the main portion of the library; and they require a high level of service to scholars who will use the collections if they are lively and functional ones. Clearly, the financial support which black college libraries receive hardly justifies separate and special collections as an added expense to library budgets.

Special collections in black literature constitute the principal claim to advanced research status that a few of the black college libraries can make. Although special black collections have emerged in some institutions almost simultaneously with the burgeoning curricular programs in black studies, the collections at such institutions as Howard, Fisk, Atlanta, and Tuskegee had reached great stature long before this newer curricular emphasis. These collections have supported research efforts of scholars who were preparing dissertations and theses for graduate school as well as research efforts of seasoned scholars who continued to write and publish on black subjects. The results of two early research activities undertaken in these collections are Arna Bontemps's *Chariot in the Sky: A Story of the Jubilee Singers* (1951), which utilized the Fisk Collection, and Dorothy Porter's *North American Negro Poets, A Bibliographical Checklist of Their Writings, 1760-1944* (published in 1945), which utilized the collection at Howard. Also during this early period, papers of scholars or groups of scholars who were engaged in research activities while employed in the black colleges frequently were deposited in these libraries and helped to strengthen their original source materials. Examples of such collections are the files of the Social Science Research Center at Fisk, which issued, among other publications, *God Struck Me Dead* (1945), a compilation of interviews with former slaves, and the files of Monroe Nathan Work, who published his *Bibliography of the Negro in Africa and America* (1928) while at Tuskegee. The collections also contain examples of publications from the university presses which Fisk, Howard, and Tuskegee maintained during this early period.

The strength of the special collections of black materials housed in black libraries and the extent to which significant items are collected generally in black libraries can be determined through various union lists or checklists. Logically, this can be done on a regional as well as a national basis. Perhaps the best effort to produce such lists may be seen in the work of the African-American Materials Project, discussed in Chapter 3, which attempts to provide bibliographical control over black materials in six southern states. The union lists of black newspapers and periodicals, master's theses on black subjects, and pre-1950 imprints by black authors are examples of AAMP's work in the region. This project serves as a model for identifying and locating black materials, shows what can be done in other regions, and suggests the need for extending this approach to include all black libraries as well as other libraries that collect black materials.

Librarians are often asked to compare the special black collection at Moorland-Spingarn to the one at Fisk or at the Schomburg Center. Little do they realize that there are necessarily variations in the content of these three collections. While each contains many materials that are basic to the support of general research on the black experience, they differ vastly in the scarce items which they contain and are especially different in the nature of the original research materials which they collect. For example, the researcher who is interested in Jean Toomer, Charles Waddell Chesnutt, or Scott Joplin would study at Fisk; the researcher who is interested in Blanche Kelso Bruce, E. Franklin Frazier, or P. B. S. Pinchback would study at Moorland-Spingarn; and the researcher who is interested in Alexander Crummell, Claude McKay, and Richard Wright would study at Schomburg. However, the researcher who is interested in Alain LeRoy Locke would study at both Moorland-Spingarn and Schomburg, while the researcher who is studying Langston Hughes would visit Schomburg, Fisk, Lincoln (Pennsylvania), and perhaps other libraries. The logical question should be, "What makes a special black collection distinguished?"

Measures of the excellence and comprehensiveness of special black collections can be determined by using the following sample checklist to examine such collections. Emerging collections can also use the checklist as a guide to their development.

SAMPLE CHECKLIST FOR DETERMINING ADEQUACY OF SPECIAL
COLLECTIONS OF BLACK LITERATURE

Divide materials that have been collected or are to be gathered into five
categories: (1) type, (2) form, (3) matter or content, (4) period, and (5)
place.[5] Materials must relate to the black experience either by authorship
or by subject matter. As this checklist is followed, make certain that there
is something unique—in information (subject) and in record (duplication)
—about the collection in question; and develop the unique areas extensive-
ly. The list is suggestive, giving samples of materials to be collected or evaluated under each category. Materials may be appropriately found within
more than one category.

I. Type

A. Primary
   1. Archives of the institution
      a. Papers of former presidents, deans, and officers of the institu-
         tion
      b. Records of committees
      c. Minutes of Faculty meetings
      d. Records of student activities
      e. Minutes of meetings of trustees and administrative committees
      f. Charter of the institution
      g. Student publications (journals, yearbooks, and so forth)
      h. Research reports and theses prepared at the institution
      i. Student and faculty directories of the institution
      j. Papers of alumni groups and former students
   2. Institutional related works
      a. Works by and about alumni and former students
      b. Works related to the institution but published elsewhere
      c. Histories of the institution
   3. Local archives
      a. Papers of local groups or corporate bodies (for example, the local
         NAACP, the local Urban League, and early black churches)
      b. Papers of state or regional groups or corporate bodies (such as
         black teachers' organizations no longer in existence)
   4. National archives
      a. Papers of national organizations (for instance, religious groups,
         fraternities, or women's organizations)

    b. Private papers: unpublished works and/or items by persons who made some notable contribution to the black experience, regardless of their ethnic or national origin or of the period in which they lived

B. Secondary
  1. General
    a. Extensive numbers of published works by and about black people. Include especially the following:
      (1) First editions
      (2) Limited editions
      (3) Autographed copies
      (4) Personal libraries of notable people
  2. Reference
    a. Extensive or complete runs of serial publications covering a wide range of subjects of local, state, regional, national, or international concern. Include current items as well as those no longer published. Examples are
      (1) Journals

        African Arts
        African Music
        African Religious Research
        African Studies Bulletin
        Beta Kappa Chi Bulletin
        Black Academy Review
        Black Collegian
        Black Enterprise
        Black Perspective in Music
        Black Politician
        Black Scholar
        Black Sports Magazine
        Black Theatre Magazine
        Black World
        Civil Rights Digest
        CLA Journal
        Crisis
        Drum
        Ebony
        Encore

Essence
Freedomways
Integrated Education
Journal of African History
Journal of African Languages
Journal of Afro-American History
Journal of African Languages
Journal of Black Poetry
Journal of Black Studies
Journal of Negro Education
Journal of Negro History
Journal of Religious Thought
Kappa Alpha Psi Journal
Message
Missionary Seer
Negro History Bulletin
New South
Opportunity
Phylon
Présence Africaine
Race Relations Reporter
Sepia
Southern Patriot
Studies in Black Literature

(2) Newspapers

Afro-American
Amsterdam News
Atlanta Daily World
Black Panther
California Eagle
Chicago Daily Defender
Cleveland Call and Post
Dallas Express
Denver Star
Informer
Journal and Guide
Kansas City Call
Los Angeles Sentinel
Michigan Chronicle

Muhammad Speaks (now *Bilalian News*)
Negro World
New York Age
Philadelphia Tribune
Pittsburgh Courier
St. Louis Argus
(3) Consumer Magazines
Black America
Tuesday

b. Wide range of bibliographic aids (retrospective and current) for selecting or identifying items, including
(1) Miller, Elizabeth W., and Fisher, M. *The Negro in America: A Bibliography.* 2d ed., rev. and enl. Cambridge, Mass.: Harvard University Press, 1970.
(2) Porter, Dorothy B. *The Negro in the United States: A Selected Bibliography.* Washington, D.C.: Library of Congress, 1970.
(3) ——. *A Working Bibliography of the Negro in the United States.* Ann Arbor: Xerox, University Microfilms, 1969.
(4) Work, Monroe N. *A Bibliography of the Negro in Africa and America.* New York: Wilson, 1928. Reissued, New York: Octagon, 1965.

c. Catalogs of other black collections, such as
(1) Fisk University. Library. Nashville, Tennessee. *Dictionary Catalog of the Negro Collection of the Fisk University Library.* 6 vols. Boston: G. K. Hall, 1974.
(2) Hampton Institute. Collis P. Huntington Library. Hampton, Virginia. *Dictionary Catalog of the George Foster Peabody Collection of Negro Literature and History.* Westport, Conn.: Greenwood Press, 1972.
(3) Howard University. Washington, D.C. *Dictionary Catalog of the Arthur B. Spingarn Collection of Negro Authors.* 2 vols. Boston: G. K. Hall, 1970.
(4) ——. *Dictionary Catalog of the Jesse E. Moorland Collection of Negro Life and History, Howard University.* 9 vols. Boston: G. K. Hall, 1971.
(5) Lincoln University. Vail Memorial Library. *Catalog of the Special Negro and African Collection.* Lincoln University, Pa.: Lincoln University, 1970.

(6) ——. Supplement, 1972.

(7) New York (City). Public Library. Schomburg Collection of
Negro Literature and History. *Dictionary Catalog.* 9 vols.
Boston: G. K. Hall, 1962.

(8) ——. Supplement I, 1967. 2 vols.

(9) ——. Supplement II, 1972. 4 vols.

d. Guides to collections of manuscripts and archives in other libraries
or research centers, such as

(1) Ash, Lee. *Subject Collections.* 4th ed. New York: Bowker, 197

(2) *National Union Catalog of Manuscript Collections.* Ann Arbor:
Edwards, 1959-72.

(3) Schatz, Walter. *Directory of Afro-American Resources.*
New York: Bowker, 1970.

(4) U.S. National Historical Publications Commission. *A Guide
to Archives and Manuscripts in the States.* Edited by Philip
M. Hamer. New Haven: Yale University Press, 1961.

e. Indexes to black periodicals and newspapers, such as

(1) *Black Information Index.* Herndon, Va., 1970-.

(2) *Index to Periodical Articles By and About Negroes.* (Title
varies) Boston: G. K. Hall, 1950-.

f. Other reference tools, including directories, encyclopedias, handbooks, guides, fact finders, books on black authors and authorship, and similar items; for example

(1) Davis, John P. *The American Negro Reference Book.* Englewood Cliffs, N.J.: Prentice-Hall, 1966.

(2) Ebony. *The Negro Handbook.* Chicago: Johnson Publishing
Company, 1974.

(3) *International Library of Negro Life and History.* 10 vols. New
York: Publishers Company, 1967-68.

(4) Loggins, Vernon. *The Negro Author, His Development in
America to 1900.* Port Washington, N.Y.: Kennikat Press,
1964, copyright 1959.

(5) *National Cyclopedia of the Colored Race.* Montgomery:
National Publishing Co., Inc., 1919.

(6) *The Negro Heritage Library.* Yonkers: Educational Heritage,
Inc., 1964.

(7) Ploski, Harry A., and Brown, Roscoe L. *The Negro Almanac.*
New York: Bellwether, 1967.

    (8) Salk, Erwin A. *A Layman's Guide to Negro History.* Chicago: Quadrangle Books, 1966.

    (9) Shockley, Ann A., and Chandler, Sue P. *Living Black American Authors: A Biographical Directory.* New York: Bowker, 1973.

    (10) Whiteman, Maxwell. *A Century of Fiction by American Negroes, 1853-1952.* Philadelphia: Saifer, 1955.

    (11) *Who's Who in Colored America; A Biographical Directory of Notable Living Persons of Negro Descent in America.* New York: Who's Who in Colored America Corp., 1927-50.

II. Form

A. Printed: published and unpublished materials in typewritten or printed form, including books, music scores, reports, broadsides, programs, handbills, invitations, postcards, calendars, and ephemera.

B. Handwritten: early as well as contemporary documents that are handwritten (may be included in archives and other papers), such as
    1. Autograph books
    2. Diaries
    3. Early drafts of research reports and books
    4. Notes
    5. Plantation records

C. Nonprinted: materials often regarded as audiovisual, such as
    1. Films
    2. Filmstrips
    3. Microform (that is, microfilm and microfiche)
    4. Photographs
    5. Recordings
    6. Slides
    7. Tapes (including oral history)
    8. Transparencies
    9. Videotapes

D. Memorabilia
    1. Coins
    2. Medals
    3. Personal effects
    4. Scrapbooks

III. Matter or Content

A. Materials should be extensive, intensive, and diverse, covering such
   subjects as
   1. Various languages (particularly French, Spanish, Arabic, and various
      African languages)
   2. Divergent philosophy; for example, materials relating to the Black
      Panthers, the Black Muslims, and the Ku Klux Klan
   3. Genealogy

IV. Period

A. Works should be collected which begin with earlier centuries and continue to the present time. Such materials may take various forms.

V. Place

A. Include materials which relate to the black experience in many areas,
   regions, and countries, including Africa, Germany, England, Canada,
   and the United States. Emphasize coverage of the continental United
   States.

SUMMARY OF FINDINGS AND RECOMMENDATIONS

The development of collections of black literature in black college libraries showed varying patterns, with some libraries reporting the inclusion of such materials in their libraries from the year of inception and
others reporting the establishment of collections in later years by interested benefactors. Still others, in more recent years, established such collections to support the epidemic of curricular programs in black studies
or, in some instances, as a response to the demands of students protesting
the absence of such materials in forms more visible to them.

The exceptional libraries found in the black colleges are those that have
developed rich collections in black studies materials. Although they may
be lacking in other areas, these collections have made the few libraries in
which they are found notable. Even with this achievement, the libraries
have not been without problems of underfinancing, cramped quarters,
and insufficient staffs to process materials and to serve the needs of students, faculty, and scholars who use the collections.

Collections of black literature now found in black libraries serve one
or more purposes, depending upon the nature of the resources. Some may

be geared to serve only the instructional program of the institution; some serve the curricular needs as well as the research requirements of scholars; and in almost every instance, each responds to the requirements of the community by providing resources in this area. If these needs are to be met and if these libraries are to continue to function simultaneously in their traditional roles, they will require additional and substantial financial support.

The history of black people, black colleges, and black libraries supports the conclusion that the black heritage must be preserved. Black students and others must be introduced to this heritage more completely through larger, richer collections of black literature. Black colleges and their libraries share this responsibility.

Recommendation 23. Institutions should immediately reassess their collections in black studies materials in terms of the academic and research programs that they support. Serious attention should be given to developing these collections along more desirable lines so that they will achieve greater strength. In particular, the great collections of black studies materials that are housed in some of these libraries should be significantly strengthened.

Twenty-seven of the libraries reporting in this study maintained separate or special collections of black studies materials. Only five of these were administered by full-time librarians whose primary responsibility lay in that area. Others were administered either by persons who shared the responsibility with other departments or by the head librarian. Services in these collections were hampered, however, by a shortage of professional and clerical staff. Written policies governing the administration of these collections were available in only nine libraries. Policies governing the administration and use of such collections are vitally needed.

Recommendation 24. Institutions should immediately begin to examine the administrative organization of their separate collections of black studies materials. Maintaining collections separately is not always a wise practice, particularly when budgetary, spatial, and staffing problems are present. Some of these libraries should consider merging their special collections of black literature with the general collections if conditions favor this arrangement. In addition, where policies governing the administration of special black collections do not exist, they should be prepared immediately.

Nearly half of the libraries included in the study reported that black studies were offered in their institutions. No doubt, at least one such cours is offered on each of the black campuses. Materials in black libraries include many items collected for the express purpose of serving these needs and of providing resources for the enrichment and presentation of the blac mystique.

Libraries at Atlanta, Fisk, Hampton, Lincoln (Pennsylvania), Tuskegee, and Texas Southern have, over the years, developed equally rich collections of original research materials. Black collections in libraries reporting in this study total 157,578 volumes, while 803 periodical subscriptions an 300 newspaper titles were also being collected at the time of the inquiry. Less attention has been given to collecting materials in such forms as microfilms, recordings, audio and videotapes, and other media, which are becoming increasingly important.

Some of these collections have been strengthened in the past five years through gifts of other manuscript and book collections as well as gifts of microreading equipment and microfilm; yet there remains to be collected an abundance of original black studies materials. Librarians in the black institutions are actively seeking to gather these materials from private collectors and from various agencies that are known to have such resources.

Recommendation 25. Black libraries should add increasing amounts of nonprint media on black subjects to their collections to supplement bound volumes. Although most black libraries make no effort to support research in black studies, they should collect and preserve the heritage of their institutions through college archives.

Administrators should, therefore, take immediate steps to transfer college archives to the libraries for processing and servicing, keeping in mind that staffing needs will increase. Furthermore, archives councils should be established on the campuses to encourage archival development, including the collecting of papers of faculty, alumni, local persons, and friends of the college. Holdings should be reported to the *National Union Catalog of Manuscript Collections* and other guides to collections.

Vast amounts of original research materials located in some of the black libraries have been processed and are available for use by scholars; yet an equal amount remains unprocessed. In their history, many institutions fail to recognize the value of such materials and hesitated to employ staff for processing. As few staff persons have been added to process these materials in recent years, they have been unable to complete the vast amount of work to be done.

Recommendation 26. Funds should be provided immediately to employ archivists to process the vast amounts of unprocessed manuscripts and archives in some of the black colleges, particularly at Hampton, Fisk, Lincoln (Pennsylvania), and Tuskegee. In addition, grants should be made to enable publication of calendars and guides to these collections once processing has been completed.

Facilities housing some of the collections of black materials are rated from excellent to poor, with similar ratings given to their equipment. Two of the larger collections are housed in cramped quarters, and limited seating and study space is available in others. Even in some of the more established collections, years of neglect have resulted in the deterioration of materials, much of which will disintegrate completely within a few years unless methods of preservation are employed.

Recommendation 27. Additional space should be provided as rapidly as possible to relieve the crowded conditions that exist in some libraries housing large black collections. Immediate efforts must be made to preserve the valuable research resources in these libraries, including additional archival materials that may be collected. Microfilmers should be placed in each of the large research collections, for cooperative use by libraries with smaller collections.

In each of the libraries reporting, the loss of materials in black studies through theft was a common problem. In the larger research collections, where scholars constantly seek materials for their work, this matter was even more pressing. Even with limited or restricted access to stacks, as was reported in the twenty-seven special collections, theft is not uncommon.

Recommendation 28. Greater security precautions must be taken to reduce the incidence of theft of black studies materials, both primary and secondary.

Statistics on the use of materials appear to be recorded irregularly, with few libraries able to compare use of the collections over a five-year period. The use of statistics may help justify the financial requests of special collections departments and, in many instances, may even justify their existence. Libraries need to examine the use of their collections in terms of the types of materials used, the number of patrons served, the number of items added to the collections, and the number of items lost. In addition, they must study their other problems.

Recommendation 29. Black libraries should engage in realistic record-keeping practices which will show the use made of their special collections and will provide other statistical data necessary for self-examination.

A mere handful of black academic libraries are active in consortia which involve their black studies collections. In the past few years, many libraries throughout the United States have been able to enrich their resources through cooperative programs with other libraries and have received sizable federal grants for this purpose. While a few black libraries have taken advantage of this privilege, far too many failed to do so.

Recommendation 30. Black libraries should become involved immediately in formal cooperative arrangements with other libraries, as through consortia programs, and should seek external funding for the express purpose of strengthening their collections of black materials.

A severe limitation of this portion of the study was the absence of data on financial support provided for black collection development, particularly in the special collections. A few grants were made for development of some of these collections during the period from 1964-65 through 1968-69, reaching a total of $83,961. Of particular importance to the proper development of these collections was the addition of sizable grants to support the purchase of resources as well as to accommodate other needs of the special collections departments.

Recommendation 31. Black libraries should keep more accurate records of the expenditures of their special collections departments or of expenditures in subject areas in black studies. Institutions must provide for the support of these areas, particularly as they relate to the instructional program.

Recommendation 32. Financial grants of significant amounts should be provided for the support of special collections departments in the black libraries where research resources are maintained.

Examination of collections in the black colleges revealed that many interesting, rare, or notable items have been collected. In-depth analysis of even the research collections which a few of these libraries maintain was impossible to make during the period of this study. Catalogs which describe these collections are available in some instances, and many provide brief histories of the collections. Lacking are comprehensive catalogs which describe primary as well as secondary source materials in black studies in the seven notable research collections reported.

Recommendation 33. Institutions housing special collections of black materials should immediately begin to make their resources more widely known through union lists, checklists, and comprehensive guides which record and, when possible, describe all materials included. These collections require more thorough analysis so that the strengths of particular libraries may be more properly identified.

Outstanding items that may be scattered throughout the black libraries should be identified for the purpose of scholarship.

Black libraries should attempt to trace the history of their special collections as a means of gathering and preserving this part of their heritage.

NOTES

1. McGrath, *The Predominantly Negro Colleges and Universities in Transition,* p. 129.

2. *National Survey of Higher Education of Negroes,* p. 98.

3. The Spingarn Collection represents items gathered by Arthur Spingarn over many years. Duplicates of some of these items formed the Spingarn Collection at UCLA.

4. Since this inventory was completed, many black college libraries have acquired additional and notable primary and secondary materials on black subjects. For example, the black collections at Howard and Dillard have seen exponential growth, while Bishop College has accelerated its collecting practices and has founded the Southwest Research Center and Museum for the Study of African-American Life and Culture.

5. See also "Acquisition Policy for Special Collections, Fisk University Library," Appendix D.

6

Black Academic Libraries and Research Collections: The Past, the Present, and Implications for the Future

As black colleges struggle to increase their educational effectiveness, they constantly reexamine their roles and redefine their mission in terms of their responsibility in preparing their students for professions and in meeting other needs imposed on them by society. Of fundamental importance to this self-examination is an analysis of the library program provided in each institution.

THE PAST AND THE PRESENT

The purpose of this study was to analyze the past and the present library programs, facilities, and services in black academic institutions; to provide historical data as well as current information on their development; and to serve as a prototype for ten-year follow-up studies of black academic institutions and their libraries. The study examined library programs in terms of the requirements of evaluation agencies and determined the extent to which these libraries met established standards for evaluation. It focused on the strong as well as the weak elements of library programs and attempted to identify special programs that had a direct effect on these libraries over and above those generally addressed in established standards. By putting into proper perspective the traditional function of the black academic institution as well as the conditions of these institutions that prevailed when the study was conducted, the survey attempted to examine the library in terms of the demands placed on it by the institution.

Particular emphasis was placed on black materials found in libraries in black academic institutions. Realizing that some of the best collections of black materials are located in black academic libraries, this study identified the strengths of these collections according to the information available and determined their role in curricular and research activities. When possible, it determined the history of these collections, identified their scope and content, analyzed their administrative organization, studied the quality and number of staff members serving the collections, investigated methods of housing and preserving the collections, determined staff services that were provided, examined the amount of financial support provided, and reviewed the projections which library staffs had made for the future development of these collections.

The collected and interpreted data are concentrated during the period from 1964-65 through 1968-69, with some projections given for the period from 1969-70 through 1973-74. Since the study was completed, many new developments have occurred in these institutions and in their libraries. Detailed accounts of these developments are omitted from this report; however, examples of such developments are reported through notes. The final chapter also highlights recent developments in black academic institutions and their libraries and further justifies the need for ten-year follow-up studies.

The results of the study should be of benefit to foundations, college accrediting agencies, scholars and researchers, administrators in black academic institutions, librarians, library school educators and students, and others who are interested in the problems, developments, and trends of black academic institutions and their libraries.

The investigation was limited to the eighty-nine four-year or graduate level degree-granting institutions in the United States which are traditionally black in enrollment. Any institution which did not fall within this definition at the time of the study is omitted from the report. Both publicly and privately supported institutions were included, and efforts were made to compare the development of libraries in the two types of institutions. In conducting this study, the investigator used the survey method. Questionnaires were distributed to head librarians in each of the institutions. The investigator also notified presidents of these institutions that the study was in progress and sought their support in the collection of data.

Additional data were collected through follow-up visits to the libraries, whether or not they responded to the questionnaire, and through interviews with head librarians, library staffs, faculty, students, and when possible, administrators. Publications of these libraries, annual reports of the librarians, and college catalogs were used as sources of data. Self-study reports which were prepared by these institutions for accrediting agencies were also examined, and the data reported were compared to that collected by the investigator.

Data collected through the questionnaires were analyzed through use of a computer. This procedure permitted the establishment of a data bank which will enable revision of the study periodically with minimum difficulty, particularly where statistical information is involved. In addition, an historical profile of each institution which responded to the questionnaire is available through the data bank.

In order to place black academic libraries in their proper perspective, it was necessary to give an historical overview of the black colleges. The study showed that black colleges began their development prior to the Civil War for the specific purpose of providing higher education to black people, although it was not until the end of the war that they became more stable and offered degree programs. The responsibility for founding these institutions may be credited to both black and white religious denominations, a political organization, religiously oriented groups, and the states in which some of these institutions are located. Political, economic, and social conditions of the time are reflected in their emergence, administration, curricular offerings, and development.

In their history, black colleges have changed from normal schools to colleges and from colleges to universities. Some have merged, some are no longer predominantly black in enrollment, and all have developed newer areas of concentration in their curricular programs. Greater emphasis has been placed on liberal arts programs, the sciences, and graduate education (in two instances, including doctoral programs). More recently, two additional black institutions have added doctoral programs to their curricular offerings, two have established medical schools, and two of the three library schools in black institutions have been accredited by the American Library Association. The third library school, that of Atlanta University, was already accredited at the time of the study. In addition, urban studies has become a major area of interest among these institutions This survey supports evidence found in other studies indicating that significant portions of black students enrolled in higher educational institutions at the time of the study were enrolled in black colleges. Thus programs aimed toward educating black Americans must necessarily focus on these colleges where a sizable number of black students are found.

While nearly all of these institutions were founded prior to 1900, studies show that it was not until 1917 that noticeable attention was given to analyzing the status of their libraries. Between 1917 and 1942, three major surveys relating to black academic libraries were made available. After that time, a number of smaller studies, surveys of individual libraries which were prepared as master's theses at the Atlanta University School of Library Service, and broad surveys which were conducted in 1965 and in 1970 were published. Both in 1970 and in 1976, studies which focused on libraries in historically black public colleges and universities were published, thus representing a departure from many earlier studies which embraced libraries in privately as well as publicly supported black institutions or which focused on libraries in certain privately supported institutions.

A summary of the comparative data shows that black academic libraries have continuously remained below standard. Each study reflected the growth, development, and improving status of these libraries; yet each agreed that these libraries had not reached the status that they needed to achieve in order to support the educational purposes of their institutions. These studies suggested that substantial funds were needed if these libraries were to overcome their deficiencies.

Various improvement programs have been launched to benefit black academic libraries and their staffs. Significant among these were the efforts of organized philanthropy including the Carnegie Corporation, the General Education Board, the Julius Rosenwald Fund, the Ford Foundation, and the Rockefeller Foundation. Efforts of the United Negro College Fund resulted in programs of support for a number of privately supported member institutions.

Among the various conferences which have been held since the study was completed and which were directed toward black librarians or librarians in black institutions are a colloquium on the Southeastern Black Librarian sponsored by the School of Library Science, North Carolina Central University; and an On-Line Information Retrieval Workshop jointly sponsored by the Lawrence Livermore Laboratory and the Atlanta University School of Library Service.

Libraries in black academic institutions have experienced careful and deliberate evaluation in recent years as many prepared themselves for appraisal by their regional accrediting agencies.

The early history of many of these libraries is lacking, for early record-keeping practices were poor and many records were destroyed during the passing years. The fragmented records of the past coupled with those of more recent years show that the development of these libraries has been hampered primarily because of the inadequate financial support which they have received. The consequences of this inadequate support include the small collections, the shortage of professional and clerical personnel, the lack of innovative library programs, and the lack of proper equipment, all of which were among the chief problems facing these libraries at the time of the study. Subsequently, efforts of the Council on Library Resources, through its Academic Library Management Intern Program, and the Andrew Mellon Foundation and the Association of College and Research Libraries, through an internship program for administrators in predominantly black college libraries, have enabled black academic library administrators to enhance their management skills. The results may well have far-reaching effects on these libraries.

Automated services, once hardly visible in black academic libraries, increasingly have received the attention of black institutions and their library staffs. More and more, these libraries are automating library services as they attempt to modernize their library programs.

The impact of Title III funds on library programs is yet to be measured but may well indicate that black academic libraries have been able to embark on newer projects through the support that these funds provided to their institutions. The establishment of learning resource centers, the installation of the SOLINET system, and the establishment of library-based tutorial programs are examples of activities which resulted from Title III funds. In addition, many, though not all, of these libraries were housed in inadequate buildings which hampered their offering of services. New and/or expanded facilities which may now be seen in many black academic institutions no doubt have helped to rectify this problem.

The needs of these libraries are not uniform. Of central importance among the reporting institutions, however, was the need for substantial and sustained financial support to permit them to overcome their problems. The self-study reports which were available in the majority of these institutions indicated that administrators, faculties, and library staffs were aware of the problems which their libraries faced. The reports also recommended solutions to their library problems, even though the means for the solutions may not have been available.

The distinctiveness of black academic libraries lies in the rich collections of black literature which many of them contain. Almost immediately, the incompleteness of scholarship was clearly visible as the untapped sources of black studies materials were identified in these libraries. Although lacking in other areas, the sizable black collections have made the few libraries in which they were found notable. Even with this achievement, the libraries have not been without problems of underfinancing, inadequate quarters, and insufficient staffs to serve the needs of students, faculty members, and scholars who use the collections.

While the black academic libraries have been severely hampered in their development, they have failed to succumb to their problems. The achievements of these libraries may be directly attributed to dedicated staffs who were determined to provide the best possible library service to their institutions despite the obstacles which they faced. Their interest in enhancing their effectiveness as librarians may be seen in the increasing numbers of staff persons who are pursuing or have received terminal degrees since the study was completed.

CONCLUSIONS

While most of the black colleges were founded prior to 1900, the development of the black academic library is primarily an achievement of the twentieth century. Fewer than one-third of those institutions which were founded in the 1800s indicated that their libraries were established at the same time that their institutions were founded. Some of these libraries have experienced a century of neglect, while others reflect almost continuous neglect since their founding. Black librarianship, like black education, is still between two worlds. It has yet to achieve full entrance into the mainstream of librarianship, and it must serve a group of institutions which were created to serve a purely segregated society.

Libraries in black academic institutions are faced with various problems. Chief among these are the lack of firm policies which govern their administration; a shortage of professional and supportive staff members (with the greatest need falling in the area of clerical staff); inadequate provisions for staff improvement through formal and informal training; inadequate salaries to recruit and retain qualified personnel; inadequate collections in terms of both size and content; a high incidence of obsolete materials in the collections; too little emphasis on nonprint media; inadequacies in periodical holdings, in terms of both titles received and the extent of back volumes; the lack of firm policies for collection development; arrearages in cataloging and processing; inadequate seating space, with little provi-

sion for individual seating; the lack of innovative programs to foster greater use of the library; and inadequate budgets. Salaries and budgets were
generally higher in publicly supported institutions; yet the greater deficiencies in the size of collections were also found among them.

While a number of these libraries were housed in fairly new buildings
at the time of the study, many of the buildings were lacking in modern
concepts of design, function, and aesthetics. Additionally, some of these
libraries were housed in quarters which were totally inadequate and which
served to impede use of the collection.

The collections of black literature that are found in the black colleges
have been faced with similar problems, particularly where separate collections have been maintained. These collections have served dual purposes:
they provide materials to support the increasing emphases on black studies curricula, and they provide a source of primary materials for scholars
engaged in research activities. The greatest problem which these collections have faced is the lack of adequate financial support to permit them
to grow and develop, to provide sufficient staff for servicing the collection,
to process and preserve valuable research materials, and to engage in activities which will promote the research functions which they have the
potential for supporting. Of the seven notable collections of black literature found in black colleges reporting in this study, six were in privately
supported institutions.

Problems surrounding special black collections are as crucial and critical today as they were when this study was made. It may be said that some
of these problems have been compounded as black libraries have engaged
in rigorous collecting practices to acquire black primary and secondary
source materials and as they have continued to establish black oral history programs in an effort to preserve the black heritage. Since this study
was completed, follow-up visits to many of these libraries as well as conferences with librarians from these institutions have helped to substanti-
ate this claim.

IMPLICATIONS FOR THE FUTURE

Problems affecting the growth and development of black academic libraries were identified in Chapters 4 and 5, and recommendations for over-
coming these problems were given. Each recommendation is being repeat-
ed here to emphasize its importance in a comprehensive plan for improving

the black academic libraries. In addition, other recommendations which were indirectly related to the two chapters on library development, but which are related to libraries in black academic institutions, are included. When some relief has been given to a problem and to a subsequent recommendation relating to it, reference is made at the appropriate point to those developments which have had an impact on that problem.

1. Institutions should immediately reassess their libraries in terms of the academic program of the college, with student, faculty, library staff, and administrative involvement. Rigorous and serious attention should be given to the library in order to upgrade it as rapidly and as systematically as possible and to provide for its continuous development once it has reached the level desired by the accrediting agencies and by the institution's academic program.

2. All institutions should review the assignment of the library in the reporting structure. Assignment to a senior officer other than the chief academic officer should be continued only for clear and justifiable reasons, and the documentation in support of those reasons should be made a part of the permanent records of the institutions.

3. All institutions should include the library committee among the standing committees of the institution, and the manner of determination of its membership and the responsibilities of the committee should be clearly stated and included among the permanent records of the institution. It is further recommended that the responsibilities include: (a) the establishment and review of policies related to the quality, scope, and size of the collection and to the quality and extent of service, (b) the evaluation of the library, and (c) self-evaluation of the committee.

4. All libraries should develop policy and operations handbooks.

5. Each institution should establish a mechanism for a thorough review of the professional status of its librarians. Such a review should include matters of level and diversity of training, faculty rank and tenure, participation in professional development programs, and salary structure.

6. Libraries should alter their staffing patterns to provide a more favorable ratio of clerical to professional persons on their staffs and should avoid relying too heavily upon student employees. Further, each library should develop a staffing pattern based on the programs which the library conducts; and working with and through the chief academic officer and the budget officer, it should develop a plan to implement an acceptable staffing pattern.

7. Provisions should be made to recruit promising black students for the library profession and to upgrade library staffs in the black colleges through scholarship and fellowship programs, workshop and internship programs, and travel programs.

   The scholarship and fellowship program for black students, many of whom are in the black colleges, should permit them to pursue degrees in librarianship at the library school of their choice. This program should be extended to clerical staff persons in the library.

   Workshop and internship programs for library administrators, supportive librarians, and library technical assistants should be launched. Special consideration should be given to administrators and library technical assistants. Year-long internship programs have now been developed for library administrators or for those who will be elevated so that position, as may be seen in the Andrew Mellon/ACRL and the CRL management internship programs; yet many institutions are unable to free staff persons to participate in the programs.

   Librarians and their staffs should be further encouraged to participate in professional meetings, especially the annual meeting of the American Library Association. This encouragement is best done through budgetary provisions.

8. Salaries of all library personnel should be reviewed to insure that they are fairly well aligned with those offered in other institutions of similar size and purpose. When staff persons have certain competencies as well as higher degrees, their salaries should be equal to those of comparable administrative officers, department heads, or teaching faculty, even though this amount may exceed that normally paid in an institution of comparable size.

9. Granting agencies should consider awarding special and sustained funds to black academic libraries. Such funds should be earmarked solely for the purpose of removing deficiencies in the content and/or size of their collections, including those that exist as a result of increased enrollments, those that exist as a result of new degree programs (especially the master's and the doctorate), and those that would exist if obsolete materials were weeded, thereby reducing volume count. A few institutions should be considered model and should receive additional and substantial funds to enable their libraries to become superior.

   In view of the fact that such grants as are necessary to remove these deficiencies and to support model institutions would require additional staff members for processing, the Cooperative College Library Center in Atlanta, Georgia, should be approached concerning its ability to process these materials for the black academic libraries.

Libraries should be required to submit a plan for systematically removing deficiencies in their collections, making judicious use of standard guides in order to evaluate their collections and involving faculty and students in the selecting process.

10. Funds should be provided to enable a greater portion of these libraries to become learning resource centers and to enable others to purchase the newer forms of library media and equipment necessary for their use. Title III grants to black institutions have enabled some libraries to move in this direction.

11. Black academic libraries should make a careful examination of their periodical collections in terms of subscriptions received as well as in back runs required. Funds should be provided to enable these libraries to remove deficiencies in their periodical collections through the addition of new subscriptions which are needed in most of these libraries as well as by providing for some retrospective volumes as required. Attention should be given to purchasing the back volumes in microform.

12. Each library in the black colleges should develop well-defined acquisition policy statements, working closely with the faculty, representatives of the student body, and the administration. The policy statement should be closely geared to the provision of those materials that support the curricular, research, and cultural programs of the colleges. Any provisions for gift books must meet the criteria set forth in the policy statement.

13. Working closely with the business office, libraries in these institutions should develop modern methods of record keeping and acquisition of materials. Ideally, orders should be sent directly from libraries to jobbers, thereby eliminating as much repetition of work as is possible in view of the limited staffs in these institutions.

14. Libraries in the black academic institutions should join duplicate exchange unions and thereby take advantage of the benefits of such programs.

15. Funds should be provided to support a study of the classification and cataloging problems and requirements of the libraries in black institutions, with some provision offered for helping them to meet these needs.

16. The writer is fully aware of the serious financial condition of higher education generally and therefore cannot recommend that inadequate

structures be replaced at this time. However, an institution having a library building which impedes the improvement of library services should consider placing a new structure very high on its list of building priorities. Other institutions, utilizing available consulting services, should explore innovative ways to increase the user's access to library materials.

As funds become available for building construction, a team of consultants should be selected to work with these institutions. Such a team should include representatives of black college libraries who have already undergone building programs or who are fully aware of the requirements of black institutions. New or renovated facilities should provide for modern concepts of function, aesthetics, and innovation.

17. Libraries in these institutions should make per capita use studies of library circulation over the past five years to determine the extent to which actual use is increasing or decreasing (as far as can be determined when open access to materials is provided). Innovative programs which closely relate the library to the instructional programs should be developed in each of these institutions, even if on modified bases. Innovative instructional programs which foster greater use of the library must be initiated.

18. Libraries in these institutions should look toward consortia or cooperative programs as a means of strengthening resources and services.

19. Computer services and automated activities should be initiated in increasing numbers of libraries according to the needs of the institution and the funds available for the support of such new programs.

20. In view of a long history of inadequate support for libraries included in this study, support well beyond the typical 5 percent of the E and G budget is required. Support for the current operation of the library, particularly for building the collection, should be given a high priority in each institution's developmental effort.

21. A percentage of certain grants and gifts to the university for educational purposes—including training programs, institutes, and the creation and/or development of specific departments—should be allocated for library development.

22. Careful study should be made of the graduate library education programs at Atlanta, Alabama A & M, and North Carolina Central, which are training the preponderance of black students. Increased and sustained financial assistance should be provided for their support.

23. Institutions should immediately reassess their collections in black studies materials in terms of the academic and research programs that they support. Serious attention should be given to developing these collections along more desirable lines so that they will achieve greater strength. In particular, the great collections of black studies materials that are housed in some of these libraries should be significantly strengthened.

24. Institutions should immediately begin to examine the administrative organization of their separate collections of black studies materials. Maintaining collections separately is not always a wise practice, particularly when budgetary, spatial, and staffing problems are present. Some of these libraries should consider merging their special collections of black literature with the general collections if conditions favor this arrangement. In addition, where policies governing the administration of special black collections do not exist, they should be prepared immediately.

25. Black libraries should add increasing amounts of nonprint media on black subjects to their collections to supplement bound volumes. Although most black libraries make no effort to support research in black studies, they should collect and preserve the heritage of their institutions through college archives, as many are now doing.

   Administrators should, therefore, take immediate steps to transfer college archives to the libraries for processing and servicing, keeping in mind that staffing needs will increase. Furthermore, archives councils should be established on the campuses to encourage archival development, including the collecting of papers of faculty, alumni, local persons, and friends of the college. Holdings should be reported to the *National Union Catalog of Manuscript Collections* and other guides to collections.

26. Funds should be provided immediately to employ archivists to process the vast amounts of unprocessed manuscripts and archives in some of the black colleges, particularly at Hampton, Fisk, Lincoln (Pennsylvania), and Tuskegee. In addition, grants should be made to enable publication of calendars and guides to these collections once processing has been completed.

27. Additional space should be provided as rapidly as possible to relieve the crowded conditions that exist in some libraries housing large black collections. Immediate efforts must be made to preserve the valuable research resources in these libraries, including additional archival materials that may be collected. Microfilmers should be placed in each of

the large research collections, for cooperative use by libraries with smaller collections.

28. Greater security precautions must be taken to reduce the incidence of theft of black studies materials, both primary and secondary.

29. Black libraries should engage in realistic record-keeping practices which will show the use made of their special collections and will provide other statistical data necessary for self-examination.

30. Black libraries should become involved immediately in formal cooperative arrangements with other libraries, as through consortia programs, and should seek external funding for the express purpose of strengthening their combined collections of black materials.

31. Black libraries should keep more accurate records of the expenditures of their special collections departments or of expenditures in subject areas in black studies. Institutions must provide for the support of these areas, particularly as they relate to the instructional program.

32. Financial grants of significant amounts should be provided for the support of special collections departments in the black libraries where research resources are maintained.

33. Institutions housing special collections of black materials should immediately begin to make their resources more widely known through union lists, checklists, and comprehensive guides which record and, when possible, describe all materials included. These collections require more thorough analysis so that the strengths of particular libraries may be more properly identified.

   Outstanding items that may be scattered throughout the black libraries should be identified for the purpose of scholarship.

   Black libraries should attempt to trace the history of their special collections as a means of gathering and preserving this part of their heritage.

Clearly, a ten-year follow-up study is needed, as consideration is given to the historical nature of the present work and the many developments that have occurred in black academic institutions and their libraries since these data were collected. Additionally, as black libraries, various organizations, governmental agencies, and others examine the historical account of black academic libraries given in this study and react to the recommendations made and the implications drawn for the future, it is possible that significant new developments may result.

A revised study may also examine the current condition of black academic institutions and their libraries and may study the impact of dwindling federal resources and other monies on their programs and services. The effect of inflation on the library dollar will require serious examination. Among those research activities under way which relate to areas of the study is the Fayetteville State University project which attempts to measure the impact of Title III monies on black academic institutions. Further attention will need to be given to the impact of external funding in general on black academic institutions and their libraries. Perhaps a definitive financial history of these institutions centering around external funding should be undertaken as a separate work.

A follow-up study of ACRL and CRL interns and the impact that they have made on black libraries may be of special interest. The present study as well as its subsequent revision may demonstrate that the Higher Education General Information Survey (HEGIS) of the National Center for Educational Statistics, the ALA standards, and standards of regional accrediting agencies are insufficient measures of the effectiveness of black academic libraries. Also, their use alone does not lead to a clear understanding of these libraries. The application of such standards to library examination should in no way lead to the conclusion that these libraries have been unable to respond positively to the demands placed on them by their institutions and by their communities, even though the level of response might not have been as high as they desired. Their ability to serve research functions, as many have done, is particularly noteworthy. What is needed most is a scheme designed to incorporate the thrust of various standards as well as to show the distinctiveness of black institutions and their libraries.

Black academe is faced with a difficult task: it must be prepared to meet the unpredictable challenges of the remainder of this century as well as the more unpredictable ones of the next century. It must now begin to redefine its mission and to establish goals which will lead to the full realization of that mission. The same is true of black academic libraries. Their ability to respond to newer missions effectively and efficiently will be the direct result of the immediate changes which they initiate, the long-range program planning in which they must engage, the program monitoring and evaluation which they must make, and well-executed action steps which they must take toward achieving new goals. Both the institution and the library must design programs which will lead to continuous self-renewal.

Appendix A:
Eighty-Nine Black Four-Year or Graduate Degree-Granting Institutions

EIGHTY-NINE BLACK FOUR-YEAR OR GRADUATE DEGREE-GRANTING
INSTITUTIONS IN THE UNITED STATES, 1969

Institution	Location	Year Founding	Level of Offerings	Affiliation	Accreditation	Total Enrollment
ALABAMA						
*Alabama A & M	Normal	1875	Master's	State	SA	2,091
*Alabama State	Montgomery	1873	Master's	State	SA	2,340
Miles	Birmingham	1902	Bachelor's	CME	S	1,006
*Oakwood	Huntsville	1896	Bachelor's	SDA	SA	600
*Stillman	Tuscaloosa	1876	Bachelor's	Presb. U. S.	SA	678
*Talladega	Talladega	1867	Bachelor's	AMA-Independ.	SA	550
*Tuskegee	Tuskegee	1881	Master's	Independ.	SA	3,000
ARKANSAS						
*Arkansas A M & N	Pine Bluff	1873	Bachelor's	State	NCA	3,728
Arkansas Baptist	Little Rock	1884	Bachelor's	NBC	S	170
*Philander Smith	Little Rock	1877	Bachelor's	Methodist	NCA	596
DELAWARE						
Delaware State	Dover	1891	Bachelor's	State	MSA	1,300
DISTRICT OF COLUMBIA						
D. C. Teachers	Washington	1873	Bachelor's	City	MSA	2,482
Howard	Washington	1867	Doctoral	Independ.	MSA	8,550

Institution	Location	Year of Founding	Level of Offerings	Affiliation	Accreditation	Total Enrollment
FLORIDA						
*Bethune-Cookman	Daytona Beach	1904	Bachelor's	Methodist	SA	1,165
Edward Waters	Jacksonville	1883	Bachelor's	AME	S	915**
*Florida A & M	Tallahassee	1887	Master's	State	SA	4,300
*Florida Memorial	Miami	1892	Bachelor's	ABC	SA	757
GEORGIA						
Albany State	Albany	1903	Bachelor's	State	SA	1,816
*Atlanta Univ.	Atlanta	1865	Doctoral	Independ.	SA	1,407
*Clark	Atlanta	1869	Bachelor's	Methodist	SA	1,168
*Fort Valley	Fort Valley	1895	Master's	State	SA	2,247
Interdenominational Theol. Center	Atlanta	1958	Master's	Independ.	P	142
Morehouse	Atlanta	1867	Bachelor's	Independ.	SA	982
*Morris Brown	Atlanta	1881	Bachelor's	AME	SA	1,495
*Paine	Augusta	1882	Bachelor's	Meth. & CME	SA	656
Savannah State	Savannah	1890	Bachelor's	State	SA	2,387
Spelman	Atlanta	1881	Bachelor's	Independ.	SA	976
KENTUCKY						
*Kentucky State	Frankfort	1886	Bachelor's	State	SA	1,610
*Simmons Bible	Louisville	1879	Bachelor's	NBC	S	119

Institution	Location	Year of Founding	Level of Offerings	Affiliation	Accreditation	Total Enrollment
LOUISIANA						
*Dillard	New Orleans	1868	Bachelor's	Independ.	SA	922
*Grambling	Grambling	1901	Bachelor's	State	SA	3,455
*Southern	Baton Rouge	1880	Master's	State	SA	8,385
*Southern - N. O.	New Orleans	1959	Bachelor's	State	SA	1,309
*Xavier	New Orleans	1925	Master's	RC	SA	1,364
MARYLAND						
Bowie State	Bowie	1867	Master's	State	MSA	1,609
Coppin State	Baltimore	1900	Master's	State	MSA	1,573
Morgan State	Baltimore	1867	Master's	State	MSA	4,653
Univ. of Md. - Eastern Shore	Princess Anne	1886	Bachelor's	State	MSA	717**
MISSISSIPPI						
*Alcorn	Lorman	1871	Bachelor's	State	SA	2,300
*Jackson State	Jackson	1877	Master's	State	SA	4,385
Mississippi Indust.	Holly Springs	1905	Bachelor's	CME	S	424
*Mississippi Valley	Itta Bena	1950	Bachelor's	State	SA	2,314
Rust	Holly Springs	1866	Bachelor's	Methodist	S	610
*Tougaloo	Tougaloo	1869	Bachelor's	AMA & UCMS	SA	694
MISSOURI						
*Lincoln	Jefferson City	1866	Master's	State	NCA	2,013

Institution	Location	Year of Founding	Level of Offerings	Affiliation	Accreditation	Total Enrollment
NORTH CAROLINA						
*Barber-Scotia	Concord	1867	Bachelor's	Presby.	SA	599
Bennett	Greensboro	1873	Bachelor's	Methodist	SA	627
*Elizabeth City	Elizabeth City	1891	Bachelor's	State	SA	1,039
*Fayetteville State	Fayetteville	1867	Bachelor's	State	SA	1,115
*Johnson C. Smith	Charlotte	1867	Bachelor's	Presby.	SA	1,209
*Livingstone	Salisbury	1879	Bachelor's	AMEZ	SA	809
*N.C. A & T	Greensboro	1891	Master's	State	SA	3,714
*N.C. Central	Durham	1909	Master's	State	SA	3,290
*St. Augustine	Raleigh	1867	Bachelor's	Protest. Episc.	SA	1,099
*Shaw	Raleigh	1865	Bachelor's	ABC	SA	1,031
*Winston-Salem	Winston-Salem	1892	Bachelor's	State	SA	1,275
OHIO						
*Central State	Wilberforce	1856	Master's	State	NCA	2,262
*Wilberforce	Wilberforce	1856	Bachelor's	AME	NCA	1,008
OKLAHOMA						
*Langston	Langston	1897	Bachelor's	State	NCA	1,225
PENNSYLVANIA						
*Cheyney State	Cheyney	1837	Bachelor's	State	MSA	2,041
*Lincoln	Lincoln University	1854	Bachelor's	Independ.	MSA	1,130

Institution	Location	Year of Founding	Level of Offerings	Affiliation	Accreditation	Total Enrollment
SOUTH CAROLINA						
Allen	Columbia	1870	Bachelor's	AME	S	608
*Benedict	Columbia	1870	Bachelor's	ABC	SA	1,259
*Claflin	Orangeburg	1869	Bachelor's	Methodist	SA	709
*Morris	Sumter	1905	Bachelor's	SBC	S	534
*South Carolina State	Orangeburg	1895	Master's	State	SA	2,025
*Voorhees	Denmark	1897	Bachelor's	Protest. Episc.	SA	715
TENNESSEE						
*Fisk	Nashville	1866	Master's	Independ.	SA	1,248
*Knoxville	Knoxville	1875	Bachelor's	United Presby.	SA	918
*Lane	Jackson	1882	Bachelor's	CME	SA	974
*LeMoyne-Owen	Memphis	1870	Bachelor's	AMA & Baptist	SA	703
Meharry Medical	Nashville	1876	Medical	Independ.	P	459
Tennessee State	Nashville	1909	Master's	State	SA	4,543
TEXAS						
*Bishop	Dallas	1881	Bachelor's	ABC	SA	1,968
*Huston-Tillotson	Austin	1877	Bachelor's	Meth. & United Church of Christ	SA	697
*Jarvis Christian	Hawkins	1912	Bachelor's	Disciples of Christ	SA	554
*Paul Quinn	Waco	1872	Bachelor's	AME	S	621
*Prairie View A & M	Prairie View	1876	Master's	State	SA	4,138
*Texas College	Tyler	1894	Bachelor's	CME	S	468
*Texas Southern	Houston	1947	Master's	State	SA	3,980
*Wiley	Marshall	1873	Bachelor's	Methodist	SA	468

Institution	Location	Year of Founding	Level of Offerings	Affiliation	Accreditation	Total Enrollment
VIRGINIA						
*Hampton	Hampton	1868	Master's	Independ.	SA	2,384
*Norfolk State	Norfolk	1935	Bachelor's	State	SA	4,411
Saint Paul	Lawrenceville	1888	Bachelor's	Protest. Episc.	SA	537
Virginia Seminary	Lynchburg	1888	Bachelor's	Baptist	S	64
*Virginia State	Petersburg	1882	Master's	State	SA	2,498
*Virginia Union	Richmond	1865	Bachelor's	ABC	SA	1,325
WEST VIRGINIA						
Bluefield State	Bluefield	1895	Bachelor's	State	NCA	843
*West Virginia State	Institute	1891	Bachelor's	State	NCA	3,063

SDA – Seventh Day Adventist
RC – Roman Catholic
UCMS – United Christian Missionary Society
* – Institutions reporting in the survey
** – 1970 enrollment

ABC – Baptist
AMA – American Missionary Association
AMA-Ind. – American Missionary Association-Independent
AME – African Methodist Episcopal
AMEZ – African Methodist Episcopal Zion
CME – Christian Methodist Episcopal
INDEPEND. – Independent
MSA – Middle States Association
NBC – Northern Baptist Convention
NCA – North Central Association
P – Professional Agency
Protest. Episc. – Protestant Episcopal
S – State
SA – Southern Association
SBC – State Baptist Convention

Appendix B:

Recommendations
of the Conference on
Materials by and about Negroes

PROCEEDINGS OF THE INSTITUTE ON MATERIALS BY AND
ABOUT AMERICAN NEGROES, OCTOBER 21-23, 1965,
ATLANTA UNIVERSITY, SCHOOL OF LIBRARY
SERVICE, ATLANTA, GEORGIA

Recommendations

Acquisition

1. Librarians in all types and sizes of libraries should
    cooperate with the Association for the Study of Negro
    Life and History to establish a historical committee for
    the purpose of collecting published and unpublished book
    and nonbook materials.

2. Adequate regional or sectional special collections should
    be established in the East, South, Midwest and West, using
    existing collections when possible and developing others
    when necessary.

Preservation

3. Librarians should begin an intensive and extensive re-
    printing program to preserve and make available the
    deteriorating titles on the American Negro.

4. The possibilities for making special materials available
    through use of the techniques of reproduction should be
    fully explored.

5. A new microfilm project for retrospective newspapers
    and journals should be undertaken.

Communication

6. Communication among librarians who are responsible for developing collections on the American Negro should be improved.

7. A quarterly newsletter for the exchange of information and ideas should be issued. Included in the newsletter would be such information as reports of outstanding acquisitions, bibliographical notes, work in progress, lists of ephemera, and descriptions of outstanding collections.

8. An annual handbook of current studies on the American Negro should be prepared. Such a handbook would include a directory of resources and a bibliography of bibliographies.

9. The Journal of Negro History should be asked to give space for news on special acquisitions and research in progress. A column devoted to such information might appear quarterly or annually.

10. A survey, through questionnaire, should be made of published and unpublished bibliographic tools for Negro source materials. The results of the survey should be published.

11. Consideration should be given to encouraging subject specialization in preparing bibliographies and sending one copy of each list to a central place.

12. More descriptive articles, indexes to, and calendars
of manuscripts should be prepared for distribution.

13. An index to retrospective Negro periodicals and newspapers should be prepared. It should indicate where
the issues are located and should include titles that
are known to have existed which do not exist today.

14. A union catalog of master's theses and doctoral dissertations relating to the Negro should be established.

15. An index to photographic materials regardless of medium
or locations should be prepared.

Institute Follow-Up

16. A committee should be organized to implement the recommendations that are feasible.

17. Financial assistance should be sought from interested
foundations to support bibliographic projects and
other activities considered worthwhile by the Institute
participants.

Appendix C:
Covering Letter and Questionnaire

FISK UNIVERSITY
NASHVILLE, TENNESSEE 37203

OFFICE OF THE LIBRARIAN

Dear

    I am currently conducting a survey of libraries in the pre-
dominantly Negro colleges, with emphasis on special Negro collections
that are in some of these libraries. The survey is being financed
through a grant from the Council on Library Resources

    The purpose of the survey is to provide up-to-date information
as well as historical data on these libraries. Among the many uses
of the results of the study to these libraries are: to stimulate
foundations and financiers to increase significantly their financial
support; to emphasize the research resources in Negro collections;
to influence greater institutional support of these libraries as
needed, and to recommend specific means of improving services and
resources.

    Upon request, colleges participating in the survey may obtain
an evaluation of their own library as compared with other libraries
in the study. Every effort will be made to involve the eighty-nine
four-year Negro colleges, and each of the colleges will be visited
during the first half of 1970.

    I solicit your cooperation in making this study successful,
and I ask that you kindly complete the enclosed questionnaire and
return it to me by April 1, 1970. Will you also send recent copies
of the following:

    1.   Self-study report for the library.
    2.   College catalog.
    3.   Annual reports, last five years.
    4.   Other documents as requested in the questionnaire.

Thank you kindly for your cooperation.

                  Sincerely yours,

                  (Mrs.) Jessie Carney Smith
                  University Librarian

JCS/vp

SURVEY OF NEGRO COLLEGE LIBRARIES

Part A

Questionnaire

Name of Institution _____

Address _____

City and State _____ Zip Code _____

Public _____ Private _____

Date of establishment _____

I. General:

1. Accredited by _____

    _____

    _____

2. Fields in which undergraduate degrees are awarded _____

    _____

    _____

    _____

    _____

3. Fields in which master's degrees are awarded _____

    _____

    _____

    _____

    _____

    What was their nature? _____

    _____

    _____

4. Fields in which doctoral degrees are awarded _____

_____

_____

5. Fields in which professional degrees are awarded _____

_____

_____

6. Fields in which vocational certificates are awarded _____

_____

_____

7. Other fields in which special programs are offered _____

_____

_____

8. Special research programs or institutes in progress _____

_____

_____

_____

9. Enrollment fall of 1969 (FTE)

    Undergraduate _____

    Graduate _____

10. Number of faculty members, fall of 1969 (FTE) _____

11. Briefly describe projections for the educational program of the

institution during the next ten years. _____

_____

_____

_____

_____

_____

II. <u>The library</u>:

    1. Date of establishment _____

    2. Brief history of the library _____

       _____

       _____

       _____

       _____

       _____

    3. Dates on which evaluative studies and/or surveys were made _____

       _____

       _____

    4. Library administration

          To whom is the librarian responsible _____

          Is library administration centralized _____. If not,

          describe administrative organization _____

          _____

          _____

          _____

          Is there a faculty library committee _____

          Does the librarian serve on the committee _____

          In what capacity _____

          Do students serve on the committee _____

          Functions of the committee _____

          _____

          _____

          _____

Composition and method of selection _____

_____

_____

Are there written policies governing library administration

_____(if so, please attach)

5. Personnel

List the professional positions filled as of September 1,

1969 (FTE) _____

List the professional positions budgeted, but unfilled as of

September 1, 1969 _____

Number of subprofessional librarians as of September 1, 1969

(FTE) _____

Quality of staff

Degrees held by head librarian _____

Highest degree held by other librarians _____

Library schools attended by professional staff _____

_____

_____

Degrees held by subprofessional staff _____

_____

Degrees held by clerical staff _____

In-service training programs attended (e.g., workshops)

_____

_____

_____

_____

Professional development of librarians (e.g., additional

formal training) _____

_____

_____

Hours of work each week

Professional _____

Clerical _____

Number of staff needed next five years

Professional _____

Clerical _____

Total hours of student assistance, 1968-69 _____

Status of professional librarians:	Head librarian only	All librarians
Academic or faculty status	_____	_____
Faculty rank	_____	_____
Professional classification	_____	_____
Other (please explain)	_____	_____

Eligibility for:	Head librarian only	All librarians
sabbaticals	_____	_____
hospitalization	_____	_____
retirement	_____	_____
tenure	_____	_____
vote in faculty meetings	_____	_____
membership on faculty committees	_____	_____
membership on curriculum committees	_____	_____
others	_____	_____

Salaries, 1969-70:   9-10 months   11-12 months

  Director $ _____   _____   _____

  Assistant director $ _____   _____   _____

  *Department heads $ _____   _____   _____

  *Other librarians $ _____   _____   _____

  *Subprofessionals $ _____   _____   _____

  *Clerical $ _____   _____   _____

              *Indicate highest and lowest salaries

6. The collection

Number of volumes processed and ready for use, July 1,

  1969 _____

Number of volumes added during past five years

1964-65   1965-66   1966-67   1967-68   1968-69

_____   _____   _____   _____   _____

Projections in growth during next five years

1969-70   1970-71   1971-72   1972-73   1973-74

_____   _____   _____   _____   _____

Number of volumes withdrawn during past five years

1964-65   1965-66   1966-67   1967-68   1968-69

_____   _____   _____   _____   _____

Number of items of nonbook materials held as of July 1, 1969

  Microfilm _____   Microcard _____

  Microfiche _____   Microprint _____

  Recordings _____   Photographs _____

Tapes _____   Slides _____

Filmstrips _____   Films _____

Reproductions _____

Number of periodical subscriptions received, July 1, 1969

_____

Number of newspaper subscriptions as of July 1, 1969 _____

Indicate how many of these are on microfilm _____

What standard lists have been checked against library

holdings. Give title, date of latest check, and indicate

results by percentages or otherwise _____

_____

_____

_____

_____

_____

_____

What tools are used for book selection? Indicate to what

extent _____

_____

_____

_____

_____

Who has chief responsibility for book selection and

initiating orders

faculty _____

library staff _____

Is the faculty active in book selection _____

Does the library employ a professional bibliographer _____

Does the library have an acquisition policy statement ____
   (attach copy)

Procedures used for acquiring books and materials
   directly from library to publishers and/or jobbers _____
   through business office _____

Is the library a member of a duplicate exchange union with
   other libraries? _____
   How many items were sent on exchange in 1968-69 _____
   How many items were received on exchange in 1968-69 ____

Is the library a full (or partial) depository for U. S.
   government publications _____
   date of designation _____

Is the library an official depository for other government
   publications (indicate if international, provincial,
   state, or local government) _____
   _____
   Date of designation _____

7. Cataloging and classification

   Classification system(s) used LC _____

                                  DDC _____

                                  Other _____

   Are you reclassifying _____ . If yes, indicate old and
   new systems _____

   Are you converting, but not reclassifying _____. If yes,
   indicate old and new systems _____

Percentage of cataloging done through Library of Congress___

Percentage of cataloging done through other sources

(indicate sources) _____

8. Facilities (attach list with data for departmental libraries)

Date building was constructed _____

Date of addition(s) _____

Physical condition of building _____

Air-conditioned _____

Lighting _____ (footcandles; or, indicate type of

lighting used) _____

Floor covering used _____

Condition of furniture and equipment _____

Number of carrels for undergraduates _____

Number of carrels for graduate students _____

Number of carrels for faculty _____

Number of seats at tables and in lounge areas _____

Staff work space (indicate square feet) _____

Shelf capacity of building _____

Are open stacks provided

undergraduates _____

graduate students _____

faculty _____

9. Services

Scheduled hours of service each week _____

Service to faculty and students

preparation of bibliographies _____

library orientation _____

bibliographical service _____

other (please explain) _____

_____

_____

Library publications available (list and supply samples)

_____

_____

_____

_____

_____

_____

Use of library during past five years

	1964-65	1965-66	1966-67	1967-68	1968-69
Faculty	_____	_____	_____	_____	_____
Students	_____	_____	_____	_____	_____
Reserve book	_____	_____	_____	_____	_____
Interlib. loan					
Borrowed	_____	_____	_____	_____	_____
Loaned	_____	_____	_____	_____	_____
Other	_____	_____	_____	_____	_____

10. Library cooperation (please explain each)

Contributes to union lists _____

_____

Member of consortium _____

_____

Participates in cooperative acquisition programs _____

_____

_____

Special agreements with other libraries _____

_____

_____

11. Special programs or projects

Are any of the following services automated or planned

	Automated	Planned	Not planned
cataloging	_____	_____	_____
selection	_____	_____	_____
acquisition	_____	_____	_____
processing	_____	_____	_____
circulation	_____	_____	_____
fines	_____	_____	_____
inventory	_____	_____	_____
budgeting	_____	_____	_____

What computer facilities are available on campus _____

_____

_____

_____

_____

_____

_____

_____

_____

Describe any innovations in which library is involved

_____

_____

_____

_____

_____

Audiovisual services and equipment available in library

Dry carrels _____   Filmstrip projectors _____

Wet carrels _____   Overhead projectors _____

Record players _____   Opaque projectors _____

Tape recorders _____   Other _____

Film projectors _____

12. Budget

Library expenditures during past five years

	1964-65	1965-66	1966-67	1967-68	1968-69
Books					
Periodicals					
Binding					
Travel					
Salaries					
Wages					
Supplies					
Audiovisual					
Other					

Total library
expenditures____ , ____   _____   _____   _____   _____

Percentage of institution's educational and general budget

expended for library purposes during past five years

1964-65   1965-66   1966-67   1967-68   1968-69

_____   _____   _____   _____   _____

Projections for next five years

1969-70   1970-71   1971-72   1972-73   1973-74

_____   _____   _____   _____   _____

Grants and gifts received over past five years

1964-65   1965-66   1966-67   1967-68   1968-69

_____   _____   _____   _____   _____

H.E.A. Title II-A   _____   _____   _____

Are funds allocated to departments or divisions? _____

If not, what methods are used to ensure proper development

of subject areas? _____

_____

_____

13. What projections can you make for the future of the library

during the next five years _____

_____

_____

_____

14. Are courses in library science offered by the library staff___

If not, is what department are they offered? _____

Briefly describe the program (undergraduate minor; state

certification, etc.) _____

_____

_____

_____

_____

_____

_____

Name of person completing questionnaire _____

Position _____

Return: (Mrs.) Jessie Carney Smith
         University Librarian
         Fisk University
         Nashville, Tennessee 37203

SURVEY OF NEGRO COLLEGE LIBRARIES

Part B

Materials on the Negro

(Complete this part only if your library incorporates materials on the Negro in the general collection. If separate Negro collection is maintained, complete Part C instead.)

1. Scope and content

   Describe the scope and content of these materials.

   _____

   _____

   _____

   Published guides in which the materials are described (e.g.,

   National Union Catalog of Manuscript Collections) _____

   _____

   _____

2. If separate statistics are maintained, indicate the following:

   Number of volumes on the Negro as of July 1, 1969 _____

   Number of volumes added during last five years

   1964-65   1965-66   1966-67   1967-68   1968-69

   _____   _____   _____   _____   _____

   Projections for next five years

   1969-70   1970-71   1971-72   1972-73   1973-74

   _____   _____   _____   _____   _____

   Do you plan to establish a separate Negro collection _____

   When _____

Describe any special gift collections received during past five

years _____

_____

_____

3. Types of materials

Number of periodical subscriptions as of July 1, 1969 _____

Number available on microfilm _____

Number of newspaper subscriptions as of July 1, 1969 _____

Number available on microfilm _____

If possible, indicate number of items in the following categories

as of July 1, 1969

manuscripts	_____	films	_____
microfilm	_____	filmstrips	_____
microfiche	_____	reproductions	_____
microcard	_____	photographs	_____
microprint	_____	slides	_____
recordings	_____	scrapbooks	_____
tapes (audio)	_____	uncataloged	
tapes (video)	_____	pamphlets	_____
college archives	_____	prints	_____
other archives	_____		

4. Do you have an acquisition policy statement governing Negro

materials _____ (please attach)

If not, what procedures for selection are followed _____

_____

_____

What tools are used for selection of materials _____

_____

_____

_____

_____

_____

Who has chief responsibility for selecting these materials

faculty _____ several members of library staff _____

member of library staff _____ other persons _____

5. Use of materials

If separate statistics are available, indicate items circulated

during past five years

1964-65   1965-66   1966-67   1967-68   1968-69

_____   _____   _____   _____   _____

Clients served

students _____

faculty _____

community _____

researchers (please explain) _____

others _____

6. Curricular and research programs served

Are black studies offered in your institution _____

(attach copy of the curriculum)

List degree(s) offered _____ Is a minor offered _____

Are African (or Afro-American) Studies offered in your

institution _____ (attach copy of the curriculum)

List degree(s) offered _____ Is a minor offered _____

7. Organization of materials

Indicate which materials are processed

	yes	no	partially		yes	no	partially
books	___	___	_____	films	___	___	_____
manuscripts	___	___	_____	filmstrips	___	___	_____
microfilm	___	___	_____	reproductions	___	___	_____
microfiche	___	___	_____	photographs	___	___	_____
microcard	___	___	_____	slides	___	___	_____
microprint	___	___	_____	scrapbooks	___	___	_____
recordings	___	___	_____	art objects	___	___	_____
tapes (audio)	___	___	_____	paintings	___	___	_____
tapes (video)	___	___	_____				
college archives	___	___	_____				
other archives	___	___	_____				

8. Services

Services to faculty and students

Preparation of bibliographies _____

Assistance with class projects _____

Other (please explain) _____

_____

_____

Service to others (please explain) _____

_____

_____

Library publications available describing services and/or

Negro materials (list and supply samples) _____

_____

_____

9. Cooperative programs

List the cooperative programs in which use of Negro materials

is involved _____

_____

_____

10. Budget

Is a separate budget provided for the Negro materials _____

If possible, give library expenditures during past five years

	1964-65	1965-66	1966-67	1967-68	1968-69
Books					
Periodicals					
Binding					
AV					

Name of person completing this questionnaire _____

Position _____

Return to: (Mrs.) Jessie C. Smith
            University Librarian
            Fisk University
            Nashville, Tennessee 37203

SURVEY OF NEGRO COLLEGE LIBRARIES

Part C

<u>Negro Collections</u>

(Complete this part only if your library has a separate Negro Collection)

1. History of the collection

    Date of establishment _____

    Source of original collection _____

    _____

    _____

    Other historical information _____

    _____

    _____

    _____

2. Scope and content

    Describe the scope and content of the collection. Attach list if

    necessary _____

    _____

    _____

    _____

    Published guides in which the collection is described (e.g., National

    Union Catalog of Manuscript Collections) _____

    _____

    _____

    _____

    _____

3. Number of volumes as of July 1, 1969 _____

    Number of volumes added during last five years

    1964-65   1965-66   1966-67   1967-68   1968-69

    _____   _____   _____   _____   _____

    Projections for next five years

    1969-70   1970-71   1971-72   1972-73   1973-74

    _____   _____   _____   _____   _____

    Describe any special gift collections received during past five

    years _____

    _____

    _____

4. Types of materials

    Number of periodical subscriptions as of July 1, 1969 _____

    Number available on microfilm _____

    Number of newspapers as of July 1, 1969 _____

    Number available on microfilm _____

    Indicate number of items in the following categories as of July 1, 1969

    manuscripts _____   films _____

    microfilm _____   filmstrips _____

    microfiche _____   reproductions _____

    microcard _____   photographs _____

    microprint _____   slides _____

    recordings _____   scrapbooks _____

    tapes (audio) _____   uncataloged pamphlets _____

    tapes (video) _____   art objects _____

    college archives _____   paintings _____

    other archival material ____

Do you have an acquisition policy statement for the collection

_____ (attach copy)

If not, what procedures for selection are followed _____

_____

_____

_____

What tools are used for book selection _____

_____

_____

_____

Who has chief responsibility for book selection

   faculty _____   other library staff _____

   staff of Negro Collection _____   other persons _____

5. Use of materials

Indicate items circulated during past five years

1964-65   1965-66   1966-67   1967-68   1968-69

_____   _____   _____   _____   _____

Do materials circulate for room use only _____

Number of hours of service each week _____

Clients served

   students _____

   faculty _____

   the community _____

   researchers (please explain) _____

   other _____

6. Curricular and research programs served

   Are black studies offered in your institution _____

      (attach copy of the curriculum)

      degrees offered _____ minor offered _____

   Are African (or Afro-American) studies offered in your institution

   _____ (attach copy of the curriculum)

      degrees offered _____ minor offered _____

7. Administration and personnel

   Is the Negro Collection administered by a librarian (separate from

      the head librarian) _____

      Services full-time _____ Part-time _____

   To whom is the supervisor responsible _____

   Number of other professionals assigned to the collection _____

      full-time _____ part-time _____

   Number of semiprofessionals assigned to the collection _____

      full-time _____ part-time _____

   Number of clerical persons assigned to the collection _____

      full-time _____ part-time _____

   Quality of staff

      Degrees held by head librarian _____

      Highest degree held by other librarians _____

      Library Schools attended by professional staff _____

      _____

      _____

      Degrees held by subprofessional staff _____

      _____

Degrees held by clerical staff _____

In-service training programs attended (e.g., workshops) _____

_____

_____

_____

_____

_____

Professional development of librarians (e.g., additional formal

training) _____

_____

_____

Number and types of personnel needed during next five years _____

_____

_____

_____

_____

Number of hours of student assistance, 1968-69 _____

Are there written policies governing administration of use of the

collection _____ (if so, please attach)

8. Cataloging and classification

Is the collection processed _____

Classification system(s) used LC _____

DDC _____

other _____

Indicate which materials are processed

	Yes	No	Partially		Yes	No	Partially
books	___	___	___	films	___	___	___
manuscripts	___	___	___	filmstrips	___	___	___
microfilm	___	___	___	reproductions	___	___	___
microfiche	___	___	___	photographs	___	___	___
microcard	___	___	___	slides	___	___	___
microprint	___	___	___	scrapbooks	___	___	___
recordings	___	___	___	art objects	___	___	___
tapes (audio)	___	___	___	paintings	___	___	___
tapes (video)	___	___	___				
college archives	___	___	___				
other archives	___	___	___				

Describe general condition of materials in the Negro Collection _____

_____

_____

_____

How are materials preserved _____

_____

_____

_____

9. Facilities

Physical condition of quarters housing the collection _____

_____

_____

Air-conditioned _____

Lighting _____(footcandles; or, indicate type of

   lighting used)

Floor covering used _____

Condition of furniture and equipment _____

_____

Number of seats at carrels _____

Number of seats at tables _____

Number of informal seating _____

Number of study rooms available _____

Staff work space (indicate square feet) _____

Shelf capacity of quarters housing the collection _____

Are open stacks provided _____

    Undergraduates _____

    Graduate students _____

    Faculty _____

    Others _____

List equipment available (e.g., record players, etc.) _____

_____

_____

_____

_____

Describe special gifts in equipment during past five years _____

_____

_____

_____

_____

10. Services

Number of hours of service each week _____

  How many of these are at night _____

  How many of these are on Sunday _____

Service to faculty and students

    Preparation of bibliographies _____

    Other (please explain) _____

    _____

Service to visiting researchers and others

    Research service _____

    Preparation of bibliographies _____

    Other (please explain) _____

    _____

What special services do you offer in addition to those described

    above _____

    _____

    _____

    _____

Library publications available describing services and/or the

    collection (list and supply samples) _____

    _____

    _____

    _____

    _____

    _____

    _____

    _____

    _____

Use of the collection during past five years

	1964-65	1965-66	1966-67	1967-68	1968-69
Faculty	_____	_____	_____	_____	_____
Students	_____	_____	_____	_____	_____
Interlib. loan Borrowed	_____	_____	_____	_____	_____
Loaned	_____	_____	_____	_____	_____

Use of materials

room use _____ outside use _____ both _____

11. Cooperative programs

Contributes to union lists (general) _____

_____

_____

_____

Participates in cooperative acquisition programs _____

_____

Special agreements with other libraries _____

_____

Other _____

_____

List other special Negro collections located in the immediate area

_____

_____

_____

_____

12. Special programs or projects

Are any of the following services automated or planned?

	Automated	Planned	Not planned
preparation of bibliographies	_____	_____	_____
information retrieval	_____	_____	_____
other (explain)	_____	_____	_____

Describe any innovations in which the Negro Collection is involved

_____

_____

_____

_____

13. Budget

Is a separate budget provided for the Negro Collection _____

Is the collection endowed _____

If possible, give library expenditures during past five years

	1964-65	1965-66	1966-67	1967-68	1968-69
Books	_____	_____	_____	_____	_____
Periodicals	_____	_____	_____	_____	_____
Binding	_____	_____	_____	_____	_____
Travel	_____	_____	_____	_____	_____
Salaries	_____	_____	_____	_____	_____
Wages	_____	_____	_____	_____	_____
Supplies	_____	_____	_____	_____	_____
Audiovisuals	_____	_____	_____	_____	_____
Other	_____	_____	_____	_____	_____

14. Financial grants and gifts received over the past five years

    1964-65   1965-66   1966-67   1967-68   1968-69

    _____   _____   _____   _____   _____

List sources of grants and gifts during this period. If possible, indicate year of grant and the amount _____

_____

_____

_____

Are funds allocated to departments, divisions, or subject areas

_____

_____

If not, what methods are used to ensure proper development of subject areas _____

_____

_____

_____

15. List any special problems affecting the development or use of the collection _____

_____

_____

_____

_____

_____

_____

16. What projections can you make for the future of the Negro Collection during the next five years _____

_____

_____

_____

_____

_____

_____

Name of person completing this questionnaire _____

Position _____

Return to: (Mrs.) Jessie C. Smith
            University Librarian
            Fisk University
            Nashville, Tennessee 37203

Appendix D:

Acquisition Policy for Special Collections, Fisk University Library

ACQUISITION POLICY FOR SPECIAL COLLECTIONS

FISK UNIVERSITY LIBRARY

Guideline for Acquisitions

The aim of the Fisk University Library's Special Collections is twofold: to provide as nearly inclusive as possible a collection of Negroana to serve as a center for the preservation of Negro history; and to collect, on a more limited basis, significant items to enhance the research value of the other resources that are located there. These aims will be achieved only insofar as budget, grant funds, and other gifts will permit. This policy is not definitive for all time, but will be reexamined constantly with a view toward providing a policy statement which is realistic to the needs of educational and research programs.

The collection now includes rare books and items, journals, newspapers, pamphlets, manuscripts, papers, archival materials, private libraries, and some audio-visual materials. Selection of materials rests primarily with the staff of the Special Collections area, with recommendations of the staff of the Fisk University Library, the Fisk faculty, and visiting researchers.

Materials in Special Collections will present all points of view. In particular, censorship practices will be disregarded. If the budget is extremely limited, only those titles of lasting significance for scholarly research, of basic interest, and those that support curricular programs at Fisk will be considered.

Negro Collection Materials

The major portion of the Special Collections materials in the
Fisk Library are those by and about the Negro. Acquisition of materials
for this collection requires expertise and thoroughness in selection to
insure proper growth and development, and to make certain that the vast
amounts of current publications are identified for consideration. Materials in all subject areas will be acquired.

Bibliographic Aids for Selection. Materials on the Negro may be
found in numerous catalogs of publishers, announcements, bibliographies, and other sources. Those tools that are basic to the
selection of materials because of their comprehensiveness, cur-
rency, and/or reliability that must be used are:

Choice

New York Times Book Review

Library of Congress cards on the Negro (these cards
are sent to the Fisk Library periodically from the
Library of Congress)

Dictionary Catalog of the Schomburg Collection

Catalog of the Moorland Foundation, Howard University

Monroe Nathan Work, Bibliography of the Negro in Africa
and America

Dorothy Porter, A Working Bibliography on the Negro

Publishers Weekly

Ebony Magazine

Journal of Negro History

Bibliography of Caribbeana

The Journal of Modern African Studies

When reprint editions are considered for purchase, the title must
be either reviewed by a knowledgeable person or appear in a reliable bibli-

ographic aid in its first edition or in its reprint edition.

Bibliographic Services are now being offered through agencies
or through individual researchers. However, before subscribing
to them, the authority, scope, and content should be examined
carefully by both the Reference and Special Collections departments to avoid duplication of other bibliographic sources.

Types of Materials. With the exception of museum pieces, materials
on the Negro will be collected regardless of form. Art objects
and other museum pieces will be collected by the Department of
Art and will be housed either in the department or in the Carl
Van Vechten Art Gallery. Materials to be acquired are:

Books. Two copies of titles will be purchased if budget
permits. One copy will be placed in the general circulation
area and the other in the special Negro collection. This
also includes juvenile books by and about the Negro. If
only one copy can be purchased, as may be the case with
expensive items, the title will be placed in the special
Negro collection.

In a limited number of instances, three copies of a title
will be acquired. Examples are: books about such personalities as Martin Luther King, books by James Baldwin and
other noted personalities, certain materials on Black Studies,
and supplementary readings for large classes at Fisk. The
formula to be followed in the case of the latter is one copy
for every fifteen students in a particular course. In such

instances, one copy of the title will be placed in the
Negro Collection while two copies will be placed on
reserve in the general collection. Some juvenile books
will fall into this category.

Paperback books. Preference will be given to hardback
editions rather than paperback edition. Paperback editions
will be acquired only if the hardback edition is unavailable,
or if the title was published only in paperback.

Reprints. Reprint editions in hard cover will be considered,
particularly when more than one copy is desired, and when
titles are available in this form only.

First editions. First editions will be preferred to reprint
and paperback editions, and will be acquired if the price is
reasonable. If a title is of general use, reprint edition
in hard cover will be acquired.

Rarities. Rare items will be acquired if the item is of
particular interest to Fisk, if the price is reasonable, and
if funds are available.

Pamphlets. Materials in pamphlet form will be acquired if
the publications meet the general requirements of the
Acquisition Policy Statement.

Journals. All Negro journals that are basic for scholarly
use will be acquired. The popular Johnson publications of

Jet, Black World, and Ebony, will be continuous. These
journals will be acquired in duplicate, with the second
copy reserved for binding.

Mimeographed booklets. Many mimeographed booklets now
being published as "magazines" will be collected only after
they are examined closely for contents, format, and authority
with a view toward lasting value before subscribing to them.

Newspapers. Black militant newspapers such as Black Panther
and Muhammad Speaks will be subscribed to primarily because
they are the official organs of organizations whose view-
points and news can be kept on record for future research.
The old standbys such as the Afro-American and Pittsburgh Courier
should be continuous. The Pittsburgh Courier will be acquired
also on microfilm. Any black newspapers or news-sheets of
surrounding Nashville or other places in Tennessee should be
subscribed to regardless of the possible duration of the
publication or the format.

Reference Books. There are to date few Negro reference books.
Two copies of these will be purchased, one each for the Negro
Collection and the Reference Department. This will enable the
reference librarian to answer questions relating to the Negro
when the Negro Collection is closed.

Theses. The library will collect theses by and about the Negro
when they are significant to the collection practices of the
library. (See also Fiskiana Collection.)

<u>Tennessee Black History</u>. A vigorous effort is now being made to build up a Tennessee Black History Collection. The collection will include books, journals, organization publications, papers and manuscripts of individuals, and group movements which will include the Civil Rights Movement in Tennessee. All materials along these lines will be acquired, and gifts encouraged.

<u>Manuscripts</u>. The Fisk University Library has a collection of manuscripts and papers in its archives. Individual scholars, writers, and organizations will be encouraged to either give these to the University Library or make the library a deposit for them. (See contract for deposit or gift of manuscript collections.)

If a collection has to be purchased, it will be examined carefully as to the originator, importance, contents, and value to scholarly research as well as to the University library. If a collection appears to be noteworthy for purchase, the funds for this should be taken from a special fund or grant for this purpose, if at all possible.

<u>Africana</u>. A basic book collection of Africana will be acquired to supplement the Afro-American and Caribbean studies programs. Purchasing of books in this area will supplement the curricula, supply basic knowledge, and serve as reference tools. Some books on Africa can be somewhat transient because the continent has rapid government turnovers. In

view of this, books will be carefully selected with regard
to authority, scope, content, and basic information.

African newspapers and journals are to be subscribed to
in limited quantity. Primarily those of general and factual
content should be weighed.

The African collection, at this point, cannot be all inclusive.

Archives (see also Fiskiana). The Fisk University Library is
the official depository for the archives of the University.
Rules governing the collection and housing of the archives are
set forth in the Archives Charter. Archival materials to be
collected are:

> Files from the Office of the President
>
> Files from the Office of the Dean of the College
>
> Files from the Office of the Associate Dean of the
> College

Theses (see Fiskiana)

Fiskiana. The Fiskiana Collection includes materials by and
about Fisk University, its faculty, students, alumni, and
friends. An exhaustive collection policy will be employed in
acquiring materials for the Fiskiana Collection. Materials
in this part of the Negro Collection will appear in all forms
(except museum pieces, although a few such items are already
in the collection). Materials to be collected are:

> Theses. One copy will be placed in the Negro
> Collection and one in the general collection.

Reprints of articles.

Brochures.

Books. Three copies of books will be acquired. Two copies will be placed in the Negro Collection and will bear the designation "Fiskiana" on the catalog cards and on the book.

University catalogs.

University yearbooks.

Annual reports of major offices.

Minutes of meetings of the faculty.

Minutes of meetings of the executive committee of the Faculty.

Minutes of meetings of the Board of Trustees.

Minutes of meetings of the educational policy committee.

Minutes of meetings of other major committees.

The Fisk Forum.

Alumni News.

Programs (Commencement, Festival of Music and Arts, Convocations, etc.)

Reports of conventions and conferences.

Faculty handbooks.

Student handbooks.

Audio-visual materials, such as photographs, clippings, recordings, etc. The Nashville Tennessean, the Nashville Banner, will be clipped.

Audio Visual Materials. The library at this time has a small collection of audiovisual materials due to the lack of space, equipment, and staff to service and expand this collection in the past. Now with a new audiovisual center, located in the library, more concentration will be given to acquiring additional materials.

More slides, tapes and filmstrips will be purchased selectively
in line with supplementing classroom instruction as well as other
materials in the library. Preference will be given to selecting
hard copies of a title rather than microform copies.

Microfilms of the Pittsburgh Courier and the Chicago Defender are
continuous. The papers are also collected in their original edition.
Any part of the manuscript collection which is in a state of
deterioration will be microfilmed.

The library is attempting to build up an oral history program. Tapes
of this kind need not be purchased unless they are directly related
to the manuscript collection, i.e., tapes of Mrs. Jean Toomer, Mrs.
Countee Cullen, etc., or Fisk history. Speeches of all noted Negro
personalities who visit Nashville will be taped. The Oral History
Program will be almost exclusively that of the library's.

Gifts. Gifts will be encouraged. Many valuable items can be
acquired through this means. Books bearing the author's autograph
will be placed in the Negro Collection.

Additions to manuscript collections will be placed with that
collection, i.e., papers of Thomas Elsa Jones with those already
there. Books by Fisk faculty or alumni will be placed in the
Fiskiana section of the Negro Collection with designation "Fiskiana".

Other Collections

Winifred Holtby Collection. Materials in the Holtby Collection
are acquired primarily through the generosity of the founder of
the collection, noted English bibliographer Dr. Geoffrey Handley-
Taylor, in memory of his friend, the young Yorkshire author, Winifred
Holtby. Through the influence of Dr. Handley-Taylor, other
Yorkshire authors are being persuaded to add to the collection.
Books, manuscripts, clippings, correspondence, notices, photo-
graphs, and similar materials are collected.

George Gershwin Memorial Collection of Music and Musical
Literature. Materials in all forms (except museum pieces) will
be collected as they relate to the contents of the Gershwin
Collection.

Sir Ralph Perrin City of London Collection. The library col-
lects no materials on this subject. The collection of 100 books
on London will not continue under present collection practices.

Florine Stettheimer Collection. This collection was established
by Carl Van Vechten in memory of his friend, artist Florine
Stettheimer. It consists of a collection of books on the fine
arts and has 1,200 items dealing with all aspects of the graphic
arts. The collection was contributed to until 1964 when Carl
Van Vechten died.

Revised June 1, 1970

FISK UNIVERSITY LIBRARY

SPECIAL COLLECTION DEPOSIT

I, _____, hereby assign to FISK UNIVERSITY,

the _____ Collection to be placed on deposit

in the FISK UNIVERSITY LIBRARY ARCHIVES for use by bona fide scholars and

researchers.

The _____ Collection is to be used under library

restrictions. Those items in the _____ Collection

that the assignee designates to be closed for a duration of stated time, or to

be used only by permission from the assignee or heirs will have to be honored.

Permission to literary rights, photocopy, or copyright of the materials will

have to be granted by the assignee, the heirs, or the Fisk University Library

Archives if so empowered.

The assignee, heirs, or any other legal designee of the estate may withdraw

all or any part of the _____ Collection upon

written request to the University Librarian.

                              Signature of Assignee _____

                              Address _____

                              Date _____

Accepted by _____

Title _____

Date _____

FISK UNIVERSITY LIBRARY

SPECIAL COLLECTIONS

Deed of Gift

I, _____, hereby give, transfer, assign
and deliver to the Fisk University Library Speical Collections, absolutely and
unconditionally the following:

together with any and all copyright, literary and other rights therein.

Signature of Donor _____

Address _____

Date _____

Accepted by _____

Title _____

Date _____

Bibliography

THE BLACK COLLEGE: ORIGIN, DEVELOPMENT, AND PRESENT STATUS

American Academy of Arts and Sciences. *Conference on Negro Colleges: Proceedings.* Boston: American Academy of Arts and Sciences, March 6-7, 1969.

Atwood, Rufus B. "Origin and Development of the Negro Public Colleges." *Journal of Negro Education* 3 (Summer 1962), 240-50.

Bond, Horace Mann. *Education of the Negro in the American Social Order.* Englewood Cliffs, N.J.: Prentice-Hall, 1934.

_____. "Origin and Development of the Negro Church-Related College." *Journal of Negro Education* 29 (Summer 1960), 217-26.

Bowles, Frank, and DeCosta, Frank A. *Between Two Worlds: A Profile of Negro Higher Education.* New York: McGraw-Hill Book Company, 1971.

Brimmer, Andrew F. "Economic Outlook and the Future of the Negro College." *Daedalus* 100 (Summer 1971), 539-72.

Brownlee, Frederick L. "Negro Church-Related Colleges." *Journal of Negro Education* 29 (Summer 1960), 401-407.

Bryant, Lawrence C. "Graduate Degree Programs in Negro Colleges 1927-1960." *Negro Educational Review* 11 (October 1960), 177-84.

Bullock, Henry A. "Black College and the New Black Awareness." *Daedalus* 100 (Summer 1971), 573-602.

_____. *History of Negro Education in the South from 1619 to the Present.* Cambridge, Mass.: Harvard University Press, 1967.

Caliver, Ambrose. "National Survey of the Higher Education of Negroes: A Summary." Misc. no. 6, vol. 4. Washington, D.C.: Government Printing Office, 1942.

Carnegie Commission on Higher Education. *From Isolation to Mainstream; Problems of the Colleges Founded for Negroes, A Report and Recommendations.* New York: McGraw-Hill Book Company, 1971.

Corson, William R. *Promise or Peril: The Black College Student in America*. New York: W. W. Norton and Co., 1970.

Daniel, Robert P. "Relationship of the Negro Public Colleges and the Negro Private and Church-Related Colleges." *Journal of Negro Education* 29 (Summer 1960), 388-93.

Daniel, Walter S. "Liberal Arts and Teacher Education in the Negro Public College." *Journal of Negro Education* 34 (Summer 1962), 404-13.

Davis, John W. *Land-Grant Colleges for Negroes*. West Virginia State College Bulletin, series 21, no. 5. Institute: West Virginia State College, April, 1934.

––––––. "Negro Land-Grant Colleges." *Journal of Negro Education* 2 (July 1933), 312-28.

Drake, St. Clair. "Black Universities in the American Social Order." *Daedalus* 100 (Summer 1971), 833-97.

"Future of the Black Colleges." Issued as vol. 100, no. 3 of the *Proceedings of the American Academy of Arts and Sciences. Daedalus* 100 (Summer 1971), 539-899.

Gallagher, Buell. *American Caste and the Negro College*. New York: Columbia University Press, 1938.

Harris, Patricia Roberts. "Negro College and Its Community." *Daedalus* 100 (Summer 1971), 720-31.

Henderson, Vivian W. "Unique Problems of Black Colleges." *Liberal Education* 50 (October 1970), 373-83.

Holmes, Dwight Oliver Wendell. *The Evolution of the Negro College*. New York: Teachers College, Columbia University, 1934.

Jencks, Christopher, and Riesman, David. "The American Negro College." *Harvard Educational Review* 37 (Winter 1967), 3-60.

Knoxville College Bulletin, 1967-68 (Knoxville, 1968).

Logan, Rayford W. "Evolution of Private Colleges for Negroes." *Journal of Negro Education* 27 (Summer 1959), 213-20.

McGrath, Earl J. *The Predominantly Negro Colleges and Universities in Transition*. New York: Bureau of Publications, Teachers College, Columbia University, 1965.

Mays, Benjamin E. "Future of Negro Colleges." *Saturday Review* 44 (November 18, 1961), 53-54.

Nabrit, Samuel. "Reflections on the Future of Black Colleges." *Daedalus* 100 (Summer 1971), 660-77.

National Association of State Universities and Land-Grant Colleges. *Public Negro Colleges: A Fact Book*. Washington, D.C.: National Association of State Universities and Land-Grant Colleges, 1969.

"Negro Education in the United States." *Harvard Educational Review* 30 (Summer 1960) 179-305.

"Negro Private and Church-Related Colleges." *Journal of Negro Education* 29 (Summer 1960), 211-407.

"Negro Public Colleges." *Journal of Negro Education* 31 (Summer 1962), 216-428.

Office for Advancement of Public Negro Colleges. "Advancement Newsletter" 2, no. 6 (Atlanta: Office for Advancement of Public Negro Colleges, July 1970).

_____. "A Contemporary Status Report of the Libraries of Historically Black Public Colleges and Universities." Compiled by the Office for Advancement of Public Negro Colleges, a division of the National Association of State Universities and Land-Grant Colleges, in cooperation with the American Association of State Colleges and Universities (Atlanta: Office for Advancement of Public Negro Colleges, September 20, 1976).

_____. *Public Negro Colleges; A Factbook.* Atlanta: Office for Advancement of Public Negro Colleges, 1969.

Southern Association of Colleges and Schools. *Black Colleges in the South: From Tragedy to Promise; An Historical and Statistical Review by the Commission on Colleges.* Atlanta: Southern Association of Colleges and Schools, 1971.

Thompson, Charles H. "Present Status of the Negro Private and Church Related College." *Journal of Negro Education* 29 (Summer 1960), 227-44.

U.S. Department of the Interior. Bureau of Education. *Negro Education: A Study of the Private and Higher Schools for Colored People in the United States.* Vols. 1 and 2, Bulletin 1916, nos. 38 and 39. Washington, D.C.: Government Printing Office, 1917.

U.S. Department of the Interior. Bureau of Education. *Survey of Negro Colleges and Universities.* Section of Bulletin, 1928, no. 7, chaps. 1-3. Washington, D.C.: Government Printing Office, 1928.

U.S. Office of Education. Federal Security Agency. *National Survey of Higher Education of Negroes.* Vols. 1-4, Misc. no. 6. Washington, D.C.: Government Printing Office, 1942.

Virginia Union Bulletin 64, no. 3 (Richmond, December 1968).

Wilberforce University Bulletin 52 (Xenia, Ohio, November 1969).

Woodson, Carter G. *The Education of the Negro Prior to 1861.* 2d ed. Washington, D.C.: Associated Publishers, 1919; New York: Arno Press and *New York Times,* 1968.

Wright, Stephen J. "Negro College in America." *Harvard Educational Review* 30 (Summer 1960), 280-97.

THE BLACK COLLEGE LIBRARY

Atkins, Eliza. "A History of the Fisk University Library and Its Standing in Relation to the Libraries of Other Comparable Institutions." Master's thesis, University of California, 1936.

Baker, Orestes Jeremiah. "Improvement of the Negro College Library." *Journal of Negro Education* 16 (Winter 1947), 91-100.

Barcus, Thomas R. *Carnegie Corporation and College Libraries.* New York: Carnegie Corporation, 1943.

Caliver, Ambrose. "National Survey of the Higher Education of Negroes: A Summary." Misc. no. 6, vol. 4. Washington, D.C.: Government Printing Office, 1942, 20-21.

Christella, Sister Mary. "Xavier University Library." *Louisiana Library Association Bulletin* 15 (Spring 1952), 43-44.

Commission on Higher Educational Opportunity in the South. *The Negro and*

Higher Education in the South. Atlanta: Southern Regional Education Board, 1967.

Federal Council for Science and Technology. Committee on Scientific and Technical Information, Task Group on Library Programs. Subcommittee on Negro Research Libraries. *Proceedings of the First Conference.* Washington: Subcommittee on Negro Research Libraries, 1970.

General Education Board. *Annual Report, 1928-29.* New York: General Education Board, 1929.

Hulbert, James. "Negro College Libraries." *Journal of Negro Education* 12 (October 1943), 623-29.

Jackson, W. V. *Library Resources of Negro Institutions in the South Offering Graduate Degrees.* Atlanta: Atlanta University, 1946.

Jordan, Casper LeRoy. "Black Academic Libraries: An Inventory." Occasional Papers, no. 1. Atlanta: Atlanta University, November 1970.

_____. "Black Academic Libraries—State of Affairs and a Selected Annotated Bibliography of Black Academe and Its Libraries." Atlanta: Atlanta University, December 1971.

Josey, E. J., ed. *Black Librarians in America.* New York: Scarecrow Press, 1970.

_____. "Feasibility of Establishing a Library-College in Predominantly Negro Colleges." *Library-College Journal* 1 (Winter 1968), 27-37.

_____. "Future of the Black College Library." *Library Journal* 94 (September 1969), 3019-69.

_____. "Negro College Libraries and ACRL Standards." *Library Journal* 88 (September 15, 1969), 3019-22.

_____. "Negro College Library and Its Disadvantaged Students." *Quarterly Review of Higher Education Among Negroes* 32 (October 1964), 189-91.

_____. "Your College Library and Your College Education." *Quarterly Review of Higher Education Among Negroes* 31 (January 1963), 9.

Lyells, R. E. S. "Library in Negro Land-Grant Colleges." *Journal of Negro Education* 14 (Spring 1945), 153-65.

McAllister, D. M. "Library Resources for Graduate Study in Southern Universities for Negroes." *Journal of Negro Education* 23 (Winter 1954), 51-59.

McGrath, Earl J. *The Predominantly Negro Colleges and Universities in Transition.* New York: Bureau of Publication, Teachers College, Columbia University, 1965, pp. 127-36.

Marshall, Albert P. "New Demands on the Negro College Libraries." *Quarterly Review of Higher Education Among Negroes* 8 (October 1940), 203-205.

_____. "Professional Needs in Negro Colleges." *College and Research Libraries* 13 (January 1952), 37.

"Negro Research Libraries' Needs Identified." *Library Journal* 95 (May 1, 1970), 1686.

Office for Advancement of Public Negro Colleges. *Advancement Newsletter* 2, no. 6 (Atlanta: Office for Advancement of Public Negro Colleges, July 1970), 1-5.

_____. "A Contemporary Status Report of the LIbraries of Historically Black Public Colleges and Universities." Compiled by the Office for Advancement of

Public Negro Colleges, a division of the National Association of State Universities and Land-Grant Colleges, in cooperation with the American Association of State Colleges and Universities (Atlanta: Office for Advancement of Public Negro Colleges, September 20, 1976).

Phinazee, Annette Hoage, and Jordan, Casper L. "Centralized Library Purchasing and Technical Processing for Six Colleges in Alabama and Mississippi: A Report." *College and Research Libraries* 30 (July 1969), 369-70.

Pollard, Frances M. "Characteristics of Negro College Chief Librarians." College and Research Libraries 25 (July 1964), 281-84.

Robinson, A. M., and Allen, F. W. "Community Service of Negro College Libraries." *Journal of Negro Education* 12 (April 1943), 181-88.

Shockley, Ann A. "Negro Librarians in Predominantly Negro Colleges." *College and Research Libraries* 28 (November 1967), 423-26.

Southern Association of Colleges and Schools. *Black Colleges in the South: From Tragedy to Promise.* Atlanta: Southern Association of Colleges and Schools, 1971, 16-17.

Totten, Herman L. "They Had a Dream: Black Colleges and Library Standards." *Wilson Library Bulletin* 44 (September 1969), 75-79.

U.S. Department of the Interior. Bureau of Education. *Negro Education: A Study of the Private and Higher Schools for Colored People in the United States.* Vols. 1 and 2, Bulletin 1916, nos. 38 and 39. Washington, D.C.: Government Printing Office, 1917, 173-76.

U.S. Department of the Interior. Bureau of Education. *Survey of Negro Colleges and Universities.* Section of Bulletin 1928, no. 7, Chap. 1. Washington, D.C.: Government Printing Office, 1928, 46-47.

U.S. Office of Education. Federal Security Agency. *National Survey of Higher Education of Negroes.* Vols. 1-4, Misc. no. 6. Washington, D.C.: Government Printing Office, 1942, 173-76.

COLLECTIONS OF BLACK LITERATURE

Ash, Lee. *Subject Collections.* 4th ed. New York: R. R. Bowker, 1974.

Bontemps, Arna. "Special Collections of Negroana." *Library Quarterly* 14 (July 1944), 187-206.

CEMBA *Newsletter.* "Collection and Evaluation of Materials about Black Americans; A Program of the Alabama Center for Higher Education." Vol. 1, no. 1. Normal, Alabama, January 26, 1971.

"Countee Cullen Memorial Collection." *Atlanta University Bulletin.* Series 3, no. 72 (December 1950), 20-21.

Dunlap, Mollie E. "Special Collections of Negro Literature in the United States." *Journal of Negro Education* 4 (October 1934), 482-89.

Leonard, Katherine Estelle. "A Study of the Negro Collection in the Trevor Arnett Library at Atlanta University." Master's thesis, Atlanta University, 1951.

McBrown, Gertrude Parthenia. "The Countee Cullen Memorial Collection of Atlanta University." *Negro History Bulletin* 17 (October 1953), 11-13.

Materials by and about American Negroes. Papers presented at an Institute sponsored by the Atlanta University School of Library Service with the cooperation of the Trevor Arnett Library, October 21-23, 1965. Edited and with an introduction by Annette Hoage Phinazee. Atlanta: Atlanta University School of Library Service, 1967.

National Union Catalog of Manuscript Collections. Ann Arbor: J. W. Edwards, 1959-69.

Porter, Dorothy B. "Library Sources for the Study of Negro Life and History." *Journal of Negro Education* 5 (April 1936), 232-44.

Reddick, Lawrence D. "Library Resources for Negro Studies in the United States and Abroad." In *Encyclopedia of the Negro: Preparatory Volume with Reference Lists and Reports,* by W. E. B. DuBois and Guy B. Johnson. New York: Carnegie Corporation, 1945, 163-82.

Schatz, Walter. *Directory of Afro-American Resources.* New York: Bowker, 1970.

Shockley, Ann A. "Does the Negro College Library Need a Special Negro Collection?" *Library Journal* 86 (June 1, 1961), 2048-50.

Smith, Jessie Carney. "The Research Collections in Negro Life and Culture at Fisk University." Paper presented before the Workshop on Bibliographic Resources for a Study of the American Negro, Howard University Library, Washington, D.C., July 22-26, 1968.

Smith, Paul. "A Critical Interpretation of Special Collections: Negro." *Journal of Negro Education* 30 (Spring 1961), 150-52.

Spingarn, Arthur B. "Collecting a Library of Negro Literature." *Journal of Negro Education* 7 (January 1938), 12-18.

Van Jackson, Wallace. "The Countee Cullen Memorial Collection at Atlanta University *Crisis* 54 (May 1947), 140-42.

Williams, Joan B. "Some Special Collections in the Fisk University Library." *Tennessee Librarian* 16 (Winter 1964), 47-52.

Wright, Dorothy. "A Comprehensive Thesaurus of Literature by and on the Negro." *School and Society* 63, no. 1642 (June 15, 1946), 430-31.

CATALOGS AND PUBLICATIONS OF BLACK LIBRARIES

Addo, Linda, comp. *The Negro in American History: A Selective Bibliography.* Greensboro, N.C.: Greensboro Tri-College Consortium, 1970.

African Art & Artifacts; Selected Works from the Lincoln University Collection, Lincoln University, Pa., April 2-30, 1967. Hetzel Union Building Gallery. Pennsylvania State University College of Arts and Architecture, n.d.

Alabama A and M University. Huntsville, Alabama. *Proceedings of the Conference for the Evaluation of Materials About Black Americans (CEMBA), April 20-25, 1969.* Sponsored by Alabama Center for Higher Education (ACHE), Southern Education Foundation, and Alabama A and M University. Huntsville, 1969.

Alabama Center for Higher Education. CEMBA. *Black Materials for Public Schools: A Study Guide.* Birmingham: Alabama Center for Higher Education, n.d.

Amistad Research Center. Fisk University. *Author and Added Entry Catalog of the American Missionary Association Archives.* 3 vols. Westport, Conn.: Greenwood [1970?].

Amistad Research Center. Dillard University, New Orleans [1971].

Bishop College. Dallas, Texas. Library. "Black Studies Paperback Project; A Selection of Paperback Books on the Black Experience." Dallas, n.d.

Cazort, Jean Elder. *A Handbook for the Organization of Black Materials.* Prepared for the Institute on the Selection, Organization, and Use of Materials by and about the Negro. Nashville: Fisk University Library, 1971.

CEMBA *Newsletter.* "Collection and Evaluation of Materials about Black Americans; A Program of the Alabama Center for Higher Education." Vol. 1, no. 1. Normal, Alabama, January 26, 1971.

Cheyney State College. Cheyney, Pa. Leslie Pinckney Hill Library. "A Bibliography of African and Afro-American Holdings." Cheyney, Pa., April 10, 1970.

Collins, L. M. *Books by Black Americans.* Prepared for the Institute on the Selection, Organization, and Use of Materials by and about the Negro. Nashville: Fisk University Library, 1970.

_____. *The One Hundred Years of James Weldon Johnson 1871-1971.* An interpretive bibliography; a publication of the Institute in Black Studies Librarianship. Nashville: Fisk University Library, 1971.

Fisk University. Nashville, Tenn. "American Missionary Association Archives in Fisk University Library." *Fisk University Bulletin* 22, no. 3, September 1947.

_____. *James Weldon Johnson: A Biographical Sketch.* Nashville: Department of Publicity, Fisk University, n.d.

Fisk University. Nashville, Tennessee. Erastus Milo Cravath Memorial Library. *The Baldridge Collection: Drawings of African Types at Fisk University.* Nashville, n.d.

_____. *Dictionary Catalog of the Negro Collection of Fisk University Library.* 6 vols. Boston: G. K. Hall and Company, 1974.

_____. *Bibliography of Charles S. Johnson's Published Writings.* Compiled by George L. Gardiner, with an introduction by Arna Bontemps. Nashville, 1960.

_____. *Edwin Rogers Embree: A Bibliography.* Nashville, n.d.

_____. *A List of Manuscripts, Published Works and Related Items in the Charles Waddell Chesnutt Collection of the Erastus Milo Cravath Memorial Library.* Nashville, n.d.

_____. *Selected Items from the George Gershwin Memorial Collection of Music and Musical Literature.* Nashville, 1947.

_____. *Special Collections in the Erastus Milo Cravath Memorial Library.* Nashville, 1967.

Fisk University. Nashville, Tennessee. Fisk University Library. Special Collections Department. *BANC,* vol. 1-. Nashville, 1970-.

Florida A and M University. Tallahassee, Florida. *A Classified Catalogue of the Negro Collection in the Samuel H. Coleman Memorial Library.* Tallahassee, 1969.

Hampton Institute. Hampton, Virginia. Collis P. Huntington Memorial Library. *African-American Studies; Periodical Holdings.* Hampton, n.d.

_____. *Dictionary Catalog of the George Foster Peabody Collection.* 2 vols. Westport, Conn.: Greenwood, 1972.

Howard University. Washington, D.C. *A Catalogue of the African Collection in the Moorland Foundation.* Boston: G. K. Hall and Company, 1970.

Howard University. Washington, D.C. [Founders Library. Moorland Foundation.] *Dictionary Catalog of the Arthur B. Spingarn Collection of Negro Authors.* 2 vols. Boston: G. K. Hall and Company, 1970.

_____. *Dictionary Catalog of the Jesse E. Moorland Collection of Negro Life and History.* 9 vols. Boston: G. K. Hall and Company, 1970.

Jackson State College. Jackson, Mississippi. *Catalog of the Negro Collection.* Compiled by the Reference Staff. Jackson, 1971.

Kentucky State College. Frankfort, Kentucky. Blazer Library. *African and African-American History and Culture.* A comprehensive bibliography compiled and edited by Cornelia A. Walker. Frankfort, 1970.

Lane College. Jackson, Tennessee. J. K. Daniels Library. "Negro Collection: A Bibliography." Jackson, 1969.

Lincoln University. Jefferson City, Missouri. Inman E. Page Library. "Bibliography of Books by and about Negroes." Jefferson City, 1970.

_____. "Pro- and Anti-Slavery Arguments Before and After the Civil War in the Lincoln University Library Collection." Jefferson City, 1968.

Lincoln University. Lincoln University, Pennsylvania. Vail Memorial Library. *Catalog of the Special Negro and African Collection.* Lincoln University, 1970. Supplement, 1972.

_____. *Slavery in America: An Epoch Ended.* Manuscripts and other items 1660-1865; selected from the Collection of Philip D. and Elsie O. Sang, River Forest, Illinois. An exhibition arranged by H. D. Gunn. Lincoln University, 1966.

_____. *The Susan Reynolds Underhill African Collection.* Lincoln University, n.d.

Materials by and about American Negroes. Papers presented at an institute sponsored by the Atlanta University School of Library Service with the cooperation of the Trevor Arnett Library, October 21-23, 1965. Edited and with an introduction by Annette Hoage Phinazee. Atlanta: Atlanta University, School of Library Service, 1967.

New York. Public Library. Schomburg Collection of Negro Literature and History. *Dictionary Catalog.* 9 vols. Boston: G. K. Hall, 1962. Supplement I, 1967. Supplement II, 1972.

North Carolina Central University. Durham. African-American Materials Project. *News Feature.* Durham, August 1971.

Roundtree, Louise Marie, comp. *"The American Negro" and "African Studies": A Bibliography on the Special Collections in Carnegie Library, Livingstone College, Salisbury, N.C.* Salisbury, 1968.

Shockley, Ann Allen. *A Handbook for the Administration of Special Black Collections.* Rev. and enl.; prepared for the Institute in Black Studies Librarianship. Nashville: Fisk University Library, 1971.

_____. comp. *A Manual for the Black Oral History Program.* Nashville: Fisk University Library, 1971.

Smith, Jessie Carney. *A Handbook for the Study of Black Bibliography.* Prepared
for the Institute in Black Studies Librarianship. Nashville: Fisk University
Library, 1971.

Texas Southern University. Houston. *Catalog of the Heartman Negro Collection.*
Houston, n.d.

"Tuskegee Institute Archives." Tuskegee Institute. Tuskegee, Alabama, n.d.

Wilberforce University. Wilberforce, Ohio. Carnegie Library. *The Benjamin William
Arnett Papers at Carnegie Library, Wilberforce University, Wilberforce, Ohio.*
Compiled by Casper LeRoy Jordan. Wilberforce, 1958.

Wiley College. Marshall, Texas. Thomas Winston Cole, Sr., Library. Technical Services Division. "A Bibliography of Books, Periodicals, and Newspapers by or
about Negroes." Marshall, n.d.

Winston-Salem State University. Winston-Salem, N.C. C. G. O'Kelly Library. "Black
Studies Paperback Book Project (Partial List), December, 1969-January, 1970.
List of Books Added to the University Library." Winston-Salem, 1970.

_____. "Library Holdings on Black Literature." Winston-Salem, n.d.

Yelton, Donald C. "A Survey of the Special Negro Collection and Related Resources
of the Vail Memorial Library." Lincoln University, Pa., 1964.

TOOLS FOR BUILDING COLLECTIONS
OF BLACK LITERATURE

Bibliographic Survey: The Negro in Print. vol. 1-. May 1965-. Washington, D.C.:
Negro Bibliographic and Research Center. Bimonthly.

Crosby, Muriel. *Reading Ladders for Human Relations.* 4th ed. Washington, D.C.:
American Council on Education, 1963.

de Lerma, Dominique-René. *Black Music in Our Culture.* Kent, Ohio: Kent State
University Press, 1971. Bibliography, 171-80.

Duignan, Peter, comp. *Africa South of the Sahara: A Bibliography for Undergraduate
Libraries.* Williamsport, Pa.: Bro-Dart, 1971.

Dumond, Dwight L. *A Bibliography of Anti-Slavery in America.* Ann Arbor: University
of Michigan Press, 1961.

Fisk University. Library. Nashville, Tenn. *Dictionary Catalog of the Negro Collection of the Fisk University Library.* 6 vols. Boston: G. K. Hall and Company,
1974.

Howard University. Washington, D.C. [Founders Library. Moorland Foundation.]
Dictionary Catalog of the Arthur B. Spingarn Collection of Negro Authors.
2 vols. Boston: G. K. Hall and Company, 1970.

_____. *Dictionary Catalog of the Jesse E. Moorland Collection of Negro Life and
History.* 9 vols. Boston: G. K. Hall and Company, 1970.

Merriam, Alan P. *A Bibliography of Jazz.* Philadelphia: American Folklore Society,
1954.

Miller, Elizabeth, and Fisher, Mary, eds. *The Negro in America; A Bibliography.*
Rev. ed. Cambridge, Mass.: Harvard University Press, 1970.

Nevins, Allan; Robertson, James I., Jr.; and Wiley, Bell I., eds. *Civil War Books:*

A Critical Bibliography. 2 vols. Baton Rouge: Louisiana State University Press, 1967.

New York. Public Library. Schomburg Collection of Negro Literature and History. *Dictionary Catalog.* 9 vols. Boston: G. K. Hall and Company, 1962. Supplement I, 1967. Supplement II, 1972.

Porter, Dorothy B. *The Negro in the United States: A Selected Bibliography.* Washington, D.C.: Library of Congress, 1970.

_____. *The Negro in the United States: A Working Bibliography.* Ann Arbor: University Microfilms, 1969.

Reardon, William R., and Pawley, Thomas D., eds. *The Black Teacher and the Dramatic Arts; A Dialogue, Bibliography and Anthology.* Westport, Conn.: Negro Universities Press, 1970.

Thompson, Edgar T. *Race and Religion; A Descriptive Bibliography Compiled with Special Reference to the Relations Between Whites and Negroes in the United States.* Chapel Hill: University of North Carolina Press, 1949.

Work, Monroe N., comp. *A Bibliography of the Negro in Africa and America.* New York: H. W. Wilson Company, 1928; Octagon Books, 1970.

GENERAL

Association of College and Research Libraries. "ALA Standards for College Libraries." *College and Research Libraries* 20 (July 1959), 274-80.

Baumol, William J., and Marcus, Matityahu. *Economics of Academic Libraries.* Washington, D.C.: American Council on Education, 1973.

Clapp, Verner W., and Jordan, Robert T. "Quantitative Criteria for Adequacy of Academic Library Collections." *College and Research Libraries* 26 (September 1965), 371-80.

Council on Library Resources. "Recent Developments," no. 17 (Washington, D.C., November 5, 1971).

_____. "Recent Developments" (Washington, D.C., November 15, 1975).

Holley, Edward, and Hendricks, Donald D. *Resources of Texas Libraries.* Austin: Texas State Library, Field Services Division, 1968.

U.S. Department of the Interior. Office of Education. *Survey of Land-Grant Colleges and Universities.* Bulletin 1930, no. 9. 2 vols. Washington, D.C.: Government Printing Office, 1930.

U.S. National Center for Educational Statistics. *Fall Enrollment in Higher Education, 1969, Supplementary Information: Institutional Data.* [Washington, D.C.: Government Printing Office, 1971.]

_____. *Library Statistics of Colleges and Universities, Data for Individual Institutions, Fall, 1969.* [Washington, D.C.: Government Printing Office, 1970.]

_____. *Library Statistics of Colleges and Universities, Fall, 1969, Analytic Report.* [Washington, D.C.: Government Printing Office, 1971.]

Wilson, Louis Round, and Tauber, Maurice F. *The University Library; The Organization, Administration, and Functions of Academic Libraries.* 2d ed. New York: Columbia University Press, 1956.

Index

About the Author

Jessie Carney Smith, university librarian and federal relations officer for Fisk University, Nashville, Tennessee, specializes in academic library administration and black studies. She has written articles for a number of journals, including *College and Research Libraries* and *Black World.*